2015

Joe –
We know you
are not a beginner
like the title says
But thought you would
enjoy al the history +
stories of various Beers!

Also – Enjoy a few 'Local'
Beers from New York!

Merry Christmas
+ Happy New Year!

Love –
John + Lynda

LET ME TELL YOU
ABOUT BEER

LET ME TELL YOU ABOUT BEER

Melissa Cole

PAVILION

DEDICATION
For Ben
Thanks for all your patience

First published in 2011 by Pavilion Books

An imprint of Anova Books Company Limited
10 Southcombe Street, LondonW14 0RA

www.anovabooks.com

A CIP catalogue for this book is available
from the British Library

ISBN 978 1 862 059146

10 9 8 7 6 5 4 3 2 1

Commissioning editor Fiona Holman
Designers Georgina Hewitt and Isobel ...
Editor Maggie Ramsay

Colour reproduction by Dot Gradat...
Printed by Times Printers Pte, Mala...

CONTENTS

INTRODUCTION

Welcome to *Let me tell you about beer*, although I suggested it should be titled *'Come in! Sit down, grab a glass. Are you comfy? Fancy a natter? Oh, you want to ask me about beer? Well, go on then, what do you want to know? And would you like a top up before we start?'* But apparently the publishers thought that was a bit long ...

OK, perhaps it is, but that is my ethos about beer: I want it to be fun and sociable and I'm always ridiculously pleased to talk about it, share a glass, watch people's reactions and generally just get very excited about all things brewed!

The other thing I'd like to say is, I'm not here to preach, I'm not here to judge you for drinking anything you like, whether it's a mass-produced brand or a craft brew I'm not fond of – far from it. I'm just here to tell you about beer as I see it and, hopefully, by giving you loads of information and inspiration, you'll come to love it as much as I do.

You see, my ethos about beer hinges on three points:

- Beer is, and always should be, fun
- Learning more about beer will help you to enjoy it more
- You may think you don't like beer; I say you just haven't met the right one yet!

And while I'm a self-proclaimed beer nerd, do you know what? It doesn't mean *you* have to be to enjoy this book.

For me, the whole point of writing this book is that for more than a decade I've had to fight through a world of beer labels that have rarely, until recently, said anything more enticing than 'a hoppy, malty beer with a bitter finish'. Wow! Really? A beer that's made with hops and malt will taste of hops and malt and have a bitter finish from the ... hops! Where's the incentive for anyone to walk away from the wonderfully described world of wine or spirits and come over to the beer side? None.

Throughout this book I want to give you clear, easily understandable descriptions of beers that reference familiar smells, flavours and sensations. Not because I think you're a bit simple, but because I feel my job is to tell you more about beer using markers you already understand.

I hope this will give you a new way of looking at beer, which will make it easier for to you make up your own mind about what you like and what you don't, and give you a deeper appreciation of this glorious drink.

Beer's variety is truly jaw-dropping. From refreshing, easy-to-drink lagers and zingy golden ales at one end of the spectrum to big, rich, vinous barley wines and sinfully dark and luscious imperial stouts at the other, there is a beer for everyone. If you want to drink mass-produced lager, it's not up to me to tell you otherwise, it's *your* choice. But let me introduce you to the wonderland of other beers out there. I've been lucky enough to try some of the world's finest beers and I'd love it if you could too.

Overcoming beer fear

Now, I'm no pyschiatrist, but there is no doubt that some people have what could be called 'issues' with beer. The world's favourite drink can evoke some very visceral reactions from people about how much they dislike it, for all manner of reasons – a lot of them based on urban myths or one or two tastes of a mass-market brand. So perhaps you'd like to lie down on my couch and we'll address your problems (with beer that is!).

#1 – it's fattening
No, it isn't. In fact, it's lower in calories than most other alcoholic drinks.

#2 – it's too gassy, it makes me bloated
As lager is the world's favourite drink, it's not surprising that some people think all beer is gassy. But if you step away from the mass-produced products, which contain quite a lot of carbon dioxide (CO_2), there's a delicious world of cask ales, craft keg and bottled beers that have significantly lower carbonation, making them far less gassy.

#3 – beer contains chemicals
It's one of those urban myths that won't go away but, unless you want to start getting picky about H_2O being a chemical, I can assure you that 99.9% of the world's beer does not contain anything sinister. The basic ingredients for any beer are water, grains, hops and yeast. These do contain 'chemicals', in the form of B vitamins and natural antioxidants called polyphenols – so let's focus on the good stuff! I've got more to say about beer and health on page 54, which also covers the next point:

#4 – it's not as good for me as wine
Despite the wine lobby's brilliant campaign to claim that wine is the 'healthy' option because it's good for the heart, there are plenty of studies showing that *any* alcohol (in moderation) is good for the heart. Also, most beer is much lower in alcohol than wine, so it is easier to regulate your alcohol intake but still enjoy yourself.

#5 – it doesn't go with food in the way that wine does
True: beer is often a much *better* match for food than wine is. I've devoted a section to matching beer with food (see pages 50–53).

Introducing

PART ONE

BEER

in all its glory

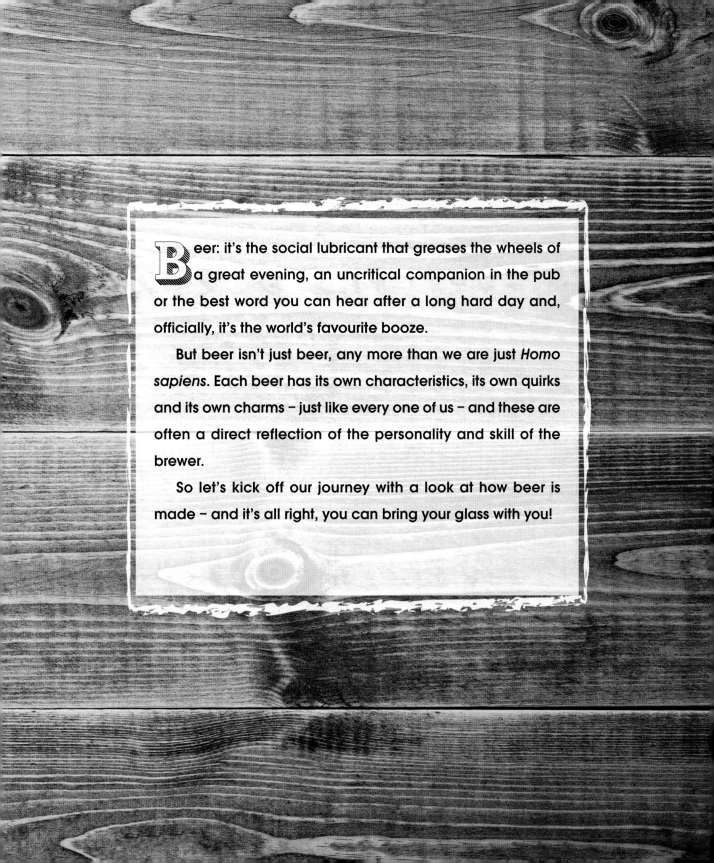

Beer: it's the social lubricant that greases the wheels of a great evening, an uncritical companion in the pub or the best word you can hear after a long hard day and, officially, it's the world's favourite booze.

But beer isn't just beer, any more than we are just *Homo sapiens*. Each beer has its own characteristics, its own quirks and its own charms – just like every one of us – and these are often a direct reflection of the personality and skill of the brewer.

So let's kick off our journey with a look at how beer is made – and it's all right, you can bring your glass with you!

THE USUAL?

Right. If you're starting at the beginning, you'll want something to drink while you're reading. So – what would you like? When I'm trying to help people find the right beer for them, my very first question is always: 'What do you normally drink?'

So, if you fancy trying a beer at the time when you'd normally be in the mood for a refreshing gin and tonic, a glass of red wine, a single-malt Scotch whisky or rich golden rum, here's my quick guide to grabbing a brew that will suit you.

IF YOU LIKE THIS	TRY THIS	SEE PAGE
Dry white wine, such as Pinot Grigio	Good-quality lager, well chilled	80
Aromatic dry white wine, such as Sauvignon Blanc	New World-style pale ale, well chilled	112
Sweet white wine, such as Gewürztraminer or Riesling	Light honey beer or flower/blossom ale	178
Dry rosé	Fruit-based wild ales, well chilled	63
Light-bodied red wine, such as young Valpolicella or Loire Valley reds	American-style bitter, lightly chilled	130
Medium-bodied red wine, such as Chilean Merlot, Californian Zinfandel	ESB (extra strong bitter), lightly chilled	130
Full-bodied red wine, such as Australian Shiraz	Porter, lightly chilled	164
Champagne	Champagne-yeast beer, well chilled	205
Prosecco	Crystal wheat beer, well chilled	68
Fino sherry	Lambic, well chilled	58
Amontillado sherry	Old ale, lightly chilled	148
Port	Belgian kriek or oud bruin (Flanders old brown)	61
Gin and tonic	Saison or bière de garde, well chilled	104
Bourbon and Coke	Smoked lager (Rauchbier), well chilled	87
Golden rum/brandy	Barley wine, lightly chilled	148
Whisky	Wood-aged beer, at cool room temperature	192

BASICALLY BEER

Fritz Maytag, the founder of Anchor Brewing in the United States, summed up the brewing process with elegant simplicity when he said: 'We brewers don't make beer, we just get all the ingredients together and the beer makes itself.' However, he's also being ridiculously modest! It is true that beer, like bread, is easy to make in principle: as long as you get the right blend of ingredients, mix them appropriately and apply the right temperatures at the right time you will end up with a finished, and hopefully tasty, article.

Here, in its simplest form, is the brewing process:

- Mill your grains and mix them with hot water in a big pot (called the mash tun)
- Strain off the resulting sweet liquid (known as wort) to a great big kettle (called the copper) to be boiled
- Boil the wort in the kettle, adding hops for bitterness and aroma at various stages over the boiling period
- Strain off the hops and transfer the liquid to another big pot; add yeast to ferment the sugars in the wort and convert them into alcohol and carbon dioxide
- After a few days, fermentation finishes and the beer is filtered off to a maturation vessel (these vary from a cask to a huge tank)
- Maturation can take anything from three days to three months, or even longer, depending on the style of your desired brew

So, that all sounded pretty darn simple, right? But, just like my baking analogy, brewing is both an art and a science: it requires the brewer to perfect that balance of art and science through the careful selection of ingredients and skilful manipulation of them. And, of course, they then need to be sprinkled with some inspiration and alchemy, to make a great end product.

And that is why there's a breathtaking variety of beers in the world today: they're the result of the detailed choices the brewer makes at every stage – which grains, water, hops and yeasts are used; temperatures, timings and the vessels used.

BEER OR ALE?

When people talk about beer, they might mean any alcoholic drink brewed from grains, whether it be lager, bitter or stout. Ale is used specifically to describe those beers made with a warm-fermenting yeast (see page 22).

The confusion over the usage of these two words is because it has changed over the centuries. 'Ale' was once the Anglo-Saxon word for brewed drinks, dating back more than 1000 years, long before hops were introduced to Britain. When brews made with hops began to appear in the 15th century, they were described as 'beer', distinguishing them from ale, made without hops.

'Beer' has come to be the umbrella term and, these days, in most parts of the world, if you ask for 'a beer' without being more specific about what you want to drink, you'll most likely be served a golden lager.

WONDERFUL WATER

Just as water is vital to humans, it is also crucial to beer, making a surprising amount of difference to the end product. Traditionally the local water determined the styles made by a brewery; today's brewers can manipulate the mineral content of their water to create a varied portfolio of beer styles, or to lend a 'house' flavour to their brews.

Most people's knee-jerk reaction when they hear about restaurants with water sommeliers is: 'For goodness' sake, it's just water!' And, while I'm equally scathing about such ridiculous affectation, we have all noticed the effects of minerals in water: 'hard' water leaves chalky deposits in pans and kettles, and creates stalactites, while water that is 'softer' than our normal supply makes soap and shampoo difficult to rinse off.

Water is hugely important in brewing because beer is about 95% water, and different water sources contain different mineral salts that can greatly affect the beer. But why? Well, first, the amount of various minerals can have a positive or negative effect on how yeast works – and the most important thing to a brewer is happy yeast!

Water with high levels of sodium chloride (salt to you and me) or magnesium, for example, kill off yeast in a heartbeat; but small traces of sodium chloride can help intensify beer's flavour, and magnesium is essential in the production of the enzymes needed for fermentation. Iron, however, is never welcome because it gives bloody, metallic flavours and impairs yeast activity.

Calcium is crucial in the brewing process, helping to control the balance of alkali and acid. Chloride makes some important contributions to various beer styles, offering heightened texture and enhancing any sweetness, and even titchy tiny amounts of various elements such as copper or zinc can have an effect on the brewing process. So you can see that water isn't just water when it comes to making beer.

The brewer can manipulate the water chemistry by adding or removing certain elements. This is nothing to be concerned about: it's no different from how water companies treat your tap water or if you run your municipal supply through a water filter; it's simply about getting the ideal balance for the perfect result.

Also, you should know, in a brewery water is for cleaning and 'hot liquor' is for brewing (it's all water, though!).

Below: Budvar's water tanks, supplied from an enormous aquifer below the Czech town of České Budějovice.

WATER'S EFFECT ON BEER STYLES

In order to get that authentic soft drinkability, one of the keys to proper pilsner lager is soft water (low in carbonates, bicarbonate and sulphates), like the local water in Plzen (Pilsen), Pilsner's birthplace in Bohemia (now the Czech Republic). Beers from the Munich area of Germany are made from sulphate-rich water, which accounts for their more intense bitterness. See lager, pages 82–3.

With its water rich in calcium sulphate (gypsum), Burton upon Trent in the UK Midlands became famous for pale ales, as the water allows for a better sugar extraction from the malts and enhances bitterness (see pale ale and IPA, page 112). And the high level of chloride in Dublin's water is perfect for brewing dark stouts, as it enhances the sweetness of this style.

Above: Lake Placid, in upstate New York, USA, from where the Saranac brewery gets its 'liquor' (the brewing term for water).

GLORIOUS GRAINS

Beer is often described as being malty, but what exactly does that mean? Well, to my mind, not a lot. It's a flavour that comes from the grains that are used as the bedrock of beer-making, but it says little about how the beer actually tastes.

From crisp, light biscuit notes through to almost burnt espresso flavours, malted grains add some of the most exciting and intense notes to a beer and form the foundation of its flavour, over which hops, yeast and water sprinkle their ephemeral magic. The choice of grains and their treatment throughout the brewing process allows brewers to make infinite subtle distinctions of flavour.

Below: Beautiful barley ready to be harvested before becoming beer.

Clockwise from top:
Pale ale malt – light biscuit and white bread notes

Amber malt – a granary bread flavour

Cara-gold malt – a light brioche flavour

Crystal malt – raisin and deep caramel/toffee

Brown malt – light chocolate flavour

Chocolate malt – bitter chocolate and rich espresso coffee flavours

WHAT IS MALT?

Put simply, malt is (mostly) barley grains that are fooled into thinking it's spring: they are steeped in water until they start to sprout, or germinate. In order to fuel the sprouting process, enzymes within the grain convert the grain's starch into sugars. At the optimum point for each style of malt (see above), the grains are kilned (malted) to halt the growth process.

The grains can be malted at low or high temperatures, and this has an effect on the flavours they bring to the beer – for example, light malts give light biscuit flavours, medium malts give caramel and raisiny notes, and dark malts give chocolate/coffee flavours. Their colour also contributes to the final hue of the brew.

To summarize, malt is a tight little bundle of brewing potential that holds the fermentable sugars the brewer will release during the mashing process and the flavour that comes from the malting process. It's

Above: The malting process is still done by hand by many maltsters. This is Warminster Maltings in Wiltshire, England.

interesting to note that, while some brewers will have the luxury of choosing their barley at farm level, most breweries rely on the skill and consistency of their malt supplier, or maltster, to provide them with a good-quality product. Before mashing the malt must be crushed to make its sugars more accessible to the hot liquor. Some breweries have their own mill to grind up the malt and grains, and some buy in ready ground, the reason for milling is to make the sugars more accessible to be dissolved in the hot liquor.

WHY USE BARLEY?

What's so special about barley that it's the brewer's most faithful companion? Well, historically, it was used more than wheat because wheat was better for making bread, and it just so happens that barley is better for making beer. This is because barley has an ample supply of an enzyme called amylase, which helps convert the grain's starches into a lovely sugary food source for yeast. Also, unlike other grains, it maintains its husk during the malting process; the husks provide a filtration bed when the wort is run off from the mash tun to the copper and this helps keep the beer clear and free of bits and bobs that might muck up the brewing process.

Beer labels and websites occasionally point out that they use something like Maris Otter or two-row barley – different varieties of barley, one common in the UK and one in the US. This isn't something I feel you should get too hung up about; it's just the brewer letting you know they've chosen their ingredients carefully, which is always nice!

OTHER GRAINS

Obviously other grains are used in brewing, otherwise the wheat beer section of this book would be pretty short! Rye, wheat, oats, maize, rice and even exotic quinoa and sorghum (see box, left) are used, both malted and unmalted, to make beer, but none of these offers the technical benefits of barley because they are low in, or completely lacking, the enzymes necessary to convert starches to sugars – and none have been found to give the taste to which we've become so accustomed. Most brewers, therefore, use a proportion of malted barley along with the other grains, in order to provide the necessary enzymes.

It's also common practice for brewers to use grains that have been kilned but not germinated, primarily for flavour purposes. Roasted barley is a good example: it doesn't go through the step where it's fooled into germination, it is just roasted at a high heat to give it strong coffee and

GLUTEN-FREE BEER

Quinoa and sorghum are both used in the brewing of gluten-free beers. The brewer must either use a huge amount of grain or, more likely, apply some additional enzymes to the brewing process.

Left: The mash tun is where the crushed grains and the hot liquor are 'mashed in' to create a porridge-like mush. Eventually, after standing and then being 'sparged' (spraying more water over it), it yields a sweet liquid called wort – which is then transferred to the copper. Sometimes there is an additional stage in here called the lauter tun, which is a wider, shallower vessel that has a rake running through it. The lauter tun's primary purpose is to maximize sugar extract from the grains by making it easier for the hot water to come into contact with as much of the grain as possible. But it's not a vital step and not every brewery has one.

chocolate flavours, and it will also help make the beer a dark colour – these malts are widely used in milds, porters and stouts.

And you might hear the word 'adjuncts' being bandied around in the beer world, mostly with disdain, but adjuncts can be good or bad, depending on how they are used. Adjuncts mean anything outside of the four core ingredients (water, malted grains, hops and yeast) that provide the brewer with a source of fermentable sugars.

For example, is it a bad thing that Cantillon's lambics (see page 62) use a high proportion of unmalted wheat? Well, the beers are stunning so in this case the answer is no. However, the rice, maize and syrups used to cut costs when making commercial lager is not a great thing, in my opinion, mostly because they make the beer rather bland. But if you like these styles of beer, who am I tell you otherwise? I can only encourage you to try something new as well as enjoying your usual!

HEAVENLY HOPS

Below: A historic way of picking hops is to use stilts, as the bines grow so high.

Hops are the essential seasoning of the brewing universe. Like salt, pepper and spices in food, the flavour benefits that hops bring to beer are almost immeasurable. And just as the winemaker has hundreds of grape varieties to choose from, the brewer has an equally wide choice of hop varieties, some delicately floral, some blackcurrant or earthy, others bursting with vibrant grapefruity zing.

THE HEART OF A GREAT BEER

There's something about the romance of hops that brings out the inner poet in every beer geek. If you ever get the chance during a tasting or a brewery tour to rub some hops between your hands and inhale their heady aroma, then please, please do so – you'll understand in an instant!

From grassy to flowery and fruity to earthy, the flavours and aromas that come from these amazing green cones (also called hop flowers or blossoms) can push a good beer into transcendent greatness. This is done either through the subtle use of a single hop variety, or through the skilful blend of several.

But what is it about the hop plant (*Humulus lupulus*) that makes it so special? Put simply, the bitter resins and aromatic oils yielded by the flowering cone of the female plant have many roles to play. Each cone looks like a little green pine cone, made up of layers of petals. At the base of each petal is a little pocket of resiny goodness called the lupulin gland. And from lupulin, the brewer gets some incredibly important substances: alpha and beta acids and essential oils. The alpha and beta acids provide bitterness to your beer and the essential oils add aroma. The alpha acids also have a very important role to play in helping to preserve beer and keep it free from infection, as they have antibacterial properties.

HOW DOES THE BREWER GET HOPS?

Brewers can obtain hops in a variety of forms. There is much debate about whether one form is better than another. In most cases, it's best to judge on the final outcome.

- **Whole flower hops** – these are dried hop flowers. Traditionally, drying was done in an oasthouse, a two- or three-storey building where hops were spread out to be dried by hot air from a wood- or charcoal-fired kiln on the bottom storey. The drying floors above were thin and perforated to permit the heat to pass through and escape through a cowl (angled chimney) in the roof. Today, hops are nearly always dried in a more industrial fashion – and many oasthouses have been converted into private homes.

- **Pelletized hops** – the hops undergo the same drying process as above, but are then milled and pressure-formed into pellets. The benefit of this is less hassle for the brewer when it comes to cleaning out the copper.
- **Fresh hops** – rather than drying the hops, they are rushed straight from the bine (the hop equivalent of the vine) to the brewer, bringing with them very fresh bitterness and aroma – they have to be used very quickly, as they soon deteriorate. Beers made with fresh hops are generally known as green-hop or wet-hop beers.
- **Hop extracts** – a liquid form of processed alpha acids and essential oils. Not considered to be part of the true brewer's craft, and they also tend to make me hiccup!

HISTORY OF HOPS

Before hops became the most widely used flavouring for beer, brewers were very adventurous and used a mixture of herbs known as gruit – kind of equivalent to a bouquet garni – which could have included pretty much anything to hand: heather, bog myrtle, yarrow, alecost, sage, rosemary, ground ivy and even spices like nutmeg and aniseed.

Unlike hops, very few of these ingredients had much of a preservative effect on the beer. Having said that, in those early days of brewing, the beer would probably have been so infected with wild yeasts and bacteria that even hops probably wouldn't have made that much difference: it would have been a pretty sour drink.

When hops were first used in beer is a matter of some debate, but it would seem the firmest evidence lies in the records of Benedictine monks (who still brew exceptional beer to this day; see Trappist beers, page 138). The abbot Adelhard, of the Corbie monastery near Amiens in France, describes in 822 how important it was for the locals, as part of their duty to the church, to gather hops for the brewing of beer. However, that may have been a bit of a localized anomaly, as we don't hear about hops again for another 300 or so years. In the 12th century the rather groovy Benedictine abbess Hildegard in the Rhineland (part of modern-day Germany) took a holistic approach to the human condition. In her treatise *Physica*, she observes that hops can replace gruit in a beer brewed with oats, although she gives little information about how they were actually used.

HOPS – NOT JUST BEER

Pliny the Elder was probably the first person to mention hops in literature (although not in relation to beer) when he talked about an edible wild plant, *lupus salictarius* – which translates as 'wolf among the willows'.

The hop plant is closely related to cannabis, but please don't try and smoke hops – the results aren't pretty!

Forage for wild young hop sprouts in spring (but please be sure you've got the right plant) and eat them Belgian-style with a warm sauce of well-seasoned butter and crème fraîche.

For as far back as records go, hops have been used as a cure for insomnia. Check out the labels of herbal sleep remedies: hops are almost certain to be in there somewhere – zzzz!

Above left: Fresh hops about to be used in a brew at Great Divide in Denver, USA.

Above right: In the middle of this hop cone you can see the lupulin gland and essential oil pockets.

FERAL HOPS

Feral hops are bitter creatures that seek to strangle other plants, creeping insidiously up and around their chosen targets, often throttling the life out of them. But when cultivated, harvested and then married to their sweet soul mate, malt, they shed their murderous edge and transform into the very essence of drinking delight.

Jump forward a couple more centuries, when the use of hops was spread by the Dutch, who wanted to emulate the hopped beers of the Hamburg area, much loved by the wealthy burghers of Holland. The Dutch were importing hopped beers from Germany by the late 1300s, and in turn started brewing them for themselves. It took around another 200 years for hops to be widely grown and used in the UK, where at first the plant was considered 'a wicked and pernicious weed'. Cultivation began in North America in the early 17th century.

In 1710, for the first time, duty was imposed on hop imports to the UK, which shows how economically important they had become, and in 1774 it became required for hop growers to put their names on the hop sacks. It was also around this time that the variety Goldings – which is still widely used today – came to the fore.

As with every other agricultural product, different hop varieties have developed over the years to improve both productivity and flavour qualities. Modern American beers are often characterized by the four Cs – Centennial, Chinook, Colombus and Cascade hops. These hops give American beers, particularly the IPAs and pale ales, their distinctive floral and grapefruit notes, as well as their biting bitterness.

And although it's widely documented that major swathes of Kent, Britain's most important hop-growing county, were covered in hop fields for hundreds of years, there was a period in the mid- to late 20th century when it looked as if British hop-growing would be wiped out as demand for traditional beers in the UK declined drastically. However, with the upturn in craft brewing, there are now more exciting styles of hops being developed all over the UK than at any other time, due to demand from forward-thinking brewers who like to mix it up a bit.

MY TOP OF THE INTERNATIONAL HOPS

Increasingly brewers are naming the hop variety used in the beer on the label, so here are some of my favourites from around the world for you to look out for:

Cascade – North America's gift to brewers all over the world. Its super-fruity/floral and spicy notes are what make so many of the USA's IPAs and pale ales so distinctive

Fuggles – the king of hops, in my opinion. Alongside its best mate Goldings, it has helped make British beer great for nearly 150 years: it was first cultivated commercially in 1875. For me, this hop evokes memories of walking through the English countryside as summer turns to autumn

Nelson Sauvin – this feisty newcomer from New Zealand was developed in 2000 and has many of the characteristics of the country's Sauvignon Blanc wines, imparting gooseberry and passion fruit aromas

Saaz – the hop that makes Czech and German pilsners so great. Used as both bittering and aroma hop, its delicate lemony and grassy aromas are soft as down and its sweet, grassy bitterness makes a beer eminently drinkable

Sorachi Ace – this astonishing Japanese hop has ginormous lemon notes with a fascinating background of earthy coconut, which makes it a very versatile aroma and bittering hop in both dark and light beers

Above: A brewer at Budvar, in the Czech Republic, adding luscious Saaz hops to the copper for both bitterness and aroma. Hops added early in the boil add bitterness while those added at the end of the boiling time provide aroma. Not always physically made from copper, these vessels are always referred to by brewers as the copper.

There is another step that the brewer can add here: it's called a hopback, where more aroma hops are added to the wort for a more aromatic finished product.

YEAST: IT'S ALIVE!

Yeast is the beast responsible for transforming the hopped wort into alcoholic beer. The fermentation stage is where beer diverges into three main types.

The choice of yeast is what makes ale different from lager, and also separates out a third category, wild ales, which are dramatically different, as these use what are termed wild yeasts during their fermentation. Within these three broad churches of beer, individual members of the yeasty congregation offer thousands of nuances of aroma and flavour.

Before I get just a tiny bit technical, let's remember that beer is fun. I happen to believe that knowing a little bit more about beer can make it even more enjoyable: my first brewery trip set me off on a fantastic journey of discovery, and I hope some of this enthusiasm will rub off on you!

Yeasts are microscopic fungi that thrive on sugar; in the process of alcoholic fermentation, yeast eats sugars and puts out alcohol and carbon dioxide. There are more than 150 species of yeasts, but only a few species are of interest to the brewer.

Below: Yeast is a frisky little beast: for every one yeast cell that's added, a brewer can get at least five back!

APPETIZING ALES

Saccharomyces cerevisiae is the yeast strain responsible for beers that are warm-fermented. They are often described as 'top-fermented' beers, because during fermentation the yeast cells rise to the top of the vessel in a foamy mass. However, the fermentation doesn't just take place on the top of the liquid, which is why I prefer to use the term 'warm-fermenting yeast'.

Why? Well, because these yeasts act at their optimum between the approximate temperatures of 15 and 24°C (60 and 75°F). They are very active beasts, so they tend to finish fermentation in between two and four days.

However, this type of yeast doesn't munch its way through as wide a spectrum of sugars as other yeasts and the resulting beers often have a slightly sweeter, more silky mouthfeel than, say, a lager.

The flavours imparted during that short, warm fermentation period by that busy little beast *Saccharomyces cerevisiae* – otherwise known as ale yeast – are found in a spectacular spectrum of beers: blonde, pale, amber and brown ales, wheat beers, porters and stouts, Trappist beers and barley wines, to name but a few.

Below: Medieval German beer being prepared for lagering.

LOW-TEMPERATURE LAGERING

Cool-fermenting yeast, *Saccharomyces pastorianus*, is a genetic hybrid of the ale yeast *Saccharomyces cerevisiae* and *S. bayanus*. It is named after the great Louis Pasteur, known to many as the father of modern brewing thanks to his seminal work *Études sur la Bière* (1876), which identified common faults in brewing and how to fix them.

However, most brewing historians agree that selective 'cropping' of yeasts (where brewers skim yeast cells to re-use) that proved effective at lower temperatures was probably started in the early 15th century by the monks of Weihenstephan in Germany.

This cool-fermenting yeast is a voracious little critter that chomps through a wide spectrum of sugars but takes its time and operates well at low temperatures, 8-12°C (46-54°F). The low temperatures prevent these hungry little bugs from blowing out big fruity notes like you find on warm-fermented beers, and help ensure the crisp, clean

Right: The iconic open fermentation vessels at the Cantillon brewery in Brussels, Belgium.

and lighter style that defines most cool-fermented beers. This cool-fermenting yeast is sometimes referred to as 'bottom-fermenting', but that's just because, unlike ale yeasts, the cells fall to the bottom of the fermentation vessel after they've done their work, which typically takes between five and 14 days.

WALK ON THE WILD SIDE

Natural yeasts are present in the air around us. For brewers, the most important is the *Brettanomyces* genus, with three main species: the mild *Brettanomyces claussenii*, named after Claussen, a Danish scientist who, at the beginning of the 20th century, was investigating spoilage in British ales that were stored for a long time; *Brettanomyces bruxellensis*, which is named for the region near Brussels famous for lambic beers; and the punch-in-the-face *Brettanomyces lambicus*, which is found in sour brown and red Flanders ales (read more about wild ales on page 58).

Brettanomyces yeasts create farmyard and barnyard notes, which can be a little sour. This might sound unappetizing, but can be deliciously refreshing: think of a squeeze of lemon or dash of vinegar in a sauce.

When brewed traditionally, lambic wort is hopped with aged hops that have lost their bitterness. They do not add aroma, but are used in huge quantities to help preserve the beer. The wort is then run off into a shallow copper vessel to cool and be exposed to the wild yeasts in the air, along with some important bacteria, before it is put into barrels to finish fermentation. You might have been marginally freaked out by the mention of bacteria there, but don't panic; the bacteria are good guys, the same as the ones that make yogurt – so what could be healthier?

These beer styles offer you a window into how beer would have tasted historically, before it was tamed in breweries, polished by science and put into shiny copper vessels.

FINAL FLOURISHES

All beer needs finishing time, and those of you who have ever home-brewed and then got a bit too excited about trying your beer before it's ready will absolutely know what I mean – everyone else will just have to trust me, it's not right!

After the initial fermentation, the brewer will transfer the beer into another container, so it is no longer exposed to the dead yeast and other debris, known to brewers as 'trub', which can create horrid flavours in the beer (see My Taste Chart on page 48 for more on off-flavours in beer).

And, just as in the initial stages, the differences in the way the three major beer styles are finished is absolutely crucial to their final flavour characteristics.

WARM-FERMENTED BEERS

In most cases these beers will be matured at temperatures around 10–12°C (50–54°F). In maturation terms this is known as warm-conditioning, compared with the icy temperatures needed to mature lager (see below).

This style of beer, particularly in the UK, can also undergo some further maturation through cask conditioning; this is where the container is re-seeded with a little sugar and some further yeast added to create a secondary fermentation in the container, to bring more complexity of flavour to the finished beer.

Exactly the same can happen in the bottle too, and if you're not sure if your beer is bottle conditioned, hold it up to a strong light source: if it has a film of sediment on the bottom, it's bottle conditioned!

However, not all warm-fermented beers are warm-conditioned; many of the stronger styles, with more complex flavours, undergo a cooler, longer conditioning.

COOL-FERMENTED BEERS

Lager alludes to both a style of beer and a method of maturation. *Lagerung* is German for 'storage' or 'laying down'. This is how cool-fermented beers are best finished: they should be cold stored, or matured, for at least four weeks (and often the longer, the better), to create the authentic dry, crisp qualities of a good lager.

Below: Beer can be matured in casks that go out to pubs for finishing; in large conditioning tanks and then kegged; or matured in bottle.

Above: Beer barrels are very rarely, if ever, made of wood these days. They are normally plastic or metal.

This is also where the finishing for lager is a bit different from ale, as it undergoes its secondary fermentation in its conditioning or maturation vessel. After initial fermentation, good lagers then have fresh yeast added before they go off to be held at near freezing temperatures for an extended period of time: some lagers take up to three months to reach their full potential and some of the very strong, 'imperial' pilsners that are being produced take even longer.

NB: It's easy to see where commodity lager brands cut corners (and flavour) in order to sell to the masses at knock-down prices. Not only do they use generally cheaper ingredients like rice and maize to replace a proportion of the malt, they also reduce maturation time drastically, meaning these beers can be in and out of the brewery in as little as 12 days.

WILD ALES

It's a bit difficult to generalize about these beers because the maturation temperatures can be dependent on the elements or on technology. There's no hard and fast rule – it's all down to the individual brewer.

However, these beers *always* take a long time to be ready, and this is mostly because of the wild yeasts and bacteria I mentioned on page 24.

Once the beer is in the barrel, the traditional *Saccharomyces* yeasts dive straight in to eating all the sugars for up to the first week. Then the *Lactobacilli* take over (lactic fermentation is what makes yogurt – it's not so scary when you think of it in those terms!). Finally, the wild *Brettanomyces* yeasts alongside other bacteria like *Pediococcus* all chime in with their unique contributions for about another year before they've finished.

A FINISHING TOUCH

Some beers can also be what's termed 'dry-hopped' – this is to add additional aroma to the beer, and the hops are added either in the maturation vessel or cask. In the same way, other flavours and aromas can be added, like ginger, elderflower or other glorious ingredients.

Warm British beer versus the rest of the world?

It's difficult to be a British beer writer and not address the issue of that quintessential British product of cask beer versus keg beer. I know we're not the only country in the world to have any real quantity of cask beer, but we are its biggest exponents, and some very short-sighted people believe it's the only 'real' beer out there. Cask beer goes through its secondary fermentation in the cask; it requires the publican to finish its maturation period in his or her cellar and has a very short 'shelf life' (usually no more than three days); it needs skilled professionals and a lot of attention to get it right (so respect your bar staff and landlord if they keep cask beer well – it's a talent).

Brewery-conditioned, or keg, beer has a longer shelf life, as it is not a living product. Basically, after the beer has finished fermentation in the brewery and has been conditioned, it is chilled and filtered to remove all the yeast. It is put in a sealed container called a keg, ready to be sent to the pub and served under pressure (which could be from carbon dioxide, nitrogen or mixed gas).

However, none of this makes cask better than keg, or vice versa. The issue is not the method of dispensing, it's the quality of the product that goes into the cask in the first place that's the basis for most people's bias.

This bias is mainly because, in the UK, unlike much of the rest of the world, virtually no artisan producers have been using keg until recently – and even now they are few and far between. What we have had, however, is a mass influx of beers from large-scale brewing companies, which led to a backlash against keg since they heavily filter and pasteurize their beers, which kills most of the flavour.

PART TWO

APPRECIATE YOUR

Beer

THAT LITTLE
BIT BETTER

From a spritzy chilled lager on a summer evening to a rich winter warmer beside a roaring pub fire, beer has a versatility and unfailing ability to suit the season and match the occasion, which is often underestimated.

Its different aromas and flavours can provide a never-ending source of epicurean adventure: beer can be immensely pleasing by itself, but it also has the power to raise an otherwise pleasant meal into something truly transcendent.

So whether you're buying beer in a pub or a shop, matching it with food or chatting about it with friends, I'd like to make your beer-drinking experience the most fun you can have with your clothes on!

BUYING BEER

Drinking beer should always be fun, but deciding which beer to order in a pub, or which bottle to choose in a supermarket, can be a scary and bewildering experience for the beginner, so here's my quick guide to buying beer.

IN A SHOP

If you are going to swop your hard-earned cash for beer, I strongly suggest that you go to an off-licence or speciality beer shop and pick the brains of the staff. Tell them what you normally enjoy drinking, mention any beers that you've really liked (or found a total turn-off) and, hopefully, they should match you to your ideal beer.

When you're buying bottled beer, steer clear of anything in a clear or green bottle. These don't protect the beer from damage by the light, which causes the lovely aromatic hop oils to degrade into wet-newspaper-smelling nasties!

Below: The array of both domestic and international beers readily available can be quite overwhelming.

Another tip, if you're going for the expensive or esoteric stuff – particularly beers that are very hop-forward – is to look at the sell-by date: if it's too near or past the date, it's best to avoid these bottles. The reason for this is that beers that rely on hops to give them their character don't always travel well, and if they are too old they will certainly have lost the zingy grapefruit, zippy lime or pine-fresh flavour that should have made them so enjoyable.

For many people, the supermarket is their first and only port of call for food and drink shopping. This is fine if you know what you're looking for, and you may be able to pick up a bargain. If this is your preferred route, I suggest you take the time to look at the back labels and read what they have to say.

A fun way to teach yourself about beer is to start with one of the beer styles described in Part Three (see pages 58–207) and buy a selection of beers in the same style to compare.

The section on tasting beer like a professional (see pages 42–44) will give you an idea of what to look for. And if you want to make a few notes on whether you like the smell and the taste of the beer you're on your way to being an aficionado!

Above: The back labels on beer bottles are much more informative nowadays, so take the time to peruse what they say.

IN A PUB OR BAR

There's one simple tip that can make your visit to any pub or bar a more enjoyable experience, and that's for you to take 30 seconds to look around at what everyone else is drinking – and follow suit.

If a bar has a reputation for good beer, then the customers will be drinking the good stuff, the artisan products, the cask ale or, if you're really lucky, the beer brewed on-site. Cask ale, mostly found in UK pubs, requires skill and care to keep well. In pubs that serve cask, other customers should be drinking it!

However, if everyone appears to be drinking a commodity lager, I would suggest you avoid any draught products and order what you find least offensive in a bottle.

If you're faced with an array of pump clips and are not sure which to choose, ask for a taster. Any pub that baulks at giving tasters of its draught beer is not to be trusted.

Above: Good bar staff aren't only friendly and efficient, they're knowledgeable about their products, too.

Seeking out great beer

- These days, pretty much everything you need to know can be found on the internet. There are sites like RateBeer.com and BeerAdvocate.com, where people give their personal scores on beers; these sites also include diaries of events going on worldwide.

- For more leisurely reading there are also some great magazines: in the UK there is the CAMRA magazine, *BEER*; in the United States there's *Ale Street News*, *All About Beer*, *Beer Advocate*, *Draft* and *Celebrator*; in Australia and New Zealand there's *Beer & Brewer*; Canada has *TAPS*; the Netherlands has *PINT Nieuws*; Sweden has *Maltesen*; and there's also the *Japan Beer Times*. If none of these are in your country, then I'm sure a swift search on the internet will yield some local results.

- Blogs are proliferating, and it would be far too hard for me to say whose is best. If you start with mine (girlsguidetobeer.blogspot.com) – and why not? – you'll find I have a list of other beer bloggers, and they will also have lists. Have a look around, and you'll quickly find people with whom you find an affinity, and to whose 'voice' you can relate.

- There are also consumer groups in nearly every country that I know of. In Europe your first stop is the European Beer Consumers Union (www.ebcu.org), which lists every consumer group from the UK's Campaign for Real Ale (which also has a branch in Canada) to Italy's UnionBirrai and Poland's Bractwo Piwne. In the US there's the Brewers Association website www.craftbeer.com.

When you receive your pint, if you have doubts, check with the bar staff. Trust your senses: if you're picking up any nasty niffs or terrible tastes (see My Taste Chart on page 48), then take it back. Make clear to the bar staff why you think it's not right, and if they don't take the beer off sale, I suggest you decamp to another venue as quickly as possible.

In the can

Until recently, beer in a can has had a bad reputation, often because it contains high-strength, cheap lager or because canned beer is often part of a supermarket 'pile 'em high, sell 'em cheap' initiative.

However, craft brewers are beginning to see the benefits of popping their brews into cans. Why? Well, for starters they are cheaper, lighter and more recyclable – meaning their carbon footprint is much smaller. There's a lining inside the can that removes all possibility of taint, and, finally, they keep beer really, really fresh. In fact, for beers that have lots of hop aroma or hop bitterness, cans are the most efficient containers for keeping them in good condition, so don't turn your nose up at all canned beers, just be a bit choosy!

STORING AND SERVING BEER

YEAST IN OR OUT?

Bottle-conditioned beers contain a yeast sediment – are you meant to drink it? Well, it won't do you any harm: far from it – there are vitamins in that yeast which are good for your hair, skin, nails and liver!

This is down to personal preference and, in my opinion, the yeast in question. For example, the super-fruity yeasts in a lot of Belgian and German beers are really very nice in the beer and are often left in when served on draught – in fact, the Belgians have a saying that the top two-thirds of the bottle are for their head and heart and the bottom bit is for their tummy!

But, for whatever yeast evolutionary reason, British bottle-conditioned beers rarely benefit from having the yeast poured into the beer, so keep back the last little bit in the bottle but, also, don't panic if some gets into your beer – it won't harm you in the least.

Most of the beer we buy in bottles or cans is intended to be drunk pretty much as soon as we get it home – or within a couple of months at most. But there are beers that continue to mature and develop over several years. Putting a little thought into how you store your beer, serving it at an appropriate temperature and – ideally – in a well-designed glass will ensure you get maximum pleasure as you sip or slurp and enjoy it the way the brewer meant you to do.

CAN I KEEP OR 'CELLAR' BEER?

Yes, and if you're lucky enough to have an actual cellar (especially one that keeps a steady temperature of around 10–12°C/50–54°F), then I'm very envious! If, like me, you're not so lucky, you'll need somewhere cool and dark.

But it's worth bearing in mind that not all beer is suitable for cellaring. Anything below about 6% ABV is meant to be enjoyed within a few months, not stored. And, also, if it's a very hop-led beer, I don't really recommend trying to cellar it, because hop oils are volatile creatures and don't last that well.

When it comes to the right types of beer for aging, there is more detailed advice on cellaring beer in the section on vintage and wood-aged beers (see page 195).

If in doubt, then call, e-mail, Tweet or Facebook the brewery in question; they'll generally tell you whether a beer is suitable for aging.

Right: If a beer bottle has a cork in it, then it should be stored on its side to keep the seal true.

**Ice cold
(0–4°C/32–39°F)**
anything you have no
interest in tasting!

**Well chilled
(4–7°C/39–45°F)**
lager, hybrids like Kölsch,
crystal wheat, fruit beer

**Lightly chilled
(8–12°C/45–54°F)**
farmhouse ale, wheat beer,
golden and blonde ale, pale
ale, IPA, British-style bitter

**Cellar temperature
(12–14°C/54–57°F)**
porter, stout, mild, wild ale,
tripel

**Cool room temperature
(14–16°C/57–61°F)**
barley wine, imperial stout,
old ale, vintage beer

SERVING TEMPERATURE

I don't want to be too prescriptive about what temperature you should
drink your beer at; it's your beer, drink it how you like! However, there's
no getting away from the fact that temperature has a major effect on the
flavour of food and drink, and beer is no exception.

Chilling dulls most flavours, bringing out dryness or bitterness, and
enhances the effect of carbonation. Warmer temperatures allow aromas
to flourish and emphasize any sweetness, while reducing carbonation:
beer – just like Champagne – seems flat when it's served too warm.

So, there are some rough guidelines (above) you can follow to get
you started, and you can adjust to your personal tastes from there.

SHOULD I STORE BEER ON ITS SIDE?

In most cases the answer is no, firstly because a lot of beers that age
well are bottle conditioned, and you don't want a huge lump of yeast
sitting halfway up the bottle when you come to pour it. Secondly, beer
will degrade the crown cap seal. However, cork-sealed bottles need to
be laid down so the cork stays moist and maintains its seal.

THE DRINKING VESSEL

What's in a glass? Well, apart from your beer of course, your choice of glassware can genuinely enhance your drinking experience, which is why nearly every brewer in Belgium has its own glass – and the rest of the world is beginning to follow suit. But, you might be thinking at this point, surely this is all just marketing? Actually it isn't, and there has been some detailed research into this subject.

When it comes to drinking beer at home, few of us keep different glasses for different beers. But if you're feeling curious and fancy having a bit of fun with your senses, try putting a subtle beer into two glasses, one with a wide mouth and one with a narrower top. Then have a sniff and see if you can sense anything different between the two.

Sometimes you'll get no choice about what your beer is served in. In the UK, we've been drinking beer in pint (20 fl oz/570ml) measures for at least 300 years, and it is illegal to sell draught beer in unmeasured glasses. You don't have to order a full pint: half pint (and sometimes one-third pint) glasses are available. But the same rules don't apply in other parts of the world; for example, the US pint is 16 fl oz (450ml), but bar staff may serve your beer in a 14, 16 or 18 fl oz glass. In Australia ordering a 'pint' or a 'schooner' means different things in different territories and in France a pint can mean 500ml, so as you can see it's a bit of a minefield.

Wheat beer glass

This design of this tall glass accentuates the exotic banana and clove aromas and flavours naturally found in both German- and Belgian-style wheat beers. The beer should be poured slowly and gently at first, and when the glass is almost full, pour more directly, to create a thick, creamy foam.

Stemmed glass

The tulip-shaped glass, with a stem for you to hold so your beer doesn't warm in your hand, suits a variety of styles, in particular sparkling pilsner-style lagers and golden or blonde ales. The slightly closed mouth allows for an intense release of flavours. I also like using this for stronger beers such as barley wines and Scotch ales, so you can swirl them gently, almost like a brandy balloon.

Wide-mouthed goblet

A style often used by Trappist breweries, this is great for stronger beers with massive aroma and wood-aged beers. The wide mouth allows all the rich aromas in these beers to assault your sense of smell before you've even taken a sip.

Lager glass

Recognizable as the standard beer classic, its mouth is slightly wider than its foot, and it is a pretty good all-rounder for all types of easy-drinking beer, such as lower-ABV ales, Helles lagers and Kölsch-style beers.

Spotting common faults

Acetic – this is when a beer has the odour or flavour of cheap malt vinegar. Vinegary smells are desirable only in small doses in wild ales (page 59) and some old ales (page 150)

Cloudy – cloudy beer can mean a whole host of things, some of which aren't exactly faults but which, to the untrained eye, can appear unpleasant:

- *Bits and pieces* – sometimes cask-conditioned beer is put on sale too early and hasn't 'dropped', meaning that the yeast that's in there for secondary fermentation hasn't been allowed to

settle after doing its job. Sometimes this indicates that it's come to the end of the barrel, which is not generally a good sign, as the bar staff should have noticed. Occasionally, however, it can just mean that some clumsy oaf has knocked the barrel in the cellar – the bar staff should check if this is the case.

- *Hop/chill haze* – this is when the beer has a slight cloudiness that's almost ribbony: if it's very cold and is very aromatic, it's likely to be what's known as a hop haze or chill haze; if it smells and tastes fine, then drink on!
- *Of the style* – sometimes beers are intended to be cloudy, for example most wheat beers (see page 68). If it tastes fine, I wouldn't worry too much, but it pays to check with the bar staff: if they seem unsure, it's probably wise to ask for a different beer.

Diacetyl – a compound created during fermentation. In small amounts, it can offer a pleasing sweet, or toffee-like, aroma. However, at higher levels it becomes what's known as 'caramel bomb', making the beer smell more like a chewable sweet than a refreshing drink

Light strike – a smell of damp dog or wet newspaper – which you can detect only when the beer is a couple of inches from your nose – created when hop oils degrade in bottled beers. Usually a result of using a clear bottle, although green bottles are also susceptible to this fault

Oxidized – oxygen can be beer's enemy and you will usually pick up this fault on the nose: it generally smells like stale black pepper, or a bit 'muddy'. On the palate you'll just instinctively know that the beer isn't as fresh as it could be

BEER JARGON

It may sometimes seem like you need to learn a whole new lexicon just to order a glass of decent beer, and this is partly because the majority of breweries seem to want to make it as difficult as possible for you to guess what the liquid in the bottle tastes like, either through a lack of tasting notes or unnecessary use of jargon.

So, I'm going to try to make things a little easier for you and furnish you with some easy tasting note tools to assist you in identifying those flavours that are literally on the tip of your tongue!

And, just as importantly, I'll also be letting you know how to express why you believe a beer has a fault, a good skill to have when you're out in a pub or bar and you're less than impressed with the beer!

THE MOST USELESS PHRASES IN BEER

While I'd like to be able to fully explain all the terms you'll see on a back label or hear in the pub, there are two words that make this an impossibility: 'malty' and 'hoppy'. What's the problem? Well, it's because they mean everything and nothing in one fell swoop …

Take the word 'malty'; what immediately springs to mind? For most people it would be the smell of either Horlicks or bread, which is all fine and dandy until you realize that when brewers use the term 'malty' they can mean any one of these flavours: dark chocolate, milk chocolate, toffee, caramel, raisin, smoke, whisky, liquorice, tar, molasses.

And what about the word 'hoppy'? For people who have tried beer and not liked it, that word may bring to mind bitterness, but for most brewers it's not just about bitterness, it's also about the aromatics: lemon, lychee, coconut, orange, nettle, autumn leaves, geranium – I could go on, but it would fill the rest of the page!

There's another commonly used word that isn't very helpful – 'bitter'. Given that bitterness, in varying degrees, is a key component in 95% of beer styles, saying a beer is bitter without elaborating is a bit like saying fish is fishy, fruit is fruity and air is airy! Unless you use some further hyperbole – for example, strong bitter finish, lingering bitter end, or, in the case of some US-style IPAs, punch-you-in-the-throat bitterness – it's not a lot of use!

Which is why, much as I'd love to, I'm afraid I can't tell you what those phrases mean when they are on any given beer label. But there are loads of phrases that I *can* demystify for you (see overleaf). There's also a more general Beer Vocabulary on pages 218–220.

Above: Some bottles deserve to be thrown out for their lack of information on the back label!

BASIC BEER TERMS

ABV – alcohol by volume, which tells you how much alcohol there is in comparison with the rest of the ingredients. Beer is generally relatively low in alcohol in comparison to other alcoholic drinks, but there are exceptions, so watch out!

Bottle conditioned – a little sugar and yeast are added to the bottle to create a secondary fermentation process, which adds more complexity to the finished beer. Look for a layer of sediment in the bottom of the bottle: this will tell you whether it's bottle conditioned

Carbonation – bubbles of carbon dioxide. Created naturally during fermentation or added to make the beer fizzy

Cask conditioned – like bottle conditioned except that the secondary fermentation takes place in a barrel. A UK speciality, occasionally seen in other countries, generally served at around 10–12°C (50–54°F) and nearly always served via hand-pull pumps

Draught/draft beer – beer that is served from a cask or keg rather than a bottle. Confusingly the word draught/draft is also used as a marketing term on some canned and bottled beers, to imply that they taste like freshly drawn beer

Head – mousse-like top to a beer, vital for delivering aroma as it contains a lot of the hop oils

Hand pull – the traditional long-armed pumps you see on bars, traditionally British

Keg – container in which beer is stored under artificial pressure from carbon dioxide (CO_2) or a mixed CO_2 and nitrogen system

Nitrokeg – method of serving kegged beer, commonly used by Guinness worldwide. Nitrogen has smaller bubbles than carbon dioxide, creating a smoother, less fizzy, drinking experience, but is often used to serve very cold beer with limited flavour, relying on mouthfeel over taste. Some craft brewers are experimenting with nitrokeg

Original gravity – this is the measurement of both the unfermentable and fermentable substances in the wort prior to fermentation; it gives the brewer a good idea of what the ABV of the beer will end up at

Top and bottom fermented – phrases used to describe how different beer styles are brewed. You will hear lager referred to as bottom fermented and ale as top fermented. It's nonsense because the yeast doesn't only eat the sugars in the wort from the top or bottom layers in the vessel, so it's more accurate to use the phrases warm and cool fermenting, as I do throughout the book.

GET YOUR INNER GEEK ON

Here are some slightly more advanced phrases to show off a bit with ... but make sure you use them right!

Adjunct – a source of fermentable sugars other than malted barley

Attenuation – this refers to the extent to which the yeast consumes the available sugars; saying that something is 'a well-attenuated beer' means you've got the right balance of sweetness against the rest of the ingredients that's appropriate to the style

Burton snatch – the distinctively sulphurous nose found on certain British and British-style ales, as a result of the brewer either using naturally gypsum-rich water, as found in the Burton upon Trent area of the UK, or treating their water to create this effect

Dry-hopping – a process to add more aroma to a beer by adding hops to the fermentation vessel, keg or cask

EBU/IBU – European Bitterness Units (EBU) and International Bitterness Units (IBU) scales are primarily a brewer's tool to express the extraction of alpha acids from the hops (see page 18). Bitterness units are not definitive because everyone experiences bitterness differently; also other elements of the beer, for example how sweet it is, will affect how you experience this bitter component

Esters – volatile compounds created during fermentation, that offer up fruity and floral aromas. However, they can become over-powering in some beer styles, and can smell almost artificial or cloyingly like overripe fruit

Zymurgy – the science of brewing beer.

TASTE BEER LIKE A PRO

Above: Beer judging is a serious business, as winning awards can make a big difference to a brewery's future.

Beer is first and foremost a social lubricant, and I believe that, to be at its best, it should be enjoyed with friends, in the pub, at a restaurant, or at home with a loved one. But that doesn't mean you shouldn't pay attention to the quality of your beer at the same time; now, more than ever, there's a plethora of great beers available, which will repay any attention you give them ten-fold.

I don't expect you to become an expert beer taster overnight, but I hope the following pages will give you some insight into the science of taste (without having to read through any boring bits) and other information to help you more quickly recognize the beers you like and dislike *and* be able to express why.

You may think that the why is pretty moot; why do I need to know why I enjoy something? But if you think about it, when you are next in a pub, bar or off-licence and you can say with confidence that you didn't enjoy X beer because of Y reasons then, with half-decent staff and even a small range of beer, you should be on your way to getting the beer you really *do* want, and avoiding disappointment.

HAVE SOME TASTE

Odd as this may sound, you 'taste' with all your senses. Drinking beer should be a pleasure for the eye, nose, mouth, tummy and heart; it should evoke anticipation and pleasure, bring back memories or help create new ones.

There's also a lot of science in tasting and much we just don't know about yet. This is because it involves one of the most hotly debated areas of human physiology, the olfactory system or, put more simply, the sense of smell. Without really thinking about it, we already recognize how closely linked sense of smell is to taste. When you inhale fabulous food scents, you start salivating; but when you have a stinking cold you can't taste anything, because your nose is blocked.

THE NOSE KNOWS

When it comes to the role of smell in tasting, science still doesn't have it all worked out, but we do know that there are between 6 and 9 million olfactory neurons between the upper part of the nasal cavity and the back of the throat. These neurons are divided between two systems: the ortho-nasal system for the perception of sniffed odours, and the retro-nasal system for the perception of flavour during eating and drinking.

The purposes of these two systems, it was quite recently discovered, are quite separate. The first is an analytical tool for your brain to identify and catalogue smells. The second, it would seem, is the opinion former: it converts aromas into flavours and imprints the memory of taste through scent – put simply, it's the system most people can blame for being captivated by chocolate or hating Brussels sprouts! This is because it isn't hard-wired straight into the cognitive, or thinking, part of the brain but takes a slightly meandering route through the ancient seats of appetite, anger, fear and memories – or, more prosaically, the hippocampus, hypothalamus and amygdala.

This is thought to have developed through evolution: at one time, tasting foods and liquids was a bit like playing Russian roulette and humans learnt to inherently fear that which would make them ill or kill them. In fact, the human race is rare in that it actively seeks out bitterness – which often indicates poison – rather than shunning it.

TONGUE TIED

Do you remember the old 'tongue map' we learnt in school, showing the very front of the tongue being responsible for sweet sensations, and the sides of the tongue for salt, then sour, and the back of the tongue for bitter? Well, it's largely complete hooey!

In reality, you perceive all taste sensations equally on the front half of your tongue, through receptors called the filiform papillae. These are the little red bumps and lumps you can see when you poke your tongue out at the mirror; they aren't taste buds, but they do provide a mechanical feedback system to the taste buds.

Packed around these to the sides and back of your tongue are other receptors called fungiform papillae (because they are shaped like mushrooms), along with your taste buds, and foliate papillae, which are extra sensitive to sourness. So the reason why the back and sides of the tongue fire off when we're eating sour things is due to these little guys; we can all experience this sensation by sucking a lemon.

At the very back of your tongue you have a group of receptors called circumvallate papillae, which are more sensitive to bitterness. That's why you should never spit when tasting beer, because bitterness is an integral part of beer tasting.

Right, that's the science part done. Now grab that glass of beer.

1. GIVE IT THE EYE

The first thing to do is to look at your beer by holding it up to the light. Admire it, check whether it's clear and, even in the case of very dark beers like stouts and porters, that light glows through it. In most cases you also want beer to have an attractive head of foam (the head shows good condition, offers a pleasing texture and also contains a lot of hop aroma); and it should be screaming 'drink me!'

Obviously, if you are looking at a cloudy wheat beer, a lambic (where there isn't supposed to be any head retention), or a clumsily poured or deliberately up-ended bottle-conditioned beer, you need to take this into account, but the next step will generally let you know whether the beer is meant to be cloudy, or whether it is just bad.

2. GIVE IT A SNIFF

The best way to get a good sniff is to pour a small amount of your beer into a glass (or ask the bar staff for a taster if it's on draught), put your hand over the top and swirl, then put your nose next to your glass and inhale deeply as you lift your hand up*.

You should sniff your beer quickly as some of the aromas dissipate fairly rapidly. The volatile notes from the hops or other botanicals in the beer are delicate scents that will flit off into the night like a will-o'-the-wisp if not appreciated in short order.

Inhaling the heady odours from your beer will also give you an idea of its condition and heighten your readiness to take that first glorious sip.

A point to note: if you like to wear a lot of perfume/aftershave or use heavily scented hand cream, this will affect what you're smelling.

3. TAKE A SLURP

Right, dive in. Take your first sip, or mouthful, and savour it. Let it work its way all round your mouth and assess what the texture and tastes are. The tongue is a miraculous organ, so give it a chance to do its work. You will be able to identify different flavours at different stages, partly through the physiology of your tongue and partly due to the order in which your brain processes them. With that first sip you are assessing the bits you like and, perhaps, the bits you don't like about a beer all in a matter of seconds.

You should also engage your retro-nasal system: blow some air back up your nose from the back of your throat. This area of your olfactory system perceives aroma as flavour and helps further analyse the beer's characteristics and store them in your memory.

Texture is also an important part of your drinking experience. Sometimes beers can taste nice but lack 'body' (in other words, they feel a bit thin); others seem almost oily (there's no fat in beer, however, or there certainly shouldn't be!). Does your beer taste bright and refreshing or rich and smooth?

4. AFTERTHOUGHTS

Once you've tasted your beer, consider the texture or 'mouthfeel' – is it silky and rounded, chewy and full-bodied or clean and fresh?

Finally, it's worth remembering that everyone's palate is utterly individual, or we'd all like the same things. So just because you can or can't smell or taste something, this doesn't mean you're wrong; it just means the other person is right about what they can sense. Please, make your own decisions; everything else (including this book) is just a guide.

Basic flavours

The tongue is a marvellous machine and has the ability to distinguish sweet, salty, sour, bitter and umami flavours.

Sweet

With so many sweet things that are so bad for us easily to hand these days, it's remarkable to think that sweetness was once a mechanism by which we identified much-needed nutrients.

You will almost always find some sweetness in your beer, even if it is a scarcely perceptible hint of biscuit, a tweak of marmalade or a mild molasses flavour. Sweetness has a very important role to play in bigger, richer styles like milk stouts, Scotch ales and barley wines, but is more of a background player in other, more quaffable styles, as a balance for the bitterness of hops or the astringency of heavily roasted malts. It is especially important when you start delving into the realms of sour beers, where the level of sweetness will often dictate whether you like a beer or not – also depending on your penchant for puckered cheeks!

Salty

It may sound like an odd one when it comes to beer, but sometimes the 'perception' of sea air is a very valid tasting note, even if there isn't actually a raised salt level in the beer.

On the other hand, you may not notice any saltiness at all, but when sodium (and to a lesser extent potassium) is present – just like the reason for using salt in your food – it enhances flavours, making them bolder and deeper. I often find this in beers made from natural mineral water sources.

Sour

This is a gauge for acidity in food and drink, an ancient sensation we have recognized since humans were hunter-gatherers and needed to check whether fruit was ripe (is there anything more disappointing than biting into an unripe peach, for example?). Sourness is also a key indicator in spoilt food.

It's not all bad, though. Sourness can be mouthwateringly refreshing (like lemon sherbet or sour cherry sweets) and can balance out other flavours (like a dash of vinegar in your salad dressing, a squeeze of lime on your Thai curry). As it's an extreme flavour experience, it varies wildly from individual to individual, which is why some people will happily down sour beers like wild ales and some can't.

Bitter

Bitterness is a key note in all beers. This bitterness comes from the oils in hops called alpha acids (more about those can be found in the section on how beer is made, on page 18, in case you skipped it), and for some drinkers extreme hop bitterness is the holy grail of beer-drinking. For others, bitterness is just nasty.

For most beer lovers, it's all about balance. A beer that has very little residual sugar but uses a huge amount of hops is likely to taste unpleasantly bitter and astringent, but if that alpha acid hit is balanced with good residual sugar and, as a general rule, a decent level of alcohol, your tongue will cope better with that bitterness.

Clockwise from top: Umami-packed soy sauce, bitters, sea salt, sour limes and sweet honey.

Umami

Umami was first identified as a separate taste in 1907 by Kikunae Ikeda of the Tokyo Imperial University. More recent research at Oxford University in 2000 confirmed umami as the fifth flavour.

Umami is a savoury, 'meaty' flavour found in, among other things, aged meats like Parma ham and bresaola, cheeses like Parmesan, seaweed and soy sauce, and you're probably wondering how it pertains to beer ...

Well, it only really applies to aged beers, which are nearly always strong in flavour. For example, old ales (see page 150) and wood-aged beers (see pages 196–198) often have a balsamic vinegar, Marmite-like or soy sauce note to them, which makes them deliciously moreish to some people but repulsive to others – it's that love it or hate it effect!

MY TASTE CHART

It is not always easy to translate into words what your nose and tongue are telling you unless you're used to doing so – so I've drawn up a list on the facing page to try and help you do just that! I've created what I hope is a user-friendly table of tasting terms that I use on a regular basis to describe the aromas and flavours in beer, but bear in mind that this list is just the tip of the iceberg. I use many other words, too, which you will come across in my tasting notes in the beer style chapters that follow.

It's partly to help you crystallize in your mind what it is you're tasting and, if you like to keep beer-tasting notes, make that process easier for you.

It's also designed so that when you go into the pub, off-licence or supermarket you can read tasting notes and translate them back to your experiences and gauge more quickly what it is that you like, or don't.

I'll admit I've used a bit of creative licence in how I've described things – for example, a nettle isn't exactly a flower, and a tomato is, botanically, a fruit rather than a vegetable – but while not everything is scientifically accurate, I think it's often more helpful to be instinctive.

I've included a section of what to look out for that's bad (see box, left); with some things this is very subjective.

For example, I dislike beers that have too much caramel in aroma and flavour (the fancy word for this is 'diacetyl') because I happen to be particularly sensitive to it; and I never drink beer from clear bottles because I always pick up light strike (where the hops degrade into a nasty whiff of damp dog in the bottle).

Weirdly, though, I'm not as sensitive to some of the sulphur compounds as my American counterparts – perhaps because a lot of British cask ale has a slightly sulphurous edge to it (comedically known as Burton snatch) and I've grown used to it.

And also, please feel free to add your own ideas to this list – it's *your* book, after all!

NASTY NIFFS, TERRIBLE TASTES AND SICKLY SENSATIONS

Cat's pee
Garlic/Rotten onion
Paper/Cardboard
Damp dog
Mouldy
Cheap malt vinegar
Cheesey
Rancid fat
Rotten egg
Over-boiled cabbage
Bad shrimp
Burning rubber tyre
Off meat
Granular
Oily

FRUITS AND FLOWERS

Lemon	Pear	Blackcurrant	Geranium	Prunes
Lime	Lychee	Blackberry	Elderflower	Raisins
Grapefruit	Passion fruit	Redcurrant	Marigold	Dates
Orange	Melon	Cherry	Nettles	Candied Peel
Apple	Raspberry	Pomegranate	Grass	
Banana	Strawberry	Rose	Hay	

VEGETABLES AND NUTS

Canned sweetcorn	Parsnip	Walnut	Coconut
Tomato vine	Celery	Almond	Baked beans
Stewed tomatoes	Onion	Pecan	

WOODS, HERBS AND SPICES

Pepper/Chilli	Cinnamon	Mahogany	Parsley
Coriander seed	Sandalwood	Pine	Fresh coriander/cilantro
Nutmeg/Mace	Pencil shavings	Resin	Bay leaf
Allspice	Oak	Sage	Garlic

SWEETIES AND PASTRIES

Juicy fruit	Corn syrup	Coffee	Sherbet
Bubblegum	Demerara sugar	Caramel	Cherry drops
Vanilla	Milk/dark chocolate	Toffee	Pear drops
Honey	Maltesers/Hershey's	Marshmallow	Fresh/Stale bread
Molasses	Whoppers	Liquorice	Toast/Burnt toast
Golden syrup	Mocha	Cola bottle sweets	Fruit cake

WINES AND SPIRITS

Sherry	Red wine	Riesling	Light/Peaty whisky
Madeira	Oaky white wine	Golden/Dark/Spiced rum	Brandy
Port	Muscat wine	Bourbon	

VINEGARS, SPREADS AND SAUCES

Balsamic vinegar	Soy sauce	Bovril	Marmalade
Sherry vinegar	Marmite	Jam	Quince/Membrillo

MOTHER NATURE AND MAN-MADE

After the rain	Autumn leaves	Leather	Nail polish remover
Sea air	Metallic	Plastic/Solvent	Tar

MOUTHFEELS

Silky	Astringent	Bitter	Salty
Warming	Mouth-coating	Sour	Sweet
Refreshing			

BEER AND FOOD

Now, I have to just say one thing here, I don't love beer and food because I'm biased, I love beer with food because, when it's done correctly, it's a transcendent gastronomic experience.

And because I'm a caring, sharing kind of person, I'd like to impart some of the finest pairings I've discovered over the past ten years. I've started with some generic suggestions, and you'll find hundreds of beer and food recommendations throughout the book so that you can experiment.

To me, beer is the most versatile alcoholic drink around: it enlivens sporting occasions, creates riotous nights out with friends and helps you relax after a hard day at work – what's not to adore about this glorious brew? But when I'm waxing really lyrical about beer, do you know what I love most about it? The way it can elevate food.

One of the reasons for my love affair with beer and food is that I'm a bit greedy! I adore the finer things in life when it comes to food and I'm lucky enough to have a modicum of skill in the kitchen. But while I'm passionate about sourcing top-quality produce for my dinner and treating it with respect, I'm also equally fond of a takeaway curry.

The great thing about beer is that it can go with everything from the simplest of dishes to haute cuisine. Sometimes a plate of cold meats and cheese is all you need.

Below: Chocolate and beer can be the best of friends, particularly rich old ales or barley wines.

MATCHES MADE IN HEAVEN

Many people believe that wine is generally a better match with food than beer is – I disagree.

Take cheese: it's a myth that wine is cheese's best friend. When you drink wine with cheese (though there are some exceptions) you end up with sensory overload, as your mouth is coated by the fats from the cheese. Beer, on the other hand, has a good, cleansing carbonation and a higher proportion of water, so it continually refreshes your palate.

Chocolate is difficult to match with wine for similar reasons, yet many beers go beautifully with chocolate. However, you do have to keep an eye on bitterness levels when dealing with higher cocoa solids chocolate – it's always best to steer towards the sweeter end of the beer spectrum, and the best partners I've found are beers like old and Scotch ales, barley wines and strong stouts. Having said that, some pale ales and IPAs are surprisingly good with white chocolate.

BASIC PRINCIPLES

The uniqueness of every palate is something to be celebrated – but it doesn't half make my job difficult sometimes! Mostly, when it comes to matters of taste, I will offer only guidelines. However, to help you discover some great gastronomic experiences, I would suggest that you stick to the following rules:

Cut, complement and contrast

- Cut – think about the way a sharp fruit- or vinegar-based sauce cuts through the richness of duck or pork belly and choose a beer style accordingly: it could be a citrussy pale ale or wheat beer to go with sashimi or a sharp geuze with a ripe blue cheese
- Complement – a creamy stout or coffeeish imperial porter goes brilliantly with a tiramisu, while a Trappist ale with a Flemish carbonnade (beef and beer stew) is a match made in heaven
- Contrast – a bold cherry wild ale is a delightful contrast to a chocolate mousse, while a shy, English-style mild is a surprising foil for rich pâté

Match strength of flavour in your beer with strength of flavour in your food. Delicate beer styles such as pilsner lager, golden ales and Kölsch will go well with delicate dishes, like steamed fish, whereas more robust beasts like IPAs and bocks will be needed for dishes like curries and barbecued or smoked meats

Try seasonal beers with seasonal foods: light blonde ales are delicious with asparagus, whereas deeper, richer old ales and winter warmers are excellent with rich casseroles

My final tip for matching beer and food is to try your beer first and then think about food. That's what I do when I'm planning a beer-and-food matched meal because, unless you are 100% familiar with your beer and your dish, it's all too easy to miss the mark.

Above: You can easily match a whole meal with beer, creating a perfect pairing for each course – yummy!

MATCHING BEER STYLES AND FOOD

Attempting to be definitive about beer and food pairing is a bit like herding cats: you will be successful at times but will inevitably be hissed at! You can't get it right every time because people's palates are so wildly different. So all I can do is share some of the beer and food partnerships that have worked well for me, either at home or when I've done a tasting for a room full of people.

In the table below I have suggested some of the best – and worst – food partners for the beer styles in Part Three (pages 56–207). I haven't included fruit and spiced beers or wood-aged beers because the vast array of flavours within each of those categories is too diverse to encapsulate here.

And, even within the main beer styles, the sheer diversity of how styles can be interpreted on a regional basis, combined with the inventiveness of brewers, means you will find variations all the time, so this is only a general guide, but I hope it will inspire you to experiment.

Bon appetit!

Left: Beer and cheese is a heavenly partnership of the highest order, from lambics with blue cheese to vintage ales paired with ripe brie.

BEER TYPE	GREAT WITH	THREE BEST FRIENDS	AVOID
Lambic, geuze	Rich fatty meats, smoked fish, smelly cheese, charcuterie	Blue cheese, oysters, air-dried hams	Heavy spices, Cheddar cheese, tomato-based sauces, yogurt, custard
Wheat beer	Thai food, sushi, sashimi, salty cured meats, shellfish	Thai green curry, tuna sashimi, mussels (both with and cooked in)	Chocolate, salty cheeses, berries
Lager, Kölsch	Gently spiced food, barbecued meat, tapas	Tagines, frittata, lemon meringue	Heavy spices, most cheese other than mild ones
Blonde ale (UK and US styles)	Light cheeses, fried chicken, Cajun/jerk spices, seafood	Chicken Caesar salad, fresh prawns, jerk salmon	Hot curries, red meats, game, duck, goose, venison

BEER TYPE	GREAT WITH	THREE BEST FRIENDS	AVOID
Belgian-style blonde ale and tripel	Dry curries, woody herbs, white chocolate, strong hard cheeses, asparagus	Malaysian beef rendang, griddled asparagus, salty hard cheeses like Cheddar	Salads, white fish, creamy desserts, mild cheese
Saison, bière de garde	Rich meats, rind-washed cheeses, oily fish	Pork belly, duck cassoulet, Port Salut cheese	South-east Asian spices, shellfish, chocolate
New World-style pale ale	Tropical fruits, shellfish, burgers	Steamed lobster, tropical fruit salad, fried bar snacks	Sharp cheese, creamy sauces, aniseed flavours
IPA	Game, hot and spicy dishes, rich meats, smoked fish and meats, white chocolate	Smoked duck or goose, citrus cheesecake, mature goat's cheese	Dark chocolate, delicate seafood, caramelized onions
Bitter and British-style pale ale	Roast red meat, salty/nutty cheeses, granary bread, cold meat, ham	Roast beef, Lancashire hotpot, ploughman's lunch (crusty bread and mature British cheese/Comté)	Creamy spicy food, almost anything sweet, anything strongly vinegary
Strong ale, e.g. Trappist and Scotch ale	Slow cooked beef stews, black pudding, Stilton and other blue cheese, crème caramel	Ox cheek stew, blue cheese soufflé with chicory and walnut salad, cherry pie and custard	Bananas, delicate seafood, chicken, Chinese and Thai flavours
Barley wine	Caribbean spicing, strong cheese, figs, candied fruits	Jerk pork, blue cheese, fruit cake	Shellfish, creamy curries, milk/white chocolate
Old ale	Vinegar-based sauces, soft cheese, berry fruits, dark chocolate	Balsamic glazes, strawberries dipped in chocolate, Vacherin	Tropical fruit, seafood, heavy spices
Mild	Seared meats, pâté, milk chocolate, candied fruits, medium-hard aged cheeses	Aged Gouda, strong liver pâté, milk chocolate mousse	White fish, seafood, dark chocolate, strong cheese, strong spices
Porter, stout	Caribbean spices, coffee, berries, game, offal	Venison, cherries, dark chocolate	Meaty fish, goat's cheese, acidic fruits, veal

BEER IS GOOD FOR YOU!

Above: He's smiling because he knows that beer, in moderation, makes you both happy and healthy. Painted by Petrus Staverenus, 1635–1666.

With all the shrill headlines and scaremongering about alcohol and health, it's sometimes difficult to remember that, when taken in moderation, some drinks can offer positive health benefits – and beer is certainly one of them.

Good-quality artisan beer contains vitamins and minerals that, in combination with a healthy diet and exercise, will do you some good – but that doesn't mean you can use beer's benefits as an excuse to skip the gym, or you'll get me in trouble!

HISTORICALLY HEALTHY

For millennia, until the advent of modern medicine, beer played a vital role in keeping whole nations healthy. Long before we knew what bacteria or viruses were, people were aware that drinking beer (which is boiled during its creation process) was much safer than drinking water, which was often contaminated with unmentionable horrors!

And, incredibly, it would appear that the Nubians (an ancient African civilization) were knowingly brewing an antibiotic beer nearly 2000 years ago. Chemist Mark Nelson, lead author of a paper published in June 2010 in the *American Journal of Physical Anthropology*, says that the bones of ancient Sudanese Nubians shows they were ingesting the antibiotic tetracycline on a regular basis, and that the source of this antibiotic was most likely from a special brew of beer.

In the past decade, wine producers, vociferously abetted by wine writers, seem to have been particularly successful in promoting the message that wine is good for you. OK, it is, but so is beer, or any other alcoholic drink, as long as it's consumed in moderation.

WILL BEER MAKE ME FAT?

If you drink too much of it, yes it will. Just like every other pleasure in life, you should enjoy beer in moderation (which I will admit is easier said than done). It is, however, lower in calories than most other alcoholic drinks, but don't take this as carte blanche to drink loads of it, because it can quickly add up!

That said, beer is fat-free, contains no cholesterol, and has some positive health benefits that other alcoholic drinks don't, so keep reading.

Is beer vegetarian?

Most beers are vegetarian, with four simple ingredients: malted grains, water, hops and yeast. However, most cask ales come into contact with a product called isinglass, which is used to clarify the beer as it conditions in the cask. Isinglass has long been used in the food and drink industry, in a similar way to gelatine; while gelatine is derived from animal collagen, isinglass is extracted from the swim bladders of fish. If you are strictly vegetarian, look for bottled beers with your country's vegetarian regulatory body's stamp on the label.

HEALTH BENEFITS

Good-quality craft beer contains: B vitamins, which help prevent heart disease; niacin, which lowers cholesterol and aids sleep; soluble fibre, which is good for your heart and other parts; and polyphenols, which are natural antioxidants.

And, as if all that wasn't enough, beers containing high levels of malted barley and hops are rich in the mineral silicon – which is needed for the growth and development of bones and connective tissue. A study by the Department of Food Science and Technology at the University of California published in February 2010 (Casey et al., Silicon in beer and brewing, *Journal of the Science of Food and Agriculture*) found that beer is a rich source of dietary silicon – and may help prevent osteoporosis.

Wheat contains less silicon than barley because it is the husk of the barley that is rich in this element, while grains such as roasted barley and chocolate and black malt, which are used in brewing darker beers like porter and stout, have lower silicon contents than pale-coloured malts. So, to make the utmost of this potential health benefit, I shall continue drinking beer regularly, in moderation – and will also keep trying different types of beer!

However, I shall also continue debunking myths like the one that stout is particularly good for you over other beers: it's an urban myth with a very long history, and, bizarrely and worryingly, is still being perpetuated by some members of the medical profession even today. For more on this, see page 170.

Below: You need strong bones to hold beer mugs this big, and beer can help build them.

Beer

Styles

PART THREE

and Brand Heroes

At this point you might well have a Homer Simpson moment, as your brain says, 'Mmmmm, beer!' and sends you off to the fridge.

In this section I describe some obscenely good beers from all around the world. Sprinkled among the descriptions I've also tried to offer some insight into the history of how these brews have developed and diverged, resulting in today's ever-expanding cosmos of beer.

I have arranged the styles roughly by colour, from light to dark, but there will always be exceptions, not least because modern breweries are constantly coming up with new and often unique takes on each style. Alternatively, you can just look at the pictures and drool a little!

WILD BEER

Beers brewed with wild yeasts can be as mouthwateringly tingly as sherbet or as sour as an unripe plum, but their feral fermentation and maturation processes make them unique among beer styles.

WHERE THE WILD THINGS ARE ...

In the past ten years or so, the use of wild yeasts and other wee beasties has blossomed to become one of the most exciting categories in the world of beer. With flavours that can be akin to manzanilla sherry, cider, or even vinegar, wild beer's generally dry nature makes it the perfect apéritif: it is certain to get the taste buds racing. There are several schools of wild ales: traditional lambics, Flemish brown and red ales and new-wave sours.

To be called a lambic the beer has to be brewed in Belgium, in the area of Pajottenland around Brussels, where brewers still use the traditional method of allowing wild yeasts and other micro-organisms to spontaneously ferment the beer – which is covered by the EU as a Traditional Speciality Guaranteed (TSG).

As well as the usual warm-fermenting yeast strain of *Saccharomyces cerevisiae*, which is floating around in the atmosphere, there are also wild *Brettanomyces* yeasts and bacteria that give lambics and other sour beers their distinctive character. *Pediococcus*, or pedio as it is known in the trade, can produce some buttery, caramel flavours in a beer and *Lactobacillus*, or lacto, is the beast responsible mainly for vibrant, sour and tart flavours.

Facing page: The wild bunch: from traditional Belgian specialities to some 21st-century interpretations, their super-sour flavours set tongues tingling.

Below: The copper at Cantillon brewery in Brussels, Belgium, famous for its traditional wild beer.

WE ❤ BACTERIA!

Lactobacillus and *Pediococcus* bacteria (which are both in the *Lactobacillaceae* family) are also responsible for yogurt (fermented milk) and sauerkraut (fermented cabbage); this bacterial fermentation creates a sour flavour and has a preservative effect, greatly extending the life of the milk or cabbage.

UNIQUE LAMBICS

Lambics are generally made with both malted barley and unmalted wheat, the latter of which can account for between 30 and 40 per cent of the grist. Lambics also contain a huge amount of hops, but these hops are generally old and stale. The lambic brewer uses hops for preservative purposes rather than for flavour, as the beers are matured for up to three years; by allowing the hops to lose all their bittering alpha acids and essential oils, the brewer ensures that the beers don't become undrinkably bitter.

The way lambic is fermented, in open shallow vats that allow maximum exposure to the elements and the local wild yeasts, accounts for a big chunk of its character, but much of its unique nature is also down to how it's aged. Still fermenting, the brew is transferred to barrels; as the yeast action wanes, the bacteria take over.

Below: Barrels play a huge role in traditional lambic brewing. These ones are at the Cantillon brewery in Brussels.

While many beer enthusiasts are raving about barrel-aging (see pages 196–198) as a cracking innovation for the beer sector, the boys from Belgium are shrugging their shoulders and failing to see what all the fuss is about because they've been doing it for centuries. Some breweries use new oak, which means there aren't any bacteria or yeasts in them from previous alcoholic residents, and others take containers from wine, sherry and port producers that are rife with additional natural beasties from the production of those drinks.

As the beer ages, a certain amount – known as the 'the angel's share' – evaporates. Lambic brewers don't top up the barrel, which means that after three years as much as 30 per cent of the barrel may be empty. Although topping up the barrels would allow the breweries to make more money, they prefer to preserve the beer's complexity and concentration of flavours (something to bear in mind if you are blanching at the price tag).

The talented Tomme Arthur of Lost Abbey, both saint and sinner!

THE FERAL FRATERNITY

It's not just lambics that employ these disorderly micro-organisms. Flanders brown (Oud Bruin) style and Flanders red-style beers (whether from northern Belgium or further afield) use them in either the long first fermentation and maturation in wood or the secondary fermentation in bottle.

In America and other areas of the world, however, brewers really aren't that keen on feral yeasts invading their breweries, as these sour-faced little beasts and their bacterial buddies will spoil their other beers with their bumptious flavours. Instead, they brew the beer in exactly the same way as any other ale (nearly always ale; I haven't heard of a sour lager yet, but if anyone is doing it, it's the Americans). Then they carefully select bacteria and various cultivated wild yeast strains (I know that's an oxymoron, but it's what the term is in the brewing world) and inoculate the beer with them.

Even the beer heaven that is the Trappist monastery of Orval (see page 143) has tamed one of these savage beasts to give this divine beer its distinct edge.

CANTILLON GUEUZE 100% LAMBIC BIO

Website: www.cantillon.be
Brewed in: Brussels, Belgium
First brewed: 1900
Grains: Malted barley, unmalted wheat
Hops: Fuggles
ABV: 5%

Appearance: Cloudy, light orange-yellow, no foam
Aroma: Sherbet, bread starter, wood
Flavour: Lemon juice, sourdough bread, fino sherry
Great with: Cold smoked fish, soft blue cheese, berry sorbet

THE BEER

Full of spritz and sparkle, this beer seems like every bottle comes with a lemon sherbet fairy who pops out and shakes her zingy dust over your nose and then zips around distributing a robust sourness on your palate. But it's not all aggressive flavours, as the beer is softened slightly by a pleasant fino sherry-like mustiness before the magical nature of the spontaneous fermentation's flavours reassert themselves to tingle all over your tongue.

THE BREWERY

The Cantillon brewery in Brussels is literally a working museum; run by the amazing Van Roy family, this brewery would stop producing and championing these incredible beers only over their dead bodies!

Started in 1900 by Paul Cantillon in the Anderlecht area of Brussels, it was one of hundreds of breweries in the Belgian capital at the time, but is now Brussels' only surviving example of a lambic producer. After World War II, Paul's sons Robert and Marcel took over the brewery and it soared to an annual production of 2,500 hectolitres (55,000 gallons). Marcel's son-in-law Jean-Pierre Van Roy entered the business in 1968 and can still be found there today, pretending to look stern but with a twinkle in his eye for those who love Cantillon's beers. His children have followed in his footsteps: Jean is now the main creative force behind the beers, and has produced some truly original and stunning seasonal releases such as Pinot d'Aunis, made from grapes of the same name, and Fou'Foune, made with French Bergeron apricots. Jean-Pierre's daughter Julie is also involved in the business.

The brewery has, by its own standards, undergone quite a radical overhaul, and there is now a new tasting hall and visitors' centre, which will showcase some of the machinery previously left lying around the brewery gathering dust, cobwebs and wild yeast cells in equal measure. But the brewery retains much of its former charm, with its original open vats up in the eaves and rickety stairs everywhere; this isn't a squeaky-clean laboratory, this is a place where wild yeasts need to dwell, along with the other beasts that give Cantillon's beer its character: there are known to be 86 different micro-organisms in Cantillon's lambic.

The sour family

Lambic

Unblended, single-vintage, sour, cloudy, scary-looking stuff that can produce some of the most extreme sensations on your tongue! As it has been maturing quietly in its barrel for a year or more, it is totally flat – and you'll hardly ever find it in a bottle, only on tap in the beer cafés of Belgium. Many people's first reaction to straight lambic is that it's a bit like licking a battery while under a horse blanket (I know that's not selling it to you very well, but it's weirdly pleasant), but a second sip allows you to admire its bracing brilliance. Truly magnificent with blue cheese.

Geuze

Sometimes spelt gueuze, this is generally a blend of one-, two- and three-year-old lambic which is then bottled. It undergoes a secondary fermentation in the bottle to produce a vibrant, sparkly, slightly less sour drink than straight lambic. It can be cellared well for more than a decade.

Faro

This is sweetened lambic, for those who find that sharp, sherbet aspect a bit too much. Generally softened with brown sugar, caramel or molasses, it is very easy drinking and is lovely enjoyed as a summertime pre-dinner palate livener.

Fruit

Kriek, made from cherries, is probably the best-known fruit style of wild beer, with framboise/frambozen, made from raspberries, a close second. However, there are wild and sour ales that use everything from cloudberries to grapes and lychees to lemons. Often a bed of these fruits is added to the barrels in which the beer will finish its fermentation and maturation, providing not only flavour but also some sugars for the bacterial fermentation to work on. Generally you'll find that these tart, tangy beers are fabulous accompaniments to rich chocolate desserts or even rich meats like duck.

Flanders brown

Often described as Oud Bruin (old brown), these ales either naturally pick up *lactobacillus* bacteria, or have them introduced, to give a sour edge. The classic Belgian example is Liefmans Goudenband. From Oregon, Deschutes' The Dissident is a great New World take on the style.

Flanders red

Using a special reddish malt in their brewing process and aged for over a year in oak, these beers have very little bitterness but a noticeable tannic astringency, along with a sourness from the introduction of lactobacillus. Rodenbach Grand Cru and Duchesse de Bourgogne from the Verhaeghe brewery (see page 67) are my favourites in this style.

Off piste!

Just like any other beer category, these days the only limit on the flavours in wild beer is the brewer's imagination. Cantillon in Belgium produces one-off lambics from time to time, using rare ingredients like sea buckthorn berries.

American brewers such as Russian River in California (see page 67), Destihl from the wonderfully named town of Normal, Illinois, and Colorado's New Belgium, will use any mix of grains that takes their fancy and select any number of wild yeasts and bacteria, then blend them with fruit, age them in various spirit or wine barrels and, finally, blend the final beer offering.

LOVIBONDS SOUR GRAPES

Website: www.lovibonds.co.uk
Brewed in: Henley on Thames, Oxfordshire, UK
First brewed: 2009
Grains: Malted wheat, carapils malt, lager malt, acidulated malt
Hops: Hallertauer Hersbrucker

ABV: 4.8%
Appearance: Pinky red, low foam
Aroma: Spiced plums, cinnamon, apple sherbet
Flavour: Ripe berries, oak, quality red wine vinegar, green apple finish
Great with: A few squares of very good dark chocolate

THE BEER

As lip-smackingly satisfying and tongue-tingling as any of its Belgian counterparts, Lovibonds Sour Grapes is a genuine flavour sensation, and a rare wild beer on Britain's shores.

With an intriguing aroma like cinnamon and plum pie, it leads through to a beautifully acidulated flavour, full of earthy spice and finishing off on an unexpectedly clean, high note of green apple.

The beer itself is the result of a happy accident. In 2008 a batch of the brewery's Henley Gold wheat beer, which is very lightly hopped, became infected with *lactobacillus* and turned into something resembling a Berliner Weisse (see page 74). Owner Jeff Rosenmeier discarded most of it, but not before he and his right-hand man Jason Stevenson had decided they rather liked it. Then about 100 batches later the same thing happened. Jeff sourced some casks from a Sussex winery that had previously been filled with Pinot Noir and decided that it would be a good idea to add some *Brettanomyces* too, using three separate strains; Sour Grapes was born nine months later.

Now, given the beer's popularity, the brewery is operating a sherry solera-style system, topping up the three Pinot barrels alternately with fresh Henley Gold and any further spoilt beer. Rosenmeier plans to release it more widely at the end of 2011.

THE BREWERY

In June 2005, Jeff Rosenmeier left a successful career in software engineering to pursue his passion for brewing. He set up a small brew plant on his property and began piloting his flagship beers on a small scale. The inspiration for the Lovibonds name came when Jeff was looking for a home for his brewery in Henley on Thames; he found a site that had previously been home to John Lovibond & Sons, Brewers and Merchants, and moved right in.

The popularity of his Henley Dark and Henley Gold, as well as some special Reserve versions, has seen the team expand, and you can expect some more exciting developments from the brewery in coming years.

One eagerly awaited project is the result from a bottle of the old Lovibond brewery's Yeoman Ale, circa 1950, which literally dropped on Jason's head during a clean-out of old racking. Experts at the University of Sunderland are attempting to isolate the original yeast strain for brewing.

THE LOST ABBEY CUVEE DE TOMME

Website: www.lostabbey.com
Brewed in: San Marcos, California, USA
First brewed: 1998
Grains: Pale, crystal, chocolate and special B malts; unmalted wheat
Hops: German Magnum

Adjuncts: Sour cherries
ABV: 11%
Appearance: Ruby red, rocky foam
Aroma: Sour cherry, vanilla, wood
Flavour: Cherry, digestive biscuit, vinous
Great with: Best enjoyed by itself

THE BEER

Cuvee de Tomme takes a whole raft of influences from the world's brewing scene and adds a California twist. Rich, rounded, tart and balanced, the firm foundation of flavour and richness of mouthfeel is from the use of darker malts, which along with the astringency from the wood, creates as pleasing a flavour as a chocolate-coated digestive biscuit dunked in strong tea. The faint tinkly hop character combines with the gloriously refreshing sourness to lift the almost sticky cherry and red wine flavours and prevent the vanilla-like bourbon and brandy notes becoming too cloying.

Interestingly even the brewery doesn't know exactly what is in the mix. The yeast for the primary fermentation comes from the Trappist abbey of Westmalle (see page 147) and then, in barrel, head brewer Tomme Arthur adds *Brettanomyces* and some other secret organisms. In 2010 the brew was split across bourbon barrels, red wine and brandy barrels for aging, resulting in a more rounded character.

THE BREWERY

Lost Abbey is a sister operation to Port Brewing, which grew out of the Pizza Port brewpubs owned by brother and sister Vince and Gina Marsaglia. They asked their director of brewing operations, Tomme Arthur, to join them in setting up Port Brewing – and the beer world has been grateful ever since. Port Brewing produces a range of hop-led beers, with a few seasonal strongs and other specialities; but the Lost Abbey label, inspired by Belgian brewing traditions, is where the magic truly happens. Lost Abbey's slogan is 'Inspired Beer for Sinners and Saints Alike', and the divine beers they produce are sinfully good.

Tomme says his biggest inspiration for brewing his range of wild ales, and Cuvee de Tomme in particular, was, 'the sheer amount of Rodenbach I was drinking, I wanted something with the essence of Flanders but the balls of American craft brewing.'

MORE TO TRY ...

Boon Geuze Mariage Parfait

Website: www.boon.be
Brewed in: Lembeek, Belgium
ABV: 8%
Appearance: Cloudy orange, little to no head
Aroma: Lemon peel, biscuit, crushed autumn leaves
Flavour: Candied peel, fresh bread, overripe lime skin
Great with: Smoked mackerel pâté, tarragon-butter monkfish, ash-covered goat's cheese

This hand-selected blend of one-, two- and three-year old lambics varies year by year but is always magnificent. More rounded than many other geuze beers, it has a strong underpinning of soft wheat and biscuit, which balance out the typically sharp, sour and almost vinegary aspects of the beer.

Drie Fonteinen Oude Geuze

Website: www.3fonteinen.be
Brewed in: Beersel, Belgium
ABV: 6%
Appearance: Pale cloudy lemon, short-lived head
Aroma: Yogurt, lemon peel, earthy
Flavour: Sherbet, autumn leaves, metallic
Great with: Smoked duck, spicy salami, well-aged blue cheese

This is not a beginners' beer. Complex, funky, dairy farm aromas absolutely dominate the nose, with just a mere hint of citrus poking through, and on the palate nothing much changes apart from the fact that it's joined by a super-sour sherbet flavour, finishing in a clean metallic/mineral end. Basically, this beer will dance on your tongue and mess with your head!

Liefmans Cuvée Brut Kriek

Website: www.liefmans.be
Brewed in: Oudenaarde, Belgium
ABV: 6%
Appearance: Cloudy cherry juice, head with a hint of palest pink
Aroma: Cherry drops, marzipan, vanilla
Flavour: Sour cherry, burnt caramel, oak
Great with: Blue steak, roast duck, dark chocolate ice cream

This is made by macerating fresh whole cherries in old brown ale, and with 13kg (29lb) of cherries to every 100 litres (22 gallons) of beer, it's not surprising that the fruit is a predominant character. However, this doesn't make it a one-note drink: the sourness of both the fruit and the beer itself, and the fact that it's blended with some of the brewery's excellent Goudenband – a stronger Flanders old brown – offers an additional sweet and woody note to the whole affair.

Lindemans Pecheresse

Website: www.lindemans.be
Brewed in: Vlezenbeek, Belgium
ABV: 2.5%
Appearance: Sunlit peach, soft rocky cream head
Aroma: Peach, apricot, underripe raspberry
Flavour: Peach, brioche, cherry sherbet
Great with: Coronation chicken, red mullet, peach cobbler

The most gentle introduction to the world of wild ales you could wish for, with a pretty label, too! While this beer may sound too sweet for some, it is saved from being cloying by that sharp edge that the wild ale base brings to the party. A very straightforward beer, pleasing for its fruity honesty.

Rodenbach Grand Cru

Website:	www.rodenbach.be
Brewed in:	Roeselare, Belgium
ABV:	6%
Appearance:	Ruby red, light fluffy head
Aroma:	Oak, biscuit, underripe raspberry
Flavour:	Red Bordeaux, raisin, burnt toast
Great with:	Caviar on blinis, Singapore spicy noodles, Brie-like cheeses

Often described as the wine of the beer world, this is a great introductory beer to the sour side. Full of oak, biscuit and fruit notes on the nose, it blossoms on the palate into strong red wine, raisin and roasty, toasty notes, with just a hint of sourness, to create some complexity and cleanliness at the end. I often use this as an apéritif to an evening's beer and food matching, as it get the taste buds going without being overwhelmingly sour.

Russian River Temptation

Website:	www.russianriverbrewing.com
Brewed in:	Santa Rosa, California, USA
ABV:	7.25%
Appearance:	Subdued orange colour, low foam
Aroma:	Vanilla, green grapes, oak
Flavour:	Underripe green apple, soft apricot, wood sap
Great with:	Young Gorgonzola, roast chicken, sheep's milk ice cream

Temptation is aptly named, and was owner Vinnie Cilurzo's first experiment with Belgian wild ales – it turned out to be a very successful experiment. He begins by inoculating a Belgian-style blonde ale with Brettanomyces yeast before aging it for 12 months in French oak Chardonnay barrels from local wineries. He then re-ferments it in bottle to create a spritzy refreshing ale with mouth-wateringly sour green apple and vanilla aromas and flavours.

Verhaeghe Duchesse de Bourgogne

Website:	www.brouwerijverhaeghe.be
Brewed in:	Vichte, Belgium
ABV:	6%
Appearance:	Chocolate brown with ruby highlights, soft rocky head
Aroma:	Balsamic vinegar, sour cherries, bitter chocolate
Flavour:	Mixed berries, cocoa powder, aged balsamic vinegar
Great with:	Chargrilled ribeye steak, Toulouse sausages, aged Camembert

The Duchesse is definitely a regal beer; an ideal apéritif, it activates every part of your tongue with its super-sour, vinegary attitude. However, this sourness is partly balanced by the lovely fruitiness and bitter chocolate notes that come through. When you first try this beer, I recommend you do so with some food, cheese in particular, as its intense vinegary notes can come as a bit of a shock!

Others to try

Alken-Maes Mort Subite Oude Gueuze, Belgium
De Molen Vlaams & Hollands, Netherlands
Deschutes The Dissident, Oregon, USA
Destihl Flanders/Oud Bruin, Illinois, USA
Goose Island Sofie, Illinois, USA
Liefmans Goudenband, Belgium
LoverBeer BeerBera, Italy
New Belgium Tart Lychee, Colorado, USA

WHEAT BEER

As cloudy as a winter morning or as clear as a spring afternoon, wheat beers are as diverse as the brewer's imagination can make them. But wherever they're from, wheat beers are spicy little numbers to challenge your senses and awesome food matches for nearly any kind of cuisine.

WHY WHEAT?

Over the centuries wheat beers have developed their own regional identities, but the thing that unites them as a category is the use of one specific grain – wheat! However, wheat is never used exclusively: the brew will always include malted barley and the ratio of wheat to barley is generally between 30 and 70 per cent. Depending on the recipe, the wheat may be malted or unmalted.

Wheat itself doesn't actually contribute masses of flavour, but it does add to the body and mouthfeel of a beer, and creates excellent head retention, often leaving you with a lovely foam moustache! The proteins in wheat also contribute to the predominantly cloudy style of this beer; the cloudiness is even more pronounced if the brewers choose not to filter their beer, leaving the yeast in for flavour.

When it comes to the history of wheat beer, it's fair to assume that wheat has been used in the brewing process for at least 4000 years, as archaeological evidence puts the development of wheat as a crop in the same area as the birthplace of brewing, the Fertile Crescent in western Asia, modern day Iran and Iraq.

In more recent history, two countries, Belgium and Germany, have emerged as major exponents of the wheat beer style, so I'm going to give you a short introduction to these two countries' relationship with this beer.

BRING ON THE BELGIANS

The Belgian style of wheat beer is generally cloudy and lemony in colour. The local strains of yeast tend to be less aggressive in aroma and flavour than their German counterparts. Most of the strong spice and fruit notes come from the addition of spices and other flavourings like orange peel, often from the Curaçao orange, which is particularly bitter and helps offset the sweetness of the malts used in the beer.

The renaissance of Belgian wheat beer was driven by the Hoegaarden brand. Its success swept the world and inspired many other craft brewers in this small country with a big brewing history to take up this incredibly refreshing and enjoyable style. Often flavoured with orange peel and coriander seed, it is nearly always a lovely light lemony colour and slightly cloudy.

Hoegaarden Witbier is named after its birthplace, a small town in the province of Flemish Brabant in Belgium, formerly part of the Netherlands. As early as 1445, monks took advantage of the local wheat and barley crops to make beer and at that time, before the widespread introduction of hops, the monastery brewers would have used herbs and

Facing page: Wheat beers cover a wide spectrum of colour and flavour.

Below: A large head is a classic part of the European wheat beer pour.

spices to disguise sour and stale flavours in their beers. It is not known precisely when coriander seed and orange peel were first used in Hoegaarden's beers, but as Belgium was part of the spice-trading Netherlands until the mid-18th century it's likely this had an influence.

Over the years the town's brewing industry expanded: in 1709, Hoegaarden boasted 12 breweries and by the 1750s there were 38, serving towns for miles around.

Sadly, though, in the 1950s the market turned its back on these cloudy, perfumed beauties and towards pale, sparkling lagers – and in 1957 the last wheat beer brewery in Hoegaarden, Tomsin, closed its doors.

However, one man was determined to revive the style. Pierre Celis had worked in the Tomsin brewery as a lad, and after his early 'garage' brews were well received, he opened his first commercial brewery in the mid-1960s. By 1985, he was producing 300,000 hectolitres (6.5 million gallons) a year. Unfortunately, he was ultimately the victim of a fire, which destroyed his vastly under-insured brewery. Enter Stella Artois with an offer to buy 45 per cent of the brewery, which was fine for a few years until that company merged with another and everything became about economies of scale. Hoegaarden is now part of A-B InBev, the world's largest brewing group.

Pierre Celis went on to create Grottenbier (a dark beer originally matured in caves) and a wheat beer for the St Bernardus brewery. He became a brewing icon all over the world. He died in 2011 at the age of 85.

Celis's determination to fight for the style captured the beer world's imagination and has ensured that wheat beer is still here to refresh us today. Today's Hoegaarden is sadly lacklustre, but Blanche de Namur from the Bocq brewery and Blanche de Bruxelles (see page 76) are just two of many fine examples of the style.

Please don't garnish your beer

I have just one thing to ask of you: please don't put slices of citrus fruit in your wheat beer. It kills the head and masks the true flavours, it's a bad idea that was developed by bad marketing people and it makes for a bad drinking experience. There, I'm done, carry on!

GERMAN WEISSE BEERS

In Germany, the warm-fermenting yeast used for wheat beers has mutated to give quite aggressive flavours of overripe fruit, bubblegum and clove. These are particularly apparent in the unfiltered style known as Hefeweizen – which directly translates as yeast-wheat.

The history of wheat beer in Germany is an interesting one. Basically, as with so many things in life, being able to drink wheat beer separated the haves from the have-nots.

In 1516 the now-famous Reinheitsgebot (see below), or Purity Law, was introduced, requiring brewers in Bavaria in southern Germany to use only barley, water and hops.

Reinheitsgebot – the German beer purity law

These days the Reinheitsgebot, literally 'purity law', is little more than a marketing tool used by brewers the world over to emphasize the 'purity' of their beer, but it played a huge role in shaping one of the largest beer-drinking and beer-producing nations in the world.

The Purity Law was drawn up by a Bavarian ruler and introduced in 1516. It decreed that the only ingredients to be used in brewing beer must be barley, hops and water. They didn't understand much about yeast back then; that was added later. A key motive for the law was to prevent brewers from using grains that were needed for breadmaking, like wheat and rye.

As Bavaria expanded and become a large and important kingdom, the rules were implemented in other parts of Germany. With the unification of the country in 1871, the Reinheitsgebot gave government the tools to regulate the ingredients and quality of beer sold to the public (and to levy taxes on beer!). Later, the law was modified and updated, with the addition of yeast as a basic ingredient and malted wheat as an allowable ingredient in top-fermented beers such as Weissbier.

In 1988, a European Court of Justice ruling effectively wiped out the Reinheitsgebot by insisting that anything permitted in other foods was also allowed in beer. Beer is now subject to regular food additives laws, athough beer brewed according to the Reinheitsgebot (using only water, malt, hops and yeast) receives special treatment as a protected, 'traditional' food.

Meet the family

Rather like the characters in a Russian novel, wheat beers use a number of similar-sounding but slightly different names. Brewers often label these beers as 'white' (*weiss* in German, *blanche* in French, *wit* in Dutch and Flemish) and certainly many of them have a cloudy haze – but there are also crystal-clear wheat beers and dark brown versions.

Dunkelweizen
German for 'dark wheat' – you will also see beers labelled Dunkle Weisse or Weissbier Dunkel (yes, that's 'dark white' or 'white beer dark'). All beers were dark before pale malts were developed and many brewers now make both dark and light versions.

Hefeweizen
German for 'yeast wheat'; also known as Hefeweissbier. As this as unfiltered, it has a lot of the strong clove/banana/bubblegum aromas and flavours thrown off by German wheat beer yeasts.

Kristall/Crystal
A clear, filtered wheat beer, from which the yeast and much of the wheat protein has been removed. It is fresher-tasting and lighter of body than Hefeweizen, less overwhelming and less full of those banana/clove flavours.

Weissbier
'White beer', or Bavarian-style wheat beer, which may be pale or dark.

Weizenbock
A dark wheat beer that's higher-strength than the average Dunkelweizen.

Witbier
Belgian-style wheat beer.

However, the nobility considered themselves well above this law and Munich's royal brewhouses continued to use wheat to brew beers for the landed gentry and aristocracy. Throughout the 16th to 18th centuries the brewing of wheat beer was strictly controlled and licensed by the dukes who ruled Bavaria. In 1872, royal control was loosened to move wheat beer brewing rights into the public domain. Georg Schneider was the first to acquire these rights. He was followed by others such as Erdinger, founded in 1886 and now the largest wheat beer brewer in Germany. Schneider's family brewery still produces a range of wheat beers, including the wheat doppelbock Aventinus (see page 77).

The modern story of German wheat beer is just as intriguing. It's hard to believe now but, just as in Belgium, the 1950s and early 1960s saw German wheat beer nearly disappear and then, for reasons no one seems able to explain, it suddenly became sexy again! Both men and women were enjoying it and it now accounts for around 35 per cent of the domestic market and has spread all around the world in exports and influence.

Above: How I imagine an idle nobleman cooling his wheat beer away from the commoners in olden times. In fact, this is an advertisement for Schneider Weisse beer.

Two wheat beers to try, Velvet Fog from Canada (below) and IJWit from the Netherlands (right).

BERLINER WEISSE

A northern German speciality, this beer is made with a less assertive strain of yeast than south German-style wheat beers and is also fermented with *Lactobacillus*. This bacterial fermentation gives it an exceptionally sour, slightly creamy edge. It is something of an acquired taste and, while I'd urge you to try it 'au naturel', it is traditional to add a dash or two of woodruff (a slightly bitter herb) or raspberry syrup.

OTHER WORLD WHEAT BEERS

The characteristic flavours of German and Belgian wheat beers have inspired brewers in other parts of the world to come up with their own versions. Some use regular warm-fermenting yeast, like the UK's Otley O-Garden (see facing page); others choose the very aromatic German wheat beer yeast, such as the UK's Bristol Beer Factory's Bristol Hefe; the more restrained Belgian yeast is used elegantly in the easy-drinking Coors Blue Moon from North America. It all depends on how the brewer wants their beer to taste.

OTLEY O-GARDEN

Website: www.otleybrewing.co.uk
Brewed in: Pontypridd, Wales
First brewed: 2007
Grains: Pale malt, torrified wheat
Hops: Amarillo, Celeia
Additional ingredients: Clove, coriander, orange peel

ABV: 4.8%
Appearance: Hazy light amber, open foamy head
Aroma: Passion fruit, citrus, spice
Flavour: Earthy orange, full spice, zingy citrus finish
Great with: Marmalade-glazed ham, roast goose, tiramisu

THE BEER

There are few other beers of this strength that throw out this much aroma and still manage to be superbly drinkable.

When you pop the cap off the bottle-conditioned version or stand close enough to the bar when O-Garden is being poured, you cannot mistake that there is orange and clove in the beer, topped by some tropical fruit – it's utterly enticing. When you take your first sip, you get a slightly sweet clove spice up-front, then a more earthy note from the coriander and then a super-zingy finish from the orange and a refreshing bitterness from the hops.

Like so many of the world's great beers, O-Garden was a bit of a happy accident, as co-owner of the brewery Nick Otley explains: 'Initially we were trying to make it like Weissbier, but the yeast didn't arrive in time and so we used our normal ale yeast and we decided to turn it into a crystal by roughly filtering it.

'The only thing we've changed from the original recipe are the hops: originally we used Styrian Goldings but we just couldn't get our hands on any, so we now use Celeia.

'The idea of using clove is a bit unusual, as many wheat beers derive their clove-like aroma from the yeast, but we spent quite a long time researching old recipes and some of them really did use clove as an ingredient.

'We've been quite surprised at its success: it's our third biggest seller and has won many awards, taking Champion Beer of Wales in 2010 and winning the Champion Beer of Britain Specialist category in 2008.

'And as for the name, we came up with it because we thought it was like walking through a kitchen into a herb garden ... or something like that.' I believe him, although thousands wouldn't!

THE BREWERY

They're a tight-knit family of Welshmen, so when Nick, Charlie and Matthew Otley come to town it's like being hit by a whirlwind of Celtic enthusiasm!

They dreamt up the idea of a brewery in 2005 over a few pints at one of their family's pubs in Pontypridd. As Nick says: 'We'd been involved in beer for as long as we could remember, and we all had a mid-drinking session moment of clarity that we should be brewing our own.

'A few weeks later three men fuelled with enthusiasm acquired an industrial unit and some kit, and with an aging Toyota pick-up and a couple of bags of hops and malt we founded our own little brewery.'

O-GARDEN
ABV 4.8%
500ML

BRASSERIE LEFEBVRE
BLANCHE DE BRUXELLES

Website: www.brasserielefebvre.be
Brewed in: Quenast, Belgium
First brewed: 1989
Grains: Pilsner malt, unmalted wheat
Adjuncts: Sugar
Hops: Styrian Goldings, Hallertauer
Additional ingredients: Coriander, Curaçao orange peel

ABV: 4.5%
Appearance: Cloudy lemon yellow, fluffy white head
Aroma: Lemon, biscuit, floral
Flavour: Lavender, biscuit, lemon zest
Great with: Sushi, simple chicken dishes, lemon posset

THE BEER

With the Mannekin Pis on the label you couldn't mistake this for anything other than a Belgian beer – and its refreshing, zingy character is almost as cheeky as the image.

A beautifully sweet, lemon meringue-like nose with underlying biscuit and a little floral touch leads into an initial flavour almost like lavender, until the citrus reasserts itself and the wheat lends a silkiness of mouthfeel. This refreshing beer is definitely an easy summer quaffer.

THE BREWERY

The more I research the history of Belgian brewing, the more I'm amazed there is one! Brasserie Lefebvre is the fifth brewery I've discovered that was almost brought to a shuddering halt by the Germans in World War I when they invaded and commandeered all the metal brewing vessels.

However, it's a testament to the indomitable Belgian spirit that what his father Jules started in Quenast in the Senne valley in 1876, Auguste Lefebvre

re-established in 1921 on a less flood-prone neighbouring hill. The third generation of Lefebvres, Gaston, joined the company soon afterwards and started bottle-conditioning the beers. After a period of growth and installation of the most modern equipment available, the brewery was hit by another world war. Although the brewery wasn't dismantled this time, the Germans decreed that the beer couldn't be brewed to anything above 0.8% abv, which meant the business took a turn for the worse.

Pierre Lefebvre took over the brewery in 1960 and his positive attitude and the introduction of new ales reinvigorated the business. The fifth generation came armed with a background in marketing and started searching for new opportunities, creating beers specifically for the Italian market and also gaining a licence from the Abbaye de Floreffe to produce its range of five beers. Blanche de Bruxelles was launched in 1989, followed by the honey beer Barbar, known and loved the world over. The brewery continues to thrive under the sixth generation of Lefebvres.

SCHNEIDER-WEISSE AVENTINUS

Website: www.schneider-weisse.de
Brewed in: Kelheim, Germany
First brewed: 1907
Grains: Pale ale malt, wheat malt, dark roasted barley
Hops: Hallertauer Magnum
ABV: 8.2%

Appearance: Chocolate brown, ruby highlights, large white head
Aroma: Caramelized bananas, nutty, burnt toast
Flavour: Warm chocolate caramel, bananas, light spicy bitter finish
Great with: Dry curry, chilli con carne, hard/salty cheeses

THE BEER

When it comes to the history of German wheat beers, Schneider Weisse has got it all sewn up, but that's not specifically why I chose this beer: it's because I think Aventinus – described by Schneider as a wheat doppelbock – is amazing!

I'm not the biggest fan in the world of sweet beers, so to find a sweet-ish beer that ticks all the boxes is brilliant.

The nose is a bit like those toffee bananas you get in old-school Chinese restaurants, with that wonderful crunchy caramel outside and a sprinkling of sesame seeds that adds nuttiness. All this follows through to the palate with an extra depth and warmth from the level of alcohol, the spicy clove note from the yeast and a slightly prickly zip from the hops.

It's also worth noting that this beer was invented by a woman. Despite being part of a brewing family dynasty, convincing your male counterparts in 1907 that you knew what you were doing in the brewhouse couldn't have been easy – so I doff my hat to Mathilde, wife of Georg Schneider III.

THE BREWERY

Georg Schneider I established his eponymous brewery in 1872, after he acquired the right to brew wheat beer from King Ludwig II of Bavaria. Sales of wheat beer had been declining in favour of lagers, but Schneider had a vision for the future and when he created Schneider Weisse at his newly renovated brewery in Munich he effectively reinvented wheat beer.

His successors expanded the business and bought other breweries in Munich, Kelheim and Straubing. However, in 1944 the Munich breweries – along with much of the city – were destroyed by bombs and all production was shifted to Kelheim, to the north of Munich. The role of the women in the Schneider family has always been important, and the wife of the then brewery owner Georg V coined the motto: 'Preserve the past and create for the future.'

The current Schneider at the helm of the brewery is Georg VI, who is keen to keep up the family traditions, not only brewing great beer but also naming his son Georg VII. I would imagine he too will run the brewery one day, as apparently his very first words were 'Schneider Weisse' – and I don't care if this is a made-up story, it's just too cute not to repeat!

MORE TO TRY ...

Allagash White

Website: www.allagash.com
Brewed in: Portland, Maine, USA
ABV: 5.5%
Appearance: Golden yellow, slightly cloudy, with a chunky white head
Aroma: Tomato vine, orange, coriander seed
Flavour: Ripe red apple, orange marmalade, earthy bitter finish
Great with: Sushi, tomato and basil spaghetti, herb-crusted charcuterie

This Belgian-style wheat beer, made with coriander seed, Curaçao bitter orange peel and a secret spice, is a real joy with food. Personally I like it with seafood pasta with a tomato and basil sauce, because its tomato vine earthiness really draws out the sweetness of the seafood and sauce, and the food brings out the citrus pop in the beer – perfect!

Bristol Hefe

Website: www.bristolbeerfactory.co.uk
Brewed in: Bristol, England
ABV: 4.8%
Appearance: Cloudy, primrose yellow, fluffy white head
Aroma: Raisin bread, banana, bubblegum
Flavour: Cloves, banana bread, grapefruit
Great with: Roast chicken and pink grapefruit salad, hot smoked salmon, Moroccan-spiced halloumi

I can't think of a better British version of the German-style Hefeweissbier (yeast-in wheat beer). Full of all the things every Weissbier fan will love – cloves, bubblegum and banana – but with a punchy pink grapefruit end that stops the whole thing from becoming too cloying and sweet.

Erdinger Weissbier

Website: www.erdinger.de
Brewed in: Erding, Germany
ABV: 5.3%
Appearance: Liquid sunshine, billowing white head
Aroma: Banana, bread, cloves
Flavour: Fruit bread, sweetened cream, herbal bitter finish
Great with: Chilli pumpkin soup, oysters Rockefeller, Roquefort

A slightly demure, but ever so drinkable, German Hefeweiss. I find this less cloying than other interpretations but with all the requisite banana, clove and herbal notes, and a refreshing mineral end – a lip-smacker for sure.

Brouwerij 't IJ, IJWit

Website: www.brouwerijhetij.nl
Brewed in: Amsterdam, Netherlands
ABV: 7%
Appearance: The colour of golden syrup, soft creamy head
Aroma: Flapjack, toast, orange marmalade
Flavour: Honey, earthy spice, citrus peel
Great with: Edam, cured ham, orange sorbet

A visit to Amsterdam's micro-brewery and a bottle of IJWit is more fun, and definitely more rewarding, than any of the city's cafés (cough, cough)! The sweet, flapjack and honey body with its earthy middle and citrus pow end will give you more than enough of a high to last the day – but beware the strength behind the soft flavours.

Made with a mix of Corsican herbes du maquis, Colomba has an almost gin-like juniper and lavender nose followed by a heady, perfumed and citrus aspect on both the nose and palate.

Weihenstephan Hefeweissbier

Website: www.weihenstephaner.de
Brewed in: Freising, Germany
ABV: 5.4%
Appearance: Cloudy orange with a towering white head
Aroma: Clove, bubblegum, lemon
Flavour: Brioche, clove, lemon sherbet
Great with: Smoked salmon, veal sausage

A big, bubblegum-laden wheat beer, with oodles and oodles of almost medicinal clove character from the yeast, balanced neatly with some lovely spicy notes from the hops.

Okell's Mac Lir

Website: www.okells.co.uk
Brewed in: Isle of Man, UK
ABV: 4.4%
Appearance: Winter sunshine through an early morning mist, light moussey head
Aroma: Lemon peel, heather, nettle
Flavour: Basil, banana, pine resin
Great with: Thai Massaman curry, vegetable goulash, young goat's cheese

Mac Lir (named for a sea deity in Irish mythology) is an 'almost' crystal wheat, with a refreshing herbal citrus nature and zippy piney finish.

Wild Rose Velvet Fog

Website: www.wildrosebrewery.com
Brewed in: Calgary, Alberta, Canada
ABV: 4.5%
Appearance: Cloudy honey, restrained head
Aroma: Apricot, digestive biscuit, orange
Flavour: Peach blossom, oat cake, orange
Food: Frittata, pork and bean stew, lemon meringue

A craft beer flower amid the thorns of mass-produced brands in Calgary cowboy country. It has lovely, soft peachy/apricot aromas leading into a satisfyingly wholegrain flavour that softens into sweetness, ending with a marmalade zing.

Brasserie Pietra Colomba

Website: www.brasseriepietra.com
Brewed in: Corsica, France
ABV: 5%
Appearance: Sandy yellow topped with a soft white foam
Aroma: Juniper, lavender, orange liqueur
Flavour: Blueberry, fresh bread, heather
Great with: Grilled red mullet, wild boar stew, blueberry pie

Others to try

Goose Island 312 Urban Wheat Ale, Illinois, USA
Hitachino Nest White Ale, Japan
Odell Brewing Co Easy Street Wheat Beer, Colorado, USA
Townshend Brewery Three Piece Wheat, New Zealand
Van Steenberge Celis White, Belgium

LAGER

Easily the best-travelled beer style in the world – if lager had one of those old steamer trunks, it would be so covered in stickers you'd never see the original surface! From its origins in Europe, it has hopped over the pond and become an American icon; settled throughout Australia and Asia, where it is well suited to the hot climate and even hotter cuisines; and has now returned to charm us all over again.

When brewed properly, lager is a refreshing gift to your palate; when badly made, it's an insult to your taste buds. So what separates the seasoned traveller from the poorly dressed tourist?

Well, avoiding the big brands is a great start. I don't like slating beers just because they are brewed by a certain company, but once you start drinking top-quality artisan lagers, I'll be very surprised if you want to go back to the bland mass-market commodity brands.

So, put on your sturdiest drinking shoes and warm up your drinking muscles, because we're going for a pretty long stroll through some fascinating history and a much wider beer category than you may have imagined ...

WHAT'S IN A NAME?

When you think about lager, the first thing that generally springs to mind is a golden sparkling liquid that's served as cold as the fridge, or tap, can make it – right? So what would you think if I told you that lager ranges in colour from the palest winter sun to rich mocha brown? Surprised? Well then, let me tell you a bit more about this fascinating beer and its history.

First things first: why is lager called lager? Well, while the word has become a generic term for a particular type of golden, sparkling beer, it's actually both a method of production and a family of beer – a cryptic statement that I shall now explain more clearly.

The word 'lager' derives from its method of production, not what it tasted or looked like. It comes from the German word *lagern*, which means 'to store': traditionally many beers, and not just German ones, were stored in nice cool caves to make sure they didn't spoil during the summer months.

Facing page: All lager is not golden; it ranges from palest lemon to ruby-tinted brown.

Above: Refreshing, sparkling and golden – we have the Czechs to thank for the world's favourite beer style.

Below: An American lager, Victory Prima Pils, a take on pilsner that the country has embraced as its own.

History in the brewing

Exactly when beer was first stored in caves is not known, but the oldest brewery in the world, Weihenstephan (see page 91) in Bavaria, Germany, has records showing that beer was brewed in the mid-700s, and the mountainside under the former Weihenstephan monastery is riddled with old caves, so it's fairly safe to assume that these caves have always been used to keep things cool. As a happy by-product of its months of necessary cold storage, it was found that the beer had matured in flavour and developed a pleasing carbonation.

The other by-product of this process of brewing and maturing the beer in the cold was that the ale yeast, *Saccharomyces cerevisiae*, which likes warm temperatures, had naturally mutated into a form that works best at cooler temperatures, which we now know as *Saccharomyces pastorianus*.

FIRST STEPS IN THE LAGER REVOLUTION

The next step in the story of lager is linked with two young bucks from European brewing families: Gabriel Sedlmayr II, son of the owner of Munich's Spaten brewery, and Anton Dreher, heir to the Dreher brewery in Vienna. In the 1820s and 1830s, Sedlmayr and Dreher made a number of trips to the UK, visiting breweries in Birmingham, Burton upon Trent, Newcastle and Alloa in Scotland, absorbing knowledge and pinching brewery secrets as they went.

On Sedlmayr's first trip to Scotland, he had gifted a brewer some of his cool-fermenting yeast (the Scots couldn't brew with it, and it withered and died; imagine how different the face of brewing would have been if it had worked!). More importantly, he took away some new brewing technology that he knew could make his Munich beers much better.

When Sedlmayer returned to Britain with his buddy Dreher in 1837, they were both impressed by the improvements in malting that were creating British pale ales (see page 119) and the new cooling coil technology that allowed brewers to control the temperature of the fermentation, as well as other technological advances such as brewing thermometers and saccharometers. Combining this with their knowledge of how to use the strain of cool-temperature-friendly yeast, the two men returned home armed with a much more scientific approach to brewing their own beers.

When Sedlmayr returned to the Spaten brewery, he continued to brew dark brown beers, which suited Munich's hard water and consumer demand, but as a result of his visit to the UK these were more efficiently fermented and more stable than before. Using his low-temperature-friendly yeast, he was soon producing beers that were the envy of many, some of whom adopted this same yeast strain for their own breweries, including J C Jacobsen, the founder of Carlsberg in Denmark.

Meanwhile, back in Vienna, Dreher decided to incorporate not only this clean, low-temperature fermentation process alongside the other technological advances, but also included a high proportion of the lighter malts the English were using: this turned out to be quite some plan! The coppery-red concoction that he came up with, known as Vienna lager, was a huge hit, and saw the Dreher family expand its business throughout the Austrian Empire. The Vienna style has travelled far and wide over the years, and there are echoes of the reddish lager in some Mexican beers, such as Negra Modelo. One of my brand heroes, Brooklyn Lager (see page 93), is created in this image, and jolly tasty it is too.

SEEING THE LIGHT

However, that copper-coloured Vienna lager is, after all, not what we instinctively think of when we think about lager.

For this we have to take a hop over to what is now the Czech Republic, to trace this golden beer back to a happy confluence of circumstances that allowed one man to create the beer style that has taken over the world!

In 1842 Josef Groll, a Bavarian brewer, was appointed brewmaster of the town of Plzen (Pilsen in German) in Bohemia, then part of the Austrian Empire. Using Bavarian cool-fermenting yeast and the new malts and technological advances that were creeping into his home country's brewing culture, he set about creating his own vision of what the next step in brewing should be – golden lager beer.

He was blessed with the fact that the local water of Plzen was extremely soft, which meant that not a lot of colour was extracted from the malts. He was also fortunate that, during the building of the town's new brewery, the already extensive network of underground cellars to ferment and mature beer was expanded. Of course, it helped that he was slap-bang in the middle of the finest growing country for Saaz hops at the time, and he took advantage of their excellence for both bittering and aroma (see Pilsner Urquell, page 90).

At first the style was slow to catch on, possibly because the lighter malts cost a lot more money to procure, and of course few breweries had enormous underground cellars like those in Plzen. But within

Below: The town of Pilsen in the Czech Republic is steeped in the beer's history.

50 years golden lager was on its way to world domination: breweries everywhere were making it, and in 1894 the Spaten brewery in Munich, which had stood by its dark and reddish lagers, produced its first light-coloured lager, which it called Helles (*hell* means 'clear' or 'light' in German).

BORN IN THE USA?

In the United States of America – as in many other parts of the world – if you ask for 'a beer' you are most likely to be given a golden lager. But why did beer, and lager in particular, find so much favour in the USA?

First, let's not forget that the *Mayflower* landed where it did, at Plymouth, Massachusetts, because the crew had run out of beer. *Mourt's Relation*, the journal of William Bradford and Edward Winslow, two of the first English settlers, refers to the fact that they had gone ashore to assess the possibility of temporarily settling the land, as they had not been able to reach their original destination due to high winds and low supplies:

'That night we returned again a-shipboard, with resolution the next morning to settle on some of those places; so in the morning, after we had called on God for direction, we came to this resolution: to go presently ashore again, and to take a better view of two places, which we thought most fitting for us, for we could not now take time for further search or consideration, our victuals being much spent, especially our beer, and it being now the 19th of December.'

So in the 17th century, beer was vital as a survival tool; because of its preservative hops and alcohol, it could survive a long sea voyage whereas water wouldn't.

During the 19th century, eight million Germans emigrated to the USA. Among them were many brewers, who made beer in a variety of styles,

Below: In 1902 Schlitz in Milwaukee, Wisconsin, was the largest beer producer in the world.

including ales, wheat beers and lagers – although it's unlikely that these beers were the light lagers that are so prevalent today. The first lager brewery of which I can find evidence was founded in 1840 in Philadelphia by John Wagner, who had travelled on a fast clipper ship so that his precious lager yeast would survive the journey.

And Wagner wasn't alone, as Ray Anderson points out in his excellent chapter on the history of industrial brewing in the *Handbook of Brewing* (2nd ed, Taylor & Francis, 2006). Over the next 20 years, the wave of German immigration to the United States brought with it such famous names as Bernhard Stroh, Eberhard Anheuser, Adolphus Busch, Frederick Pabst, Frederick Miller, Joseph Schlitz and Adolph Coors, and with this influx of immigrants came a shift in preference from ale to lager.

It also helped that the German immigrants settled in places like Milwaukee, with access to ice from Lake Michigan, and St Louis, with its cool natural caverns, but from the 1870s artificial refrigeration meant that breweries could be set up anywhere.

For a while the brewers used imported ingredients, but during the 1880s they looked to cut costs and increase convenience by developing beers based on local ingredients – and in the USA this meant a lot of maize (corn) or rice.

The result? Well, I can't put it better than Anderson: 'This, coupled with the development of an accelerated brewing process, where storage time was minimized and filtration used for clarification, led to the development of unique, very pale-coloured beers of unrivalled blandness.'

By 1910 the USA was producing more beer than any other country in the world. Although Prohibition in the 1920s and early 1930s put a major dent in the US brewing industry, the 'bland' lagers were able to bounce back quickly because the big breweries

Above: A graphic representation of how the Anheuser-Busch brewery would have looked in 1933.

had turned Prohibition to their advantage by diversifying their businesses. Anheuser-Busch, for example, made a range of products, from soft drinks and non-alcoholic beer to refrigerated cabinets, which came in useful for their distribution line later on. Sadly, the reduction in costs resulting from the use of cheap adjuncts, short maturation (lagering) time and pasteurization processes have all led to both the dumbing down and global domination of big lager brands.

Right: The classic Aussie lager Foster's is now brewed all over the world.

Below: Asian lagers are often brewed with a proportion of rice, making them low in flavour and therefore perfect served ice cold.

ASIAN AND AUSTRALIAN LAGERS

Australia, New Zealand, China, Japan, India, Thailand, Indonesia – all have their own large lager brands, which are served very cold and are more about refreshment than flavour. This is mainly down to the need to use local ingredients, particularly rice, as sources of fermentable sugars: and these just don't have the complex flavours of barley.

Although the Chinese had been brewing since 23BC, what we recognize as Chinese beer today was created by German brewmasters from the 1870s onwards: the Tsingtao brand is one that has survived.

Australia didn't take to brewing lager until the 1880s, when the American émigré Foster brothers opened their doors in Melbourne in 1889. They applied what they had learnt from US brewing culture about taking advantage of ingredients that grow well locally and began using cane sugar in their beers – which explains why Australian versions of lager are often on the sweeter side.

Meet the family

There's a huge amount of lager sloshing around the world. Some examples are golden-hued, elegantly flavoured and refreshingly dry, others are strong, dark and sweet and others are, let's face it, dull, boring and bland.

There are some historic lagers of note, however, with interesting variations in colour and style, often the result of local and regional traditions.

Bock

A Saxony speciality that has migrated all over the world; Amsterdam has an annual festival dedicated to Bock. Sweet, generally amber-coloured beer with little discernible bitterness and a smoothness of mouthfeel; it's usually high in alcohol – sometimes very high.

Dunkel

Dunkel means dark, and dark lager is a traditional Munich style that ranges from a deep copper colour to dark brown. *Dunkel*, the German word for 'dark', doesn't necessarily mean lager; it can also be applied to other styles, such as wheat beer.

Helles

A very light-coloured, spritzy lager – an easy-drinking Munich speciality.

Märzen/Oktoberfest

Different names, same thing: these copper-red to dark brown beers were traditionally brewed in March for consumption during Munich's Oktoberfest celebrations (Oktoberfest starts in mid-September and finishes just into October).

Right: The enormous aging barrels still used by Pilsner Urquell for its unfiltered unpasteurized lager.

Pils

This term originally comes from the style developed in Pilsen in 1842 and has grown to mean any style of lager that is golden and sparkling. It is not always a marker of great beer, however, as it has no protected status and is used by some poor-quality lagers.

Rauchbier

Meaning 'smoked beer', this uses smoked malts and, frankly, has a tendency to taste like your lager has been aged with a bit of bacon in it; very much an acquired taste. Craft brewers around the world are experimenting with the style.

Schwarzbier

This simply means 'black beer' in German. It is used to describe lagers that include a small quantity of very dark malts to add a touch of burnt, roasty flavour, but which are still surprisingly refreshing.

Vienna

A copper-coloured, slightly sweet, but not cloying, lager.

It's not just the fermentation process (cool and long for lager, warm and quick for ale) that affects the flavour of the beer; the maturation process can also influence the final style. Some beers pre-date the widespread use of cool-fermenting yeasts but were traditionally matured at cool temperatures. These can easily be mistaken for lagers, and it's not something to get terribly hung up on. These beers originate in Germany, but craft brewers in other parts of the world – especially north America – also produce beers in these styles.

Altbier – a speciality of Düsseldorf and other parts of North Rhine-Westphalia in Germany, this could be described as the missing link in the lager story: it uses dark malts and a warm-fermenting yeast but is lagered at cool temperatures. These beers have some of the flavour characteristics of ale, often being quite high in fruit notes, but also some of the refreshing characteristics of a lager because of their long, cold maturation process.

California common – the best-known exponent of this style is Anchor Steam Beer, from San Francisco. Back in the 1800s the terms 'common' and steam beer seem to have been used interchangeably in California; they fell out of fashion and had all but disappeared until Fritz Maytag revived the style and trademarked the name Steam Beer in the early 1970s. This beer is brewed with a warm-fermenting yeast right at its lowest temperature tolerance and then cold-conditioned – this helps to produce an ale-like flavour profile with the drinkability of a lager.

Cream ale – basically this is an American pilsner lager brewed with a warm-fermenting yeast at normal ale brewing temperatures and then cold conditioned. To be charitable it will be, at best, refreshing. I am told there's a Kentucky version that's dark and slightly soured, but I've not personally had a sighting of this rare beast – perhaps it could be the next near-extinct style to be revived!

Kellerbier – also known as Zwickelbier, this can be made using a cool-fermenting or warm-fermenting yeast, but it is cold matured and served unfiltered, straight from a tank in the cellar or barrel. It's a style that's increasingly being seen outside its German heartland.

Kölsch – a speciality of Cologne in Germany (beer made outside the area must be called Kölsch-*style*), this is brewed with very pale malts and a warm-fermenting yeast, then lagered at cool temperatures to create a smooth flavour profile. Great examples are Früh and Gaffel and they taste like fresh, very fruity, lagers.

ARTISAN ALL OVER THE WORLD

Although the first British lager brewery was the Austro-Bavarian Brewery and Crystal Ice Company in London in 1881, and Scotland certainly took to the style, with the Tennent's brewery beginning to make lager in 1885, the United Kingdom and Ireland generally held firmly to their ale and porter brewing traditions longer than almost any other countries. But during the 1960s a new form of 'standard lager', relatively low in alcohol and heavily advertised, marched in and nearly wiped out the traditional cask ale of the British Isles.

Fortunately, a few cask ale enthusiasts – Michael Hardman, Graham Lees, Bill Mellor and Jim Makin – decided to form an organization called the Campaign for the Revitalisation of Ale, which was changed a year later to the Campaign for Real Ale, or CAMRA. It has gathered pace ever since: in 2011 CAMRA celebrated its fortieth year.

CAMRA has not stopped the flood of lager, which currently accounts for around 60 per cent of the UK beer market. However, as in the USA, the explosion of craft beer breweries and new beer styles is gradually eroding lager's market share. And, happily, the UK now has a burgeoning craft lager scene, which is seeing the revival of properly matured beer from companies like Cotswold and Freedom (see page 94) and also some great innovations from breweries like Harviestoun, with its super-floral/fruity cask-conditioned lager Schiehallion (see page 95).

The UK is not alone in the renaissance of quality lagers: Vedett in Belgium, Christoffel Blonde from the Netherlands and Kasteel Cru (which is brewed with a Champagne yeast) from France are some of the notable exceptions to the big brand dominance seen throughout Europe.

A FINAL NOTE

As I write this, the US market dominance of Anheuser-Busch's Budweiser and its big-brand counterparts is beginning to wobble, as beer drinkers really get stuck into the wide variety of beers being made by the craft brewing movement.

Freezing cold and chuggable or interestingly artisan, there is one major redeeming factor about all lager-style beer and it's this – it's perfect for hotter climates. The lager may be really quite rubbish, but when you're relaxing on holiday, a cold lager, preferably brought to you at the mere crook of a finger, is simply the best thing ever. It's cold, it's thirst-quenching and it's all part of having fun on your travels – you don't need to think, just drink!

PILSNER URQUELL

Website: www.pilsnerurquell.com/in
Brewed in: Plzen, Czech Republic
First brewed: 1842
Grains: Pilsner malt
Hops: Saaz
ABV: 4.4%

Appearance: Liquid sunshine, small light white foam
Aroma: Soft honey, ripped green leaf, slight peppery spice
Flavour: Creamy biscuit, crisp lemony mousse, clean grassy finish
Great with: Sausages, smoked cheese, pickles

THE BEER

The original golden lager, Pilsner Urquell, just holds on to the Czech pilsner crown over Budvar (see page 94) by the merest whisker – at least, I reckon. Full of fresh biscuity flavours with just a hint of grassy bitterness, it is perfectly balanced between sweet and bitter, clean yet somehow rich and satisfying, and a perfect showcase for those fabulous Saaz hops grown in the beautiful Czech countryside.

THE BREWERY

The story of Pilsner Urquell really is the story of the pilsner style of beer that has conquered the globe. The name Urquell, meaning original source, may have been a marketing gimmick dreamt up quite early on by some German sales reps, but it's stuck and I rather like it.

The city of Plzen (Pilsen in German) is in western Bohemia, about 50km (30 miles) from the border with Bavaria. The legend has it that in 1838 the quality of its beer had deteriorated to the point where the city leaders poured it down the drains and built a new brewery, with extensive cellars. They called in a bright young brewing buck to oversee it – the, by all accounts, bonkers but brilliant Bavarian brewer Josef Groll. This proved to be the dawn of a golden era: the new Burghers' Brewery, as it was then known, started cranking out this amazing beer.

Groll, aged 29, with his knowledge of new brewing technology from the UK, combined the latest pale malts with the area's soft water, a cool-fermenting yeast strain and Saaz hops. The vast sandstone cellars meant the beer got a proper long, cold fermentation and maturation, and led to the birth of a glorious beer style, pilsner. Can you imagine what it must have been like, to see the world's first clear golden beer poured into the world-renowned Bohemian crystal glasses for the first time? Incredible.

These days the Plzensky Prazdroj (Pilsner Urquell) brewery still follows the more complicated method of making the beer that Groll used, called 'decoction' mashing; this means taking a portion of the mash from the mash tun and boiling it hard in another vessel. This portion of the mash that's been super-heated is then returned to the rest of the mash 'porridge': this gains the highest possible yield of sugars from the grains and also imparts some additional flavours. Originally decoction was probably intended to gain more sugars from badly malted barley; it worked, so brewers carried on doing it, even when malting technology improved. It also allows a brewer who adheres to the Reinheitsgebot (see page 71) to introduce caramel and toffee flavours normally only achievable by using sugars or other adjuncts in the brewing process.

WEIHENSTEPHAN ORIGINAL

Website: www.brauerei-weihenstephan.de
Brewed in: Freising, Germany
First brewed: unknown
(recipe adjusted in 2008)
Grains: Pilsner malt
Hops: Hallertau, Perle
ABV: 5.1%

Appearance: Light amber, billowing white head
Aroma: Soft lemon, zippy lime, slightly biscuity
Flavour: Freshly mineral, uplifting citrus, grassy finish
Great with: Smoked trout, fresh pretzels, lemon posset

THE BEER

Originally called Helles ('clear'), this super-refreshing beer was renamed Original in the early 1990s, and had its recipe 'tinkered' with in 2008, but the only discernible difference is that it is lighter and more refreshing than ever. With its playful aroma of happy smells like lime, biscuit and lemon and its clean, uplifting flavour, a Weihenstephan Original on a sunny day is a thing of pure beauty.

THE BREWERY

There are records of brewing on the hill of Weihenstephan from 725, when Saint Corbinian and 12 other monks founded a Benedictine monastery there (if you're a beer drinker, you have to love those monks, don't you?) – long before the foundation of the city of Munich, 40km (25 miles) to the south. The monastery was razed to the ground during the 10th century, but in 1040 the monks' love for beer bounced back and they were awarded a licence to brew and sell beer by the city of Freising – and Weihenstephan brewery was born. Unfortunately, after just 45 years of stability the monastery entered a very dark period

SINCE 1040

BAYERISCHE STAATSBRAUEREI

Weihenstephan

THE WORLD'S OLDEST BREWERY

and between 1085 and 1463 the building burned down four times and was depopulated by plague, famine and even an earthquake – which makes it remarkable that the monks kept their faith, let alone their brewing mojo. Then, in 1516, the Reinheitsgebot (see page 71) was introduced and the reputation of the beers from Bavaria started to grow.

In 1803 the monastery suffered a further blow when legislation, as the brewery's website says, achieved 'with a stroke of a pen what all the catastrophes of a thousand years failed to achieve'. All the monasteries in Germany were secularized and the state took over the Weihenstephan monastery – but kept on brewing the beer.

In 1921 it had a name change and became the Bayerische Staatsbrauerei Weihenstephan (Bavarian State Brewery). Its logo is the Bavarian state seal and it remains today incredibly well-supported and respected as one of the greatest centres for brewing excellence, for its brewing school and for producing some of the finest beers the world has ever seen: its wheat beer is held in particularly high regard (see page 79).

TEXELS BOCK

Website: www.speciaalbier.com
Brewed in: Texel, Netherlands
First brewed: 1999
Grains: Pale malt, roasted barley
Hops: Hallertau
ABV: 7%

Appearance: Coffee with ruby hints, large caramel-coloured foam
Aroma: Fudge, prune, orange
Flavour: Raisins, bitter molasses, smoky
Great with: Smoked ham, cheese croquettes, braised endive

THE BEER

I love the learning curve this job has me on: until 2010, I had no idea that Bock beer was such a Dutch obsession. Seriously, these guys love their beer, and they have a large festival dedicated to this one style of beer in Amsterdam every year, organized by the national beer consumer group PINT. That's where I first came across this Bock. It is made in a hybrid style, with a warm fermentation and long cool maturation, and even though that's not strictly within the definition of a lager, it's a great beer!

A rich, fruit-cake-like nose is the starting point, followed by a truly tremendous belt of something rich and smoky, which all follows through on the palate, along with a viscous, gooey loveliness that puts you in mind of licking the cake mixture spoon when you were a kid.

THE BREWERY

Texel (pronounced Tessel in Dutch) is named after the westernmost island of the archipelago of the Frisian Islands, where the intrepid Maurice Diks founded a brewery in 1999.

If you live on an island, making the most of local resources is the smart thing to do, so the brewery uses only island-grown barley and takes advantage of the pure dune-filtered water to make its beers so special. The brewers insist that the tranquil Texel lifestyle influences their brewing process, allowing everything its maximum fermentation and maturation time, but I've met these boys – they are party animals and I'm not sure anything stays quiet for that long around there!

It's not just their Bock that has gained acclaim; many of their other beers have won awards, too.

BROOKLYN LAGER

Website: www.brooklynbrewery.com
Brewed in: Utica, New York, USA
First brewed: 1989
Grains: Pale and Vienna malts
Hops: Hallertau Mittelfrüh. Vanguard, Cascade
ABV: 5.2%

Appearance: Ginger biscuit amber, medium white head
Aroma: Caramel, zesty, nettle-like
Flavour: Slightly gingery, mild caramel, spicy watercress finish
Great with: Lamb burger, vegetable tagine, Key lime pie

THE BEER

The best craft lager from the States that I've tried – it's got a really pleasing aroma that reminds me slightly of walking through a field where barley is just beginning to turn from green shoots to the colour of hay.

On the palate it has an intriguing spice of ginger, or maybe ginger biscuits, balanced by a very slight caramel and a truly elegant use of a traditional German lager hop, Hallertau Mittelfrüh, its US relative Vanguard, and American Cascade for an extra kick, the latter creating that lovely nettle/watercress-like end to the beer that I really adore – and as the beer is 'dry-hopped' this is a prominent part of the flavour experience.

THE BREWERY

It's possibly not surprising that such a great lager is named for an area of America that has seen so many German immigrants in its time. The lager beer is brewed in upstate New York, as it has been since the brewery began, because demand is so high; and the other Brooklyn beers are brewed in Brooklyn itself.

The brewery was started by two neighbours, Steve Hindy and Tom Potter, who commissioned fourth-generation German-American brewer William Moeller to develop a lager for them, which he did with help from his grandfather's brewing recipe book from Brooklyn. In the early days they struggled against big brewer-tied distribution, cynical tavern owners and organized crime, but eventually their fortunes turned.

In 1994 they hired now-idolized brewmaster Garrett Oliver to head their upstate brewery and then to oversee their new smaller plant in Brooklyn, which produces the exciting range of beers we see today. Brooklyn is definitely a force to be reckoned with in the brewing world. Other Brooklyn favourites are the Brooklyn Local 1 and the Brewmaster's Reserve series.

MORE TO TRY ...

Birrificio Italiano Tipopils

Website:	www.birrificio.it
Brewed in:	Lurago Marinone, Lombardy, Italy
ABV:	5.2%
Appearance:	Light lemon colour, white moussey head
Aroma:	Peach, lychee, cut grass
Flavour:	Rose, homemade lemonade, nettle
Great with:	Salted crisps, pork scratchings, candied walnuts

Tipopils is a beer I wish I could see more of. It's without doubt one of the most exciting takes on the pilsner style I've ever tasted. Full of aromatic floral and zippy green flavours, it is intensely satisfying yet easy drinking – a triumphant symphony of flavour and refreshment.

Budweiser Budvar

Website:	www.budweiserbudvar.co.uk
Brewed in:	Ceskè Budejovice, Czech Republic
ABV:	5%
Appearance:	Liquid sunshine, rocky white head
Aroma:	Honey, ciabatta, ripped green leaf
Flavour:	Pitta bread, agave nectar, mown grass
Great with:	Fresh pretzels, roast duck, nettle-wrapped cheese (Yarg)

I love the Budvar brewery, and if you are ever in the Czech Republic you must go to the beautiful town of Ceskè Budejovice and visit it. The beer itself is best enjoyed unfiltered and unpasteurized direct from the brewery, but is still very quaffable when it's not. Less bitter than its Pilsner Urquell rival, it has a softer, more rounded, sweetness: a great beer for encouraging mainstream lager drinkers to take a step up.

Freedom Organic Dark Lager

Website:	www.freedombeer.com
Brewed in:	Staffordshire, UK
ABV:	4.7%
Appearance:	Ruby, fudge-coloured low foam head
Aroma:	Caramel, fudge, mineral
Flavour:	Ozone, toffee, orange rind
Great with:	Chargrilled pork chop, rack of lamb, salty blue cheese

The addition of this organic, vegan-certified dark lager to Freedom's small portfolio was a stroke of genius. The beer strikes a great balance of freshness and sweetness, which shows the brewer's skill, and allows you to enjoy the sweet toffee and fruit notes without being overwhelmed by it all.

Grand Ridge Brewer's Pilsener

Website:	www.grand-ridge.com.au
Brewed in:	Mirboo North, Victoria, Australia
ABV:	4.9%
Appearance:	Light straw colour, fluffy foam
Aroma:	Lemon, orange, honey
Flavour:	Honey, herbal, citrus
Great with:	Thai-spiced prawns, chicken burger, honeycomb ice cream

Grand Ridge makes very good beer, in a land often unfairly renowned for choosing quantity over quality. It has a lovely light spritzy carbonation that allows its honeyed, citrus notes on both the nose and palate to sing.

Harviestoun Schiehallion

Website: www.harviestoun.com
Brewed in: Clackmannanshire, Scotland
ABV: 4.8%
Appearance: Light amber, white cloud-like head
Aroma: Passion fruit, light caramel, crushed grass
Flavour: Brown sugar, lychee, green mango
Great with: Garlic langoustines, pork goulash, tropical fruit salad

Schiehallion is one of the most flavoursome lagers in this section. From initial aroma to your very last sip, it is full of tropical fruit, bitter green mango notes and an underlying sweet caramel.

Saranac Adirondack Lager

Website: www.saranac.com
Brewed in: Utica, New York, USA
ABV: 5.5%
Appearance: Pale copper, low white foam
Aroma: Caramel, lemon rind, straw
Flavour: Demerara sugar, pine needles, lime skin
Great with: Burger with Swiss cheese, vegetable tagine, lemon soufflé

The Saranac brewery in upstate New York, at the foot of the Adirondack mountains, makes one of the cleanest US lagers I've ever tried. While it maintains a pleasingly sweet edge, the fresh mineral nature of the water from the surrounding mountains and the pine/lime flavours finish this refreshing lager off to a tee.

Schlenkerla Rauchbier Märzen

Website: www.schlenkerla.de
Brewed in: Bamberg, Germany
ABV: 5.1%
Appearance: Garnet red, thick, butter-coloured head
Aroma: Bacon, smoked wood, caramel
Flavour: Hickory chips, smoked caramel, autumn leaves
Great with: Goulash, slow-roast lamb, smoked cheese

This is definitely an acquired taste, made with the Schlenkerla family's secret smoked malt. Some people say it's like a fine cigar, to others it's like having bacon in your beer – but either way the Märzen is the most accessible beer in the Schlenkerla pack, with a nice sweetness in the middle to balance the otherwise dominant smoky flavour.

Victory Prima Pils

Website: victorybeer.com
Brewed in: Downington, Pennsylvania, USA
ABV: 5.3%
Appearance: Lemon yellow, slight white foam
Aroma: Thyme, golden syrup, lemon balm
Flavour: Curly parsley, light toast, lime peel
Great with: Tomato and thyme flan, prawn filo parcels, lime granita

A beast of a lager, with flamboyant, swaggering American attitude and bags of character. It is full of sweet herbal aromas and flavours and biting lime peel finish – very fresh, very clean, very addictive.

Others to try

Baird Beer Numazu Lager, Japan
Früh Kölsch, Germany
Hacker-Pschorr Münchner Dunkel, Germany
Köstritzer Schwarzbier, Germany
Meantime Helles, UK
Stiegl Goldbräu, Austria

GOLDEN & BLONDE ALE

Golden and blonde ales ... they just sound so enticing, don't they? The rich sound of the word golden and all the promise it brings, the way, when you pour one of these beers, you see the light glowing through the liquid and how this lures you in to sample its refreshing qualities again and again ...

Golden ales can be difficult to define, as so much depends on the individual brewer's interpretation, so I'm going to focus on the golden ales in the UK that have revitalized interest in craft beer on my native shores like no other style in the last 30 years.

However, I can't fail to look to Europe to Belgian blondes – and because blondes can be such fun, this cheeky style has spread across the globe with homage brews popping up wherever you go.

So, if you're looking for a bit of luxurious refreshment, here's a good place to dive in. Come on ... the beer's lovely!

GOLDEN ERA

There is a smattering of golden ales in other countries, such as Coopers Sparkling Ale in Australia and Deschutes Cascade Ale from Oregon in the USA, but they had nothing like the impact that the vanguard of golden ales in the mid-1980s had both in transforming the entire UK beer market and, frankly, probably saving cask ale from being consigned to the history books.

The very first was Exmoor Gold, brewed to celebrate the brewery's 100th birthday in 1986. It was intended to be a one-off, but it was so enormously well received that the brewery, Exmoor Ales of Somerset, had almost no choice other than to keep on brewing it. What was so exciting about this beer? Well, at a time when every other real ale was either copper, dark copper, very dark brown or almost black, the appearance of this bright, bubbly blonde that wasn't the 'real beer' drinker's hated enemy, lager (also known as Euro-fizz), Exmoor Gold was a revelation.

For a while it was alone in the British market and, as is so often the case, it doesn't get quite as much kudos as the beers that followed it, such as Hop Back Summer Lightning (see page 103) from Wiltshire, Kelham Island Pale Rider (see page 100) and Rooster's Yankee, brewed in Yorkshire – which were all a little bolder, brasher and influenced by the burgeoning American craft beer scene.

Today we'd probably call them softened-down American-style pale ales, as nearly all of this new wave of beers used American hops, but back then they were simply stupendous and a flavour sensation that took the beer scene by storm. They were christened golden ales, which is a name I rather like.

And I also have this beer style to thank for getting me into great beer. Golden ales eased me into the world of cask ale and helped me understand how a beer can uplift you. To me, golden ales hold the promise of summer in every sip – and they have a huge place in my heart.

Facing page: All that glitters may not be gold, but in the beer world the drinking public are certainly polishing off plenty of these beers.

Below: Bringing a bit of golden bling to the beer sector, Exmoor Gold started a revolution.

BELGIAN BLONDES

On top of everything else the Belgians have given to the world of beer, they are also known for their 'blonde' ales. Some beer writers don't consider there to be a difference between this style and the abbey-style blondes (see page 140), but I do; the mouthfeel is much cleaner, less sweet, and the bitterness is always much higher and more discernible; the overall effect is that they are a lot less cloying to drink.

Duvel was the breakthrough beer when it changed its recipe from using dark malts to using pale malts in the 1970s. It was first brewed after World War I, when the Belgians had much contact with British troops and, as a consequence, their preferences for beer. Albert Moortgat, owner of the brewery, went to Scotland, got an ale yeast and created a strong, dark, Scottish-style ale and then hopped the hell out of it with Saaz and Styrian Goldings. I use the phrase 'hopped the hell out of it' advisedly: originally it was named Victory Ale but was changed to Duvel when one of the owner's friends described it as 'nen echten duvel', which means 'it's a real devil' in local dialect, and it is still devilishly strong, at 8.5% ABV.

The style has influenced many brewers around the world, as you'll see from my brand hero from New Zealand, Tuatara, on page 101; other great beers in this style include Hoppenbier from Jopen in the Netherlands, Belgian-style Blonde 5 from Brouwerij West in southern California and Japan's Baird Beer's Single-Take Session Ale.

Right; The Moortgat brewery in Belgium is the home of Duvel, undoubtedly the best-known of the Belgian blonde beers worldwide.

BROUWERIJ · **MOORTGAT** · BREENDONCK

BRASSERIE DE LA SENNE TARAS BOULBA

Website: www.brasseriedelasenne.be
Brewed in: Brussels, Belgium
First brewed: 2003
Grains: Pale ale malt
Hops: Saaz, Challenger
ABV: 4.5%

Appearance: Pale amber, fluffy white foam
Aroma: Floral, grapefruit, crushed nettles
Flavour: Gooseberry, grapefruit, zingy refreshment
Great with: Meatloaf, roast chicken, goat's cheese

THE BEER

The number one reason I chose this beer is its sheer drinkability. I love the almost lily-like aroma with hints of grapefruit and lime zest. And when your nose gets closer, I adore that this becomes a more spiky nettle aroma and that when you drink it your taste buds are awash with zingy, zesty refreshment, leaving you to ponder on the dry finish and faint hint of flamed citrus peel at the back of your palate – for the few seconds before you rush back for another sip.

Taras Boulba was originally designed by the two partners in the brewery, Yvan de Baets and Bernard Leboucq, as a light but bitter, tasty and refreshing beer to drink after a hard day of work in the brewery. With an unusually low 4.5% ABV it flies in the face of the adage that Belgian blondes have to be strong to be fun. 'Then we let some friends taste it and everybody wanted to have it. Since then, it has been brewed on a regular basis, and we sell it almost without any publicity ...'

Taras Boulba is one of those underground brands that mark you out as rather cool when you're in Brussels. If you order it, or any other Brasserie de la Senne beer, when you first arrive at any speciality beer bar, I've noticed it gets you a small nod of approval from the bar staff and a few exciting suggestions about what to try next – whatever language you order in!

THE BREWERY

The brewery started in Bernard's garage, and the beers became so successful that Bernard and Yvan started using spare capacity at other breweries, becoming 'cuckoo' or 'nomadic' brewers, at times travelling up to six hours a day to get the beer out. The Brasserie de la Senne now has a fantastic new home, making it and Cantillon (where de Baets previously worked) the only full-scale breweries in the boundaries of a city famous for its beer.

KELHAM ISLAND PALE RIDER

Website: www.kelhambrewery.co.uk
Brewed in: Sheffield, South Yorkshire, UK
First brewed: 1990
Grains: Pale ale malt and a secret addition
Hops: Willamette and a secret addition

ABV: 5.2%
Appearance: Soft peach, creamy head
Aroma: Peach, raspberry, cucumber
Flavour: Creamy, apricot, underripe peach
Great with: Salmon, rabbit, soft cheese

THE BEER

With the colour of a sunset, this beer smells like a freshly baked peach and raspberry clafoutis. It tastes a bit like one too, with its rich, ripe fruit notes of zingy raspberry and apricot, and a pleasingly dry, slightly bitter finish like slightly underripe peach skin – it's a feast for all the senses.

And, as the 'pale rider' is a euphemism for death, I can honestly say that Kelham Island Pale Rider could easily be my choice for a last pint on this earth. Why? Pale Rider was the beer that got me into the world of beer and I will freely admit that when I first met the brewer, Dave Wickett, I behaved like a star-struck adolescent, stammering out ridiculous stories of how I first came across his beer.

Pale Rider was developed after Wickett noticed, during tours of his original brewery, that women, in particular, really liked the aroma hops but would often go and order a lager after the tour instead of one of the ales. So he devised a beer that was high in aroma and low in bitterness like a lager, but with the full, creamy body of an ale.

Within three months, it was the most popular beer the brewery has ever made. It took the CAMRA Champion Beer of Britain award in 2004 and has won so many others it's hard to keep count.

THE BREWERY

The story started when Wickett decided to give up his day job as an economics lecturer and in 1990 opened the Kelham Island brewery next door to his

Fat Cat pub in Sheffield – I think we can all agree that academia's loss was brewing's gain.

Now the brewery is just up the road and five times the capacity of the original, but is still turning out excellent ales. The whole UK brewing industry has a soft spot in their heart for Dave, who is terminally ill as I write this, and he gets much credit for inspiring a whole new generation of brewers and for helping other businesses like Thornbridge (see page 123) get off the ground too.

TUATARA ARDENNES

Website: www.tuatarabrewing.co.nz
Brewed in: Wellington, New Zealand
First brewed: 2001
Grains: Pilsner malt
Hops: NZ Styrian Goldings, Motueka, Saaz
ABV: 6.5%

Appearance: Bright orange, cloud-like white head
Aroma: Spicy, orange, earthy
Flavour: Sweet biscuit, orange marmalade, spicy finish
Great with: Gammon, sweet and sour chicken, blue cheese

THE BEER

It's exciting enough when a friend visits from the other side of the globe, but when they bring beer of this calibre with them, life looks even better! I was introduced to Tuatara by Scotsman Colin Mallon, who manages the Malthouse pub in Wellington, New Zealand.

Ardennes, so named because it uses a yeast strain from the Ardennes region of Belgium, is a big bold beer that truly reflects the brilliant and burgeoning New Zealand beer scene. If I had to sum it up, I'd say it was like the average Belgian blonde on steroids, but it's so easy to wax lyrical about it further that I will!

With fuller, more aggressive citrus notes than typical Belgian blondes, it has a noticeably musty but not unpleasant note that's followed up by a lovely, crushed autumn leaf spice. On the palate it sits somewhere between a chutney and a marmalade on a digestive biscuit, with a finish of spicy leaf, which is what makes it so perfect for matching with blue cheese.

THE BREWERY

Tuatara was born in 2002, when Carl and Simone Vasta joined forces with Sean Murrie of the Malthouse and Fraser McInnes of the Bar Bodega in Wellington, both of whom had sold beer from the Vastas' previous brewing ventures. They figured that with two bars as steady customers, a farm to build the brewery on and an increasingly keen beer audience in New Zealand, they would probably be onto a good thing, so Carl set about creating the brewery. With a 1200-litre (265-gallon) brew capacity they began brewing Tuatara beer.

Demand for their beers swiftly outgrew the original two outlets, so they began bottling them. In fact, it grew so much that in 2007 a German-designed brewhouse increased capacity to over 35,000 litres (7700 gallons) – but the call for Tuatara beers is not abating and there are plans afoot to expand again, which just goes to show the thirst people have for great beer in New Zealand.

MORE TO TRY...

Adnams Explorer

Website:	www.adnams.co.uk
Brewed in:	Southwold, Suffolk, UK
ABV:	4.3%
Appearance:	Light orangey gold, white open head
Aroma:	Sage, orange, grapefruit
Flavour:	Parsley stem, lemon, candied grapefruit
Great with:	Steamed citrus haddock, quiche Lorraine, New York cheesecake

A fine example of an English blonde ale that uses American hops, Columbus and Chinook. Full of herbal, citrus notes, it reminds me of a bracing sea walk – but perhaps that's because it's brewed on the coast and the pump clip looks like a sail! Whatever its secret, this grapefruity refresher is definitely one to try either in bottle or cask.

Dupont Moinette Blonde

Website:	www.brasserie-dupont.com
Brewed in:	Tourpes, Belgium
ABV:	8.5%
Appearance:	Cloudy orangeade, billowing cream head
Aroma:	Straw, tomato vine, overripe orange
Flavour:	Green tomato, honey, orange juice
Great with:	Moules à la bière, rabbit stew, Edam-style cheese

The sweet, herbal notes of Moinette Blonde are well balanced by the citric tang at the end. This beer will also age quite well if you keep it in suitable conditions (see page 195), becoming a bit thicker and sweeter over the years.

Duvel

Website:	www.duvel.be
Brewed in:	Puurs, Belgium
ABV:	8.5%
Appearance:	Cloudy yellow, fluffy white head
Aroma:	Earthy, citrus, golden syrup
Flavour:	Honey, tomato vine, orange marmalade
Great with:	Sausage and tomato bean stew, baked butternut squash, young Cheddar

Duvel, which means 'devil' in Flemish, is considered by many to be the pinnacle of Belgian blondes. Its tomato-vine and honey sweet centre is well balanced with a marmalade bitterness. However, this beer isn't called a devil for nothing, and I feel I have to warn you that its 8.5% strength is well hidden: when chilled this slides down very easily – in fact, you could say it's sinfully easy to drink!

Hop Back Summer Lightning

Website:	www.hopback.co.uk
Brewed in:	Salisbury, Wiltshire, UK
ABV:	5%
Appearance:	Lemony gold, subdued white head
Aroma:	Geraniums, lime leaves, lemon grass
Flavour:	Rose, lemon, lime
Great with:	Chicken salad, pint of prawns, young goat's cheese

The beer that created a storm in the UK brewing scene in 1988, Summer Lightning is an original and still one of the best. Full of fresh, zingy floral and citrus scents and tastes, it never fails to evoke a happy feeling of being in beautiful sunshine every time I drink it, and I hope it does the same for you.

Bières de Neuch Blonde de Neuch

Website:	www.bieresdeneuch.ch
Brewed in:	Neuchâtel, Switzerland
ABV:	6%
Appearance:	Burnished gold, rocky head
Aroma:	Fresh apple, honey, green peppercorns
Flavour:	Brioche, pepper. earthy
Great with:	Cheddar cheese on toast, honey-roast pork, tarte tatin

The Swiss beer scene is burgeoning; Bières de Neuch is one of the more established breweries, founded in 2007. This blonde, spicy ale is a deep and satisfying pour, with an excellent nose that is spicier than even most Belgian blondes and a warming honeyed flavour that will leave you feeling hugged.

Nøgne Ø Blonde

Website:	www.nogne-o.com
Brewed in:	Grimstad, Norway
ABV:	4.5%
Appearance:	Pale amber, low fluffy white head
Aroma:	Butterscotch, lemon balm, grapefruit peel
Flavour:	Honey, candied peel, lemon balm
Great with:	Steamed sea trout, asparagus, lemon sorbet

Nøgne Ø's Blonde started life as a one-off cask beer in 2003 and was so wildly popular it had to stay! Very much in the English style of blonde beers, it is designed for very easy drinking with its soft caramel sweetness, gentle herbal fragrance and tinkly citrus notes.

Others to try

Brasserie Achouffe La Chouffe, Belgium
Baird Beer Single-Take Session Ale, Japan
Coopers Sparkling Ale, South Australia
Dark Star Hophead, UK
Deschutes Cascade Ale, Oregon, USA
Exmoor Ales Exmoor Gold, UK
Holden's Golden Glow, UK
Jopen Hoppenbier, Netherlands
Little Creatures Bright Ale, Western Australia
Three Boys Golden Ale, New Zealand
Brouwerij West Blond 5, California, USA

FARMHOUSE ALE

Saison and *bière de garde* are brews with their roots in agrarian society and nutritional necessity. Once the preserve of the historic region of Flanders, the two styles have been divided by the changes in borders and differences in cultures, but both originate in farmhouse breweries in the days when farmers needed to provide refreshment for their workers, especially during the thirsty work of harvesting.

BREWED ON THE FARM

There isn't a lot of written history about farmhouse ales, which is not surprising given the circumstances in which they developed. Farmhouse breweries made beer as sustenance for their workers; it was just a part of everyday life, so no one would, or even could, write down any information about it.

Over time, as the Flanders region was divided up to form parts of Belgium, France and the Netherlands, the farmhouse styles diverged. The Belgians moved towards a lower alcohol style of beer, called *saison*, designed to keep farmworkers refreshed; records show they were given the equivalent of 4½ litres (8 pints) a day to keep them going.

Meanwhile, the heavy-drinking *paysans* of France kept their beer higher in alcohol; *bière de garde* means beer for keeping, and the escalation of the alcohol level would have happened over time as the farmer-brewers realized that the stronger beers kept and aged better.

These days, they provide a fascinating diversity of flavours, from citrus via hay and flowers to gooseberries, and a lot of scope for brewers to experiment with strong flavours and create exciting drinks.

BIÈRES DE GARDE

Beer was always to have a place in post-revolutionary France. It was the revolutionaries' drink of choice and was served at festivals and accompanied them on their marches. It was also the democratic drink readily affordable by all, being half the price of wine. In the new Republic some brewers rose to local power, becoming mayors and officers in the National Guard.

Bières de garde were brewed by farm owners in northern France. Traditionally the beers would have been made from barley grown in the nearby Champagne region or imported from France's African colonies. Other sources of fermentables like sugar may also have been added to the mix, along with local hops from French Flanders or Poperinge, just

Facing page: A traditional Belgian farmhouse. Throughout Flanders and northern France farmhouse breweries made beer as sustenance for their workers.

Below: A 1930s poster for *bières de garde*.

over the border in Belgium. These ingredients, combined with some unusual brewing techniques – such as extremely extended wort boiling times (up to nine hours!) – helped produce these distinctive beers.

Before refrigeration, brewing was not possible in the hot summer months, so enough beer had to be made and stored in cool cellars as provision for the summer. *Bières de garde* were stored in 750ml (25fl oz) bottles with a champagne cork and wire cage. Why? Well, the Champagne region is not that far away, and I would imagine it just made sense to use the same containers for their beer. So when people today talk about 'wine level' presentation of beers in Champagne-style bottles I'm sure that the French of the Nord and Pas-de-Calais regions are scratching their heads and shrugging their shoulders at this supposedly 'new' concept.

The surviving historic examples of these beers, such as the revived La Choulette's Bière des Sans Culottes (see page 108), still have that lovely, slightly aged note to them from extended cellaring, with biscuit, honeyed and sharp citrus notes. At around 5% to 7% ABV and packed full of flavour, *bière de garde* is the perfect accompaniment to French farmhouse dishes such as cassoulet or duck confit with a sharply dressed salad – or hijack a classic coq au vin to create coq à la bière!

SAISONS

The French-speaking Belgian provinces of Hainaut, Namur and Walloon Brabant are home to the *saison* (season) beers.

More thirst-quenching and lower in alcohol than their French counterparts, it would appear that, historically, pretty much anything could be chucked into the pot. *Saisons* can include a wide variety of herbs or spices, sugar or honey, and various grains – barley, wheat, spelt or rye, used as malt or unmalted grains.

These days, what really sets these beers apart is the complexity of the base beer that's then overlaid with a big whack of hops, whether they be European Saaz or English classics like Fuggles or Goldings, which add even more spiciness to the mix.

OTHER FARMHOUSE BREWS

Apart from the very few Flanders breweries that are still located on farms, probably the most active farmhouse brewing culture in the world is in Franken, Germany (home of Schlenkerla Rauchbier, page 95). Most of these farmhouses, however, are now brewing mainly light, or Helles-style, lagers to cater to local tastes.

BRASSERIE DUPONT SAISON DUPONT

Website: www.brasserie-dupont.com
Brewed in: Tourpes, Belgium
First brewed: 1844
Grains: Pilsner malt
Hops: Styrian Goldings, East Kent Goldings
ABV: 6.5%

Appearance: Bright amber, medium white foam
Aroma: Earthy, apricots, pepper
Flavour: Slightly bready, earthy spice, crisp orangey bitter finish
Great with: Crusty bread and Brie, roast duck, steamed orange pudding

THE BEER

Saison Dupont, as you can see, has been brewed for quite some time, so it's not surprising it's often considered as the archetype of the style – it also makes jolly nice drinking!

With its strongly earthy nose, soft apricot aroma and a distinctly peppery note, it is extremely intriguing before you even take a sip, but when you do you'll be happy. It's one of those beers that takes a second to develop – initially you just get a bit of a crusty bread note – and then it suddenly fills out, expanding into every corner of your mouth with rich, earthy spice, spicy orange and a very clean, dry citrus pith end.

Interestingly, the reason for the beer's delightful coppery-blond colour is that it's made in a direct gas-fired mash tun, which means that some caramelization occurs as the wort forms.

THE BREWERY

The farm on which Saison Dupont was born finally stopped being a working concern in 2000, but Saison

Dupont is still brewed in the same location, along with its stable-mates, including Bière de Miel (honey beer) and Moinette Blonde (see page 102).

In the early 19th century, the Rimaux-Deridder farm and brewery gained a good local reputation for its *saison* and honey beer. The Dupont family's involvement with the brewery began in 1920 when, to dissuade his son Louis from moving to Canada to farm, Alfred Dupont purchased the Rimaux-Deridder farm, which dated back to 1759.

Louis Dupont died in 1945; he had no children, but he bequeathed the brewery to his nephew Sylva Rosier, who was the brewer. Sylva Rosier was clearly an ambitious man. He developed the brewery, with the help of his son Marc and daughter Claude, to include a laboratory to ensure the products coming in were as good as what was going out.

Today, the business is run by the fourth generation and grandson of Sylva Rosier – Olivier Dedeycker, who succeeded his uncle, Marc Rosier, at the head of the business.

LA CHOULETTE BIÈRE DES SANS CULOTTES

Website: www.lachoulette.com
Brewed in: Hordain, France
First brewed: 1983
Grains: Pale malt
Hops: Brewer's Gold, Goldings
ABV: 7%

Appearance: Deep gold, cloud-like white head
Aroma: Bread, tea, honey
Flavour: Pear, bread, lemon curd
Great with: Wild mushrooms on toast, pot-roast chicken, mature goat's cheese

THE BEER

Utterly refreshing, designed to fuel a revolution and proudly wearing long trousers, Bière des Sans Culottes is a glorious beer.

Its nose gives you a hint of its drinkability, with subtle aromas of fresh French baguette, a little tea-like earthy freshness and lovely honeyed sweetness. Then, when you take a well-chilled sip, you get a flavour like cloudy honey spread thickly on fresh bread. This is then joined by a pleasing zesty Earl Grey note with the citrus-sweet presence of lemon curd and an ephemeral dry pear note at the end.

The name 'Bière des Sans Culottes', although directly translated as the beer without trousers or pants, refers to the fact that, during the French Revolution, the revolutionaries wore long trousers rather than the *culottes*, or knee-breeches, that were worn by the upper classes against whom they were rebelling.

THE BREWERY

Brasserie La Choulette (named after a game that predated lacrosse) is a true survivor; at the start of the 20th century there were around 300 breweries in the area around the town of Valenciennes, but now just this one remains.

In 1895 Jules Dhaussy set up a small brewery on his farm, using the barley he grew. Like other breweries in the region, he suffered during World War I, when the brewery was requisitioned and then destroyed, but the compensation they were awarded allowed them to rebuild and modernize. Jules' son, Alphonse, took over, but in the 1950s he gave up brewing, partly owing to health problems and partly because his brewery needed major investment to update it.

He kept up the farm, and his eldest son, also called Alphonse, went to work for a brewery in Valenciennes. During this period many other local breweries closed as ale-brewing went out of fashion.

Fast forward to 1977: Alphonse learnt that an artisanal brewery was up for sale just 3km (2 miles) from his family's farm. He bought it and appointed his son Alain to run it, which he does to this day, having renamed it La Choulette.

THREE FLOYDS RABBID RABBIT

Website: www.3floyds.com
Brewed in: Munster, Indiana, USA
First brewed: 2006
Grains: Pale ale malt, caramalt
Hops: Spalt, Warrior
ABV: 7.4%

Appearance: Orange-gold, rocky white foam
Additional ingredients: Camomile, white pepper, rosehips, lavender
Aroma: Floral, honey, redcurrant
Flavour: Lavender, pepper, clementine peel
Great with: Macaroni cheese, Toulouse sausage, Turkish delight

THE BEER

Described as a Franco-Belgian ale, and brewed with a yeast sourced from the Ardennes area, this is the most exciting *saison* I've ever drunk.

On the nose you get lavender and white pepper along with something slightly deeper and more berried, and a really spritzy, almost boiled sweet-like, grapefruit-orange. But, as lovely as this smells, it's got nothing on the flavour. On the palate it explodes over your senses like a Mediterranean garden: first to greet you are the sunny, joyous floral flavours of lavender and camomile, then along buzz the nectar-like honey notes and a sting of peppery heat, followed quickly by perfectly ripe satsumas that drop neatly onto your taste buds and prevent the whole thing from becoming a mélange of 'pretty flavours', bringing refreshment and a pleasingly astringent flourish to the finish.

Brewmaster and owner Nick Floyd says the beer was inspired by Fantôme (see page 110), a *saison* he greatly enjoyed during a trip to Europe – and the brewery has certainly done it justice.

THE BREWERY

If there's any brewery more rock 'n' roll than Three Floyds, then I haven't come across it. The original brewery was built in 1996 by brothers Nick and Simon Floyd, with dad Mike, in a dilapidated warehouse in Hammond, Indiana, with serious attitude and some old dairy equipment.

In pretty short order, the demand for their ales meant they had to relocate to their current location in Munster and build a proper brewhouse.

However, they have a strong commitment to keeping small and growing at a rate that will maintain their big reputation.

They have built their following not only on the success of their flagship Alpha King pale ale but also on the fact that every year beer geeks from around the United States queue for over 24 hours for the limited release of their fantastic imperial stout Dark Lord – not to mention how much people love the brewery tap with its own kitchen garden.

If you visit the website, or Three Floyds itself, you'll see that the brewery's slogan is 'not normal' – this is true, the beers, and the people, *are* abnormal, in the best possible way!

MORE TO TRY ...

Le Baladin Wayan

Website: www.birreria.com
Brewed in: Piozzo, Piedmont, Italy
ABV: 5.8%
Appearance: Hazy gold, medium fluffy head
Aroma: Jasmine, honeyed pear, porridge
Flavour: Green peppercorns, red apple, caramelized grapefruit
Great with: Red Thai curry, grilled cheese, zabaglione

Brewer Teo Musso is renowned in craft beer circles for being somewhat of a mad scientist and for breaking the boundaries of beer styles; this is his unique take on a saison (see photo on page 105). Wayan has 17 different ingredients (some of them secret) and is a fascinating beer; with its highly floral and pear-like aromas, sweet porridgey middle and spicy flavours, it is one to sit and savour.

Brasserie Duyck Jenlain Ambrée

Website: www.jenlain.fr
Brewed in: Jenlain, Nord, France
ABV: 7.5%
Appearance: Amber with a light cream head
Aroma: Autumn leaves, celery, mahogany
Flavour: Toasted bagel, Muscat grape, orange marmalade
Great with: Confit duck leg, frisée and feta salad, tarte tatin

Jenlain Ambrée is the classic bière de garde on which Brasserie Duyck built its fame. Full of sweet spice, fallen leaves and fresh celery on the nose, it mellows on the palate into toasted sweet bread and a Muscat earthiness and finishes with a pleasantly bitter punch like good-quality orange marmalade. It also has a cleansing carbonation, making it ideal to cut through unctuous foods, such as confit of duck.

Fantôme Saison

Website: www.fantome.be
Brewed in: Soy, Belgium
ABV: 8%
Appearance: Yellowy orange, large white cloudy head
Aroma: Leather, honey, orange
Flavour: Red apples, cardamom, sour apricots
Great with: Hummus, roast belly pork, mature Cheddar

Fantôme is one of the most complex of the Belgian saisons. Packed full of earthy, herbal and citrus aromas, almost farmyard in their forthright nature, but on the palate they settle into a sea of tongue-tickling flavours. A pungent spiciness, almost like Sichuan peppercorns, ending in a punch of sour fruit, can seem a little overwhelming at first, but after the first sip you are rewarded with a beer to savour.

Brasserie de Silly, Silly Saison

Website: www.silly-beer.com
Brewed in: Silly, Belgium
ABV: 5%
Appearance: Deep orange, silky white head
Aroma: Candied walnuts, hay, blackcurrant
Flavour: Resinous, parsley, underripe blackberries
Great with: Stuffed tomatoes, sautéed calves' liver, young Brie

This brewery is named for its village, which really is called Silly, making for a lovely play on words when it comes to this beer's name. This is a good introductory saison, slightly sweeter and less funky in aroma than many of its counterparts. It has some interesting blackcurrant notes on the nose, with sweet, nutty undertones; on the tongue a gently astringent resin-like quality with some fresh herb is rounded off with a dry, underripe blackberry finish.

Two Brothers Domaine du Page

Website: www.twobrosbrew.com
Brewed in: Warrenville, Illinois, USA
ABV: 5.9%
Appearance: Copper with small, cloud-like head
Aroma: Aniseed, plum, caramel
Flavour: Stewed prunes, liquorice, grassy
Great with: Baked fennel gratin, boiled bacon with Puy lentils, prune cake

Two Brothers is pretty much in the middle of nowhere, but it's worth the journey if you're ever in the Chicago area, as it has a great tap room. This French farmhouse-style beer was inspired by the brothers' time living in France; its sweet, aniseed aromas and flavours, when offset against the dried fruit notes and clean grassy end, make it a very easy beer to match to rustic Gallic dishes.

Surly Cynicale

Website: www.surlybrewing.com
Brewed in: Brooklyn Center, Minnesota, USA
ABV: 6.6%
Appearance: Peachy gold, fluffy head
Aroma: Honey, black pepper, fresh bread
Flavour: Raspberry, Sichuan pepper, elderflower
Great with: Salt and pepper squid, fried chicken, young pecorino cheese

Surly Brewing is an American craft brewery that offers its beers in cans as well as keg and bottle. This saison is something very special: full of honey and soft floral notes, it caresses your tongue and hides its relatively high alcohol under a fun and fruity bushel.

Others to try

Boulevard Brewing Tank 7 Farmhouse Ale, Missouri, USA
Flying Dog Garde Dog, Maryland, USA
Brasserie des Géants Saison Voisin, Belgium
Brasserie de Saint Sylvestre 3 Monts, France
La Brasserie à Vapeur Saison de Pipaix, Belgium

PALE ALE & INDIA PALE ALE

Encompassing warring brewers, capitalism, colonialism and adventures on the high seas, the story of these two beer styles is a fascinating one. In the following pages you will find tales of when pale ale was the drink of princes, the decline and fall of the British Empire, how pale ale was reinvented and why India Pale Ale (IPA) became the darling of craft brewing the world over.

So, grab yourself a pint, bottle or barrel of beer (depending on how quickly you read) and settle in for a tale of two beer styles that's worthy of a Hollywood blockbuster.

THE PALE REVOLUTION

As we become more and more keen to reconnect with historic cooking methods, foods and cuisines, so we have re-connected with brewing history the world over.

Over the last 30 or so years, craft brewing movements across the world have been taking local ingredients and putting their own spin on historic styles, with pale ales and India Pale Ales in particular making a huge impact – with their tremendous emphasis on hops for both aroma and bitterness.

Undoubtedly the American craft brewing movement has to take the lion's share of the credit for reintroducing highly-hopped beers to the wider market. From the lip-smackingly refreshing brews like Sierra Nevada Pale Ale (see page 129) to the more tongue-laminating IPAs such as Stone's Ruination (see page 129), the flavours coming from this part of the world are amazingly diverse and a spectacular showcase for North America's home-grown hops, and these phenomenal beers have resonated throughout the brewing world.

In Australia and New Zealand, for example, the pale ale market is awash with gloriously fruit-packed pale ales, which are as lush, vibrant and refreshing as any white wine from either of those countries and just as full of zippy tropical fruits. Japanese brewers – like Hitachino Nest, Baird Beer and Ise Kadoya, to name but three – are also making some fantastic interpretations of the pale ale style.

Roving Danish brewer Mikeller has produced myriad variations on both pale ale and IPA; in Norway Nøgne Ø makes its own, full-flavoured, versions (see page 128); and even traditional Belgian brewers are getting in on the act, with beers like Brasserie d'Achouffe's Houblon Chouffe.

And back on UK shores, where the styles originated, pale ales and IPAs in traditional and modern forms are being resurrected all over the country. The only true survivor of the original IPAs, and one with a fascinating heritage, is Worthington White Shield (see page 129). New interpretations of historic recipes include Meantime's India Pale Ale, brewed in Greenwich, London, which I would urge you to try with a board of British hard cheeses. My brand hero, Jaipur (see page 123), is a variation on the theme. From London brewers like Meantime and Kernel (see page 125), which make very different, but equally satisfying, IPAs and pale ales, to larger

Facing page: An iconic British style that developed into a cornerstone of colonial trading and intrigue on the high seas.

Below: New World takes on this classic beer style have proved tremendously popular.

regional players like St Austell in Cornwall and Marston's in Burton upon Trent, everyone is keen to brew hop-forward beers.

More and more breweries are turning out truly excellent examples of these styles. Interpretations vary wildly, but if I were forced to generalize I would say that while pale ales hover around 4 to 5.5% ABV, anything below about 6% ABV and calling itself an IPA probably isn't doing justice to the history behind those three letters.

Below: No-holds-barred flavour and marketing from the Flying Dog brewery with its Doggie Style pale ale.

PALE ALES AND IPAS – REBORN IN THE USA

Given their impact on the current face of the craft brewing scene, it's worth taking a quick look at the modern history of US pale ales and IPAs.

In the 1970s, after many decades of the North American marketplace being dominated by bland lager, it took visionaries like Fritz Maytag of Anchor Brewing, Ken Grossman of Sierra Nevada and Jack MacAuliffe of the now defunct New Albion Brewery to resurrect the American brewing movement. Pale ale and IPA were among the first styles that came onto their radar.

Their take on pale ales reintroduced the marketplace to flavour in its beer, and then they moved on to reinvent the IPA style in line with those lovely, if untrue, stories of how the historic UK brewers made their beers.

Now, English IPAs were historically packed full of flavour, but by the time the American craft beer revolution was starting in the 1970s, most British IPAs were pale imitations of their former selves. All the American brewers had to go by were a few apocryphal stories about how this beer style was made to survive the long sea journey from Britain to India and had more hops than a bag full of bunny rabbits!

The American brewers' obsession with hops has played a huge role in their rise in popularity – intensely aromatic floral, citrus and grapefruity American hops such as Cascade, Centennial and Chinook have redefined pale ales and IPAs for brewers around the world.

GOING TO EXTREMES

Unfettered by tradition, unconcerned with convention and untamed in flavour, US IPAs and pale ales are definitely the anarchists of the brewing world. Styled and promoted as the antidote to bland mass-produced lager, there is no mistaking the nakedly aggressive use of hops to produce beers that are likely to smack you in the taste buds, assault your sensibilities and leave a lot of taste in your mouth.

However, you can definitely have too much of a good thing: throughout the late 1990s and early 2000s, there was what can only

be described as the hops equivalent of an arms race to see who could use the most hops and make the most bitter beer – which rarely resulted in something good to drink.

Above: Titan IPA and Kernel Centennial Pale Ale photographed on the banks of the River Thames, where IPA was born in the 18th century.

Nevertheless, those rare examples that were good were really, really good! And that's why some of them survive today. Among these, I would include some of Stone Brewing's offerings, such as Ruination IPA (see page 129), and Pliny the Elder from Russian River (see page 129).

Another outcome of this 'my hops are bigger than your hops' competition was that the beers were also flexing their alcoholic muscles; this spawned a style that soon became known as double or imperial IPA – 90 Minute Imperial IPA from Dogfish Head, first brewed in 2001, is a great example. This style has also spread its wings across the world – Scotland's BrewDog took the 2010 crown at the World Beer Cup for its most excellent Hardcore IPA (see page 128).

Pale and interesting: the history

The founding of the British Empire – with its tales of tall ships on the high seas, adventurers and lands of untold riches – gave birth to two styles of beer that have captured the hearts and minds of beer lovers ever since. Before we get drawn into the treacherous undercurrents of IPA's history, it's worth understanding why Britain needed to send beer to its boys overseas – it's simply that you can't brew beer in hot climates without refrigeration; it just doesn't work. So, until the invention of technology for cooling, traders, administrators and soldiers posted in India relied on supplies via the sea to keep them in beer, and sea trade was controlled by the famous East India Company.

COMMERCE AND COLONIALISM

The East India Company, or to use its common sobriquet, John Company, was set up in 1600 to access the riches of the East Indies, bringing back exotic products such as spices, cotton, silk, indigo dye, saltpetre and, later, tea. As a result of its stranglehold on trade, it effectively colonized India; it was only in 1858, after the Indian Mutiny of 1857, that the British Crown assumed direct administration of India in the new British Raj.

But where does India Pale Ale fit into all of this? Well, it was a major strand of commerce for John

Below: These East India Company ships in Bombay harbour were probably rammed to the gunwhales with beer as they sailed to India.

INDUSTRY AND INVENTION

Those inventive chaps the Chinese were using coke as a fuel from around the 9th century but, as has so often been the case, the West were several hundred years behind this incredible civilization and didn't discover the method of tempering coal into a less sulphur-emitting fuel source until the early 17th century; it was first used in the malting process in 1642.

However, it took another 50 years before coke-fired kilns were widely used to create pale malts. Around 1690 pale ales started to take off: they were more expensive than darker beers and found favour with the upper classes for their paler colour. Eventually they were to spawn the global phenomena that we know today as IPA, pale ales and golden lagers.

Company because there weren't many goods going out on the ships, so it gave them an income stream from the minute they arrived at the dock.

It's a commonly held belief that the development of IPA's characteristics was the result of a calculated decision by UK brewers to make a brew strong in alcohol and with a large quantity of hops in order to preserve it during the long trip from Britain to India.

However, IPA wasn't the first pale ale and by no means was it, for quite some time, the most popular style of beer being sent out to India; in fact, it wasn't even known as India Pale Ale until the 1830s. Martyn Cornell, in his meticulously researched book *Amber, Gold & Black* (2010), uncovered evidence that other alcoholic beverages were already being exported, including cider, porter and small beer (a beer of around 2.5% ABV that wasn't normally heavily hopped). So how did IPA become such a legend in its own lifetime – a legend that has been spectacularly revived in recent decades?

THE BIRTH OF A STYLE

The beer that gave birth to IPA was made by a brewer called Hodgson's, from my home town of London. In the 1750s, around 50 years after pale malt was introduced to the wider brewing world (see box above), it was Hodgson's October beer, sold as pale ale in India, which was the first 'brand' to catch the imagination of the colonists. Described as a 'pale, well-hopped autumn-brewed stock bitter', it was loaded onto the ships alongside other beery offerings and sailed the ocean blue, with remarkable results.

The rough sea journey, with regular temperature changes as the ships crossed the Equator twice, meant all the beers underwent an accelerated maturation process and came into much more contact with the oak as they sloshed around in the barrels. This doesn't seem to have made a lot of difference to the other styles being shipped, but in the case of Hodgson's pale ale it created a smooth, complex flavour that had once been only even vaguely achievable through long cellaring. So, contrary to common belief, it was the journey that made the beer; the beer wasn't made for the journey.

While it was certainly not the first pale ale to be exported to India, the flavour qualities of this particular beer created an unprecedented buzz around this style. Hodgson's, soon followed by others, began brewing more of this highly hopped beer, because John Company was demanding ever larger volumes.

THE DECLINE AND FALL OF THE LONDON MONOPOLY

Despite Hodgson's building an excellent reputation over the next half century, this was to be undone in 1821, when the two men now running the brewery, Frederick Hodgson and Thomas Drane, made the twin errors of greed and hubris in thinking they could cut John Company out of the equation and reap the rewards of their beer's high standing themselves.

Below: The skies of Burton upon Trent in the 1850s were full of the heady smells of the brewing industry.

Hodgson and Drane took advantage of the fact that the ships leaving Britain were all but empty, thus making passage for goods incredibly cheap. They ended their long credit terms with the East India captains, sold beer for cash at the brewery gate and raised their prices by 20 per cent – not a smart move as it turns out, because the East India Company did not get to be the superpower of its time by allowing two London wide boys to turn it over.

ENTER THE BURTON UPON TRENT BREWERS

During the 1820s the Burton brewers were reeling from the loss of their export trade to Russia, after the Russian government imposed enormous import tariffs on their beers. However, their fortunes were about to change when one of the top players in the East India Company, Campbell Marjoribanks, invited Burton brewer Samuel Allsopp to dinner to discuss the possibility of replacing that lost trade with routes to India. Marjoribanks and his

colleagues were not impressed with the shenanigans of the Hodgson and Drane likely lads.

Upon hearing this, Allsopp rushed back to his Midlands brewery and quickly replicated the well-hopped pale ale from London that was so popular in India. The result? Well, the gypsum-rich water in Burton not only extracted less colour from the malt but was also more effective in the conversion of starches to sugar, creating a much drier and more palatable beer – although this was not scientifically verified until decades later. Within a year of starting to export pale ale in 1823, Allsopp was receiving letters stating that his pale ales were preferred to Hodgson's.

In 1829 William Worthington entered the fray. I mention this because, although the volumes the brewery produced aren't that notable, the brewery's White Shield brand is a survivor (see page 129) and is still brewed to a traditional recipe in the small Molson Coors-owned Museum Brewery.

However, even if Worthington wasn't a major export player, by 1832 Bass, also of Burton upon Trent, had taken over 40 per cent of the market, with Hodgson's clinging on to 28 per cent and Allsopp's holding just a 12 per cent share. One can only assume that the same business acumen which led Bass to register the world's first trademark (the Bass red triangle) saw them take this lion's share of the pale ale to India market.

THE RISE AND RISE OF INDIA PALE ALE

But, all this intrigue aside, how did IPA first become so very popular in the UK, or even come by its name? It was mostly as a result of the battle for IPA supremacy between the London and Burton brewers. The rapid development of Britain's railway network from the 1830s onwards massively reduced the cost of shipping beers around the country. And, trading on Burton's superior reputation for pale ales in the India market, the railway allowed the Midlands brewers to

Above: The Allsopp brewery in 1853. Allsopp's helped take the crown of pale ale from London to Burton upon Trent.

bring the fight to Hodgson's and other London purveyors of this increasingly popular style at a much-reduced cost. London brewer Hodgson's realized that it was in danger of going under because its pale ales were quickly deemed inferior to those coming from Burton upon Trent and that, having ticked off the East India Company, it had to do something to make up for the loss of trade.

So Hodgson's started to aim its products at those who had come home with a thirst for the style of beers they had enjoyed in India; at first, the beer for sale in the domestic market was termed only as 'pale ale brewed expressly for the India market'. According to beer writers Martyn Cornell and Pete Brown (author of *Hops and Glory*, 2009), both far greater experts on this subject than I, an advertisement for Hodgson's 'East India Pale Ale' appeared in the *Liverpool Mercury* in 1835, although it seems the term took a while to catch on.

Above: The Durbar Room at Osborne House on the Isle of Wight showed Victoria and Albert's passion for all things Indian.

Indian fever was sweeping the nation because Queen Victoria and her husband Prince Albert had a fascination with all things from India, which made IPA ever more fashionable. Britain was soon awash with amber-coloured pale ale, which was increasingly being known as India Pale Ale.

And Burton was definitely emerging as the area from which to get your pale ale; it received an excellent PR fillip in 1871. The nation was holding its breath as the Prince of Wales contracted typhoid fever, the disease that had killed his father ten years earlier, when he called for a glass of Burton pale ale and pulled through. He later visited both Bass and Allsopp but, upon his ascension to the throne in 1901, it was Worthington's that received the Royal Warrant to supply his beer – perhaps a clue that this was this beer he believed had given him the strength to battle his illness.

To show how popular this beer was, the huge demand for these beers, in both the domestic and export markets, led to a shortage of hops as early as the 1840s. While English hops were, of course, considered superior, hops were imported from Germany, Belgium and the USA; hops from the north-eastern States and from the Pacific Northwest were at various times noted as particularly fine.

PALE ALE GETS LIGHTER

From the 1860s onwards, brewing began to be recognized as a science. Louis Pasteur made the world of beer a more scientific place through his studies of yeast, published in 1876 in *Études sur la bière*, and brewers and scientists were drawn to Burton upon Trent, which by this time was the most important brewing centre in the world.

Better technology allowed brewers to produce beers that no longer needed long maturation; these beers were lower in gravity (a measure of the density of fermentable sugars in the mash), less highly hopped and lower in alcohol. Being ready much quicker, these pale ales increased the breweries' profits while satisfying the thirsty masses.

But this golden age of beer was not to last. Pressure from the national temperance movement combined with the fact that the lower middle classes were becoming less physically active and more cerebral in their working life made beer increasingly less appealing. But what really hit the brewing industry hard was taxes. Beer was traditionally taxed on the amount of malt used. As Britain was almost constantly fighting a war somewhere in the world, taxes escalated to the extent that imported wine was available for much the same price as British beer. And when in 1880 Gladstone replaced the tax on malt with taxation based on the strength of beer, it was all pretty much downhill from there. Brewers who cut the strength of their beer paid less tax. This wasn't quite the end of strong, aged, pale ales for export: when the glorious Victorian Gothic building housing St Pancras station in London was renovated, the original large cellars for Bass' export beers, dating from the 1880s, were clearly marked. However, on the domestic market alcoholic strengths fell, leaving India Pale Ales to become shadows of their former selves. The terms 'India' and IPA were often dropped altogether and 'pale ales' eventually gained a reputation for weakness. Until now ...

Prohibition – beyond the pale

The early history of pale ales and IPA in the United States is somewhat murky and Prohibition is to blame. In just 13 years this piece of legislation almost wiped out the independent brewing industry. Only those businesses that were already big enough to diversify, such as Anheuser-Busch, managed to get back into production quick-smart after the law was repealed in 1933.

Sadly, a great deal of brewery history was wiped out at the same time, but thanks to some great people in the US like Jaime Jurado of Gambrinus, beer writer Stan Hieronymous and, particularly, Mitch Steele from Stone Brewing, I've been able to uncover some of the story of IPA and pale ales in the USA. The majority of the breweries making these beers before Prohibition were based in the North East. They used traditional English brewing practices and techniques to brew their beers. Some were exported, but most were consumed domestically.

The largest brewers of these beers in the late 19th and early 20th centuries were CH Evans in Hudson, New York; Ballantine and Fiegenspan in Newark, New Jersey; Frank Jones in Portsmouth, New Hampshire; and Vassar in Poughkeepsie, New York. Ballantine IPA was the only survivor of the Prohibition era, but after being bought out by various companies it became a pale imitation of its former self from about the 1960s onwards and, as Mitch Steele puts it, died a slow death in the 1970s.

However, it wouldn't be long before IPA and pale ales got their mojo back in the US craft brewing scene. Today virtually every craft brewer in the USA has its own unique take on one of these beers, making it a diverse and exciting place to try these styles.

Below: The demise of Ballantine ale is truly sad: the only true Prohibition survivor, it was then successively dumbed down by various owners.

Enjoy the game with light refreshing Ballantine!

THAT'S ALE, BROTHER!

No other ale... no beer... has such refreshing flavor, yet is so light

NO WONDER BALLANTINE LEADS ALL ALES IN SALES!

Enjoy some soon...
Ask the man for **Ballantine ale**

P. BALLANTINE & SONS, NEWARK, N.J.

EPIC ARMAGEDDON IPA

Website: www.epicbeer.com
Brewed in: Otahuhu, Auckland, New Zealand
First brewed: 2008
Grains: English pale ale malt, caramalt
Hops: Cascade, Centennial, Columbus, Simcoe

ABV: 6.66%
Appearance: Burnished gold, fluffy white foam
Aroma: Lush tropical fruit, citrus, cut green grass
Flavour: Zesty, floral, piney
Great with: Asian-style prawn and mango salad, chilli ribs, tropical fruit salad

THE BEER

Epic Armageddon IPA is full of pizzazz and fun. Its huge aroma conjures up images of a tropical fruit buffet on the edge of a lush rainforest, and that same alluring and exotic impression is continued on your tongue, where its zesty, fruity notes are joined by some pretty, almost hibiscus, wine-like notes and a long, piney finish.

THE BREWERY

Having been immersed in the American craft brewing scene while living in California in the 1990s, and having fallen in love with British beer, Luke Nicholas took up brewing full time before buying his own brewery in 2007.

Armageddon came about in the middle of New Zealand's 2008 hop crisis, when those precious plants were unbelievably difficult to come by for many small brewers who hadn't been able to sign deals for three years in advance as the big players had done. Instead of eking out his meagre supply of hops across a range of beers, Luke in typically gung-ho style threw them all at a massive IPA, which he deliberately brewed to an ABV of 6.66% – figuring that facing the final reckoning with a joke could be the best way to go if it all went wrong!

He says with a smile: 'I just thought, "What shouldn't I do?" and did it. I figured a strapline of the "the number of the yeast" would make people smile if nothing else, and as it happens it was a huge hit. I managed to get my hands on some more hops shortly afterwards, so it was well worth that apocalyptic gamble!'

I first met Luke in England in 2009 and we spent quite some time carousing together. He went back to New Zealand inspired by English brewing tradition and Pete Brown's book about IPA, *Hops and Glory*. This led him to name two barrels of his IPA after Pete and myself and he put them on the inter-island ferry for 126 crossings in six weeks. He has since scaled up his barrel aging into new American oak.

Luke has tweaked the recipe since he first brewed it in 2008 with New Zealand Hallertau hops alongside the four US hops; you have to hope these don't run out on him any time soon – or perhaps that might not be a bad thing, as it could see another world classic ride into town.

THORNBRIDGE JAIPUR IPA

Website: www.thornbridgebrewery.co.uk
Brewed in: Bakewell, Derbyshire, UK
First brewed: 2005
Grains: Pale ale malt, torrified wheat
Hops: Chinook, Ahtanum, Centennial
ABV: 5.9%

Appearance: Amber, medium, open foam
Aroma: Grapefruit, passion fruit
Flavour: Caramelized grapefruit, honey, lime peel
Great with: Roast belly pork, curry, tomato-based sauces, white chocolate

THE BEER

As glitzy as a Bollywood epic and as seductive as a remote Goan getaway, Jaipur is a beer I've had a love affair with for a long time. It beckons you in with a shimmering haze of enticing amber that combines with an intoxicating scent of exotic citrus fruit and a hint of the tropics to dazzle the senses. And when you finally succumb, you are seduced by a rich caramelized grapefruit and sweet orange on the palate, which is softened by a caressing honeyed middle, building to a crescendo of fresh, challenging, limy bitterness at the end, which will leave you swooning and diving back for more.

To come back down to earth, maybe Jaipur is not strictly historically accurate (although Britain does have a long relationship with American hops in IPAs), but it does have an elegance, a drinkability, an appeal that almost goes beyond the explicable ...

THE BREWERY

The original 10-barrel brewery opened in April 2005, in the picturesque grounds of stately Thornbridge Hall, with the help of legendary British brewing figure Dave Wickett of Kelham Island (see page 100). In the words of head brewer Stefano Cossi, the brewery had 'low commercial expectations'. And they were very low expectations, as it turns out, as the brewery has now opened a second home just down the road, with a shiny new 30-barrel plant capable of brewing two million UK pints (or just under 11,400hl) a year! Although the first beer brewed at Thornbridge was Lord Marples, a classic British bitter, Cossi and Martin Dickie (now head brewer at the anarchic Scottish producer BrewDog) created Jaipur in 2005, and two months later it won its first award; it has gone on to win more awards than any other UK beer.

Speaking about the creation of the beer, Cossi says: 'It wasn't even a brew day. We just decided to go and brew something different. Inspiration came from home-brewing books, old brewing books and anything we could find on the web. We originally considered using honey and other flavourings but quickly rejected this idea. We knew we wanted to use pale malt, so we took Maris Otter and a touch of torrified wheat for body and built from there. The Chinook and Ahtanum hops were nothing like we'd ever used before; then we decided it needed more hops and we just kept adding them!

'At the time Martin and I were not only making but selling and delivering the beer too – so when we went out with this Jaipur, we had to get people to try it; when they did they always wanted more. When I sold my first barrel, they thought it was actually an imported beer from India – that was how little people understood what the style was supposed to be about.'

So it was the brewer's determination that saw this beer really take off, just like the IPAs in the 18th and 19th centuries.

GREAT DIVIDE TITAN IPA

Website: www.greatdivide.com
Brewed in: Denver, Colorado, USA
First brewed: 2004
Grains: Pale ale malt, caramalt
Hops: Columbus, Simcoe, Amarillo
ABV: 7.1%

Appearance: Tangerine, medium white head
Aroma: Green cooking apple skins, lime zest, pine cones
Flavour: Key lime pie, wood-sap dry finish
Great with: Massaman curry, beef Stroganoff, strong goat's cheese

THE BEER

Titan IPA (see photo on page 115) was probably the first really big American IPA I tried, in 2007; it was with fellow beer writer Pete Brown and he implored me not to sue him if my tooth enamel dropped off!

However, it's a mark of how intense many American IPAs are that, having had considerable experience with American IPAs since (damn you Brown, you got me addicted), I now consider Titan the perfect introduction to the style. It's not so gentle that you get no idea of the American hop obsession, but neither is it so extreme that it scares you off for life.

Tearing into a Titan should definitely be done sitting down; this is not a vertical drinking beer, it's a gentle sipper. Your nose will tell you immediately to expect something very full-flavoured, as it throws off huge sharp aromas like peeling cooking apples for a pie, while zesting limes in a coniferous forest (an unlikely scenario, I admit!).

Then comes the flavour: it fills your mouth entirely and, while it is what brewery owner Brian Dunn calls 'hop forward', that doesn't mean it lacks balance; there is an underpinning cheesecake-base flavour that stops the zesty, piney, woody hop flavours shouting too loud. The balanced dry finish certainly makes you thirsty for more.

THE BREWERY

In 1994 Brian Dunn decided to combine his business acumen with his homebrewing hobby and opened the Great Divide brewery in downtown Denver, hoping not simply to create a booming business but to regenerate the area as well.

Opening in an abandoned dairy processing plant, Dunn quickly gained a reputation for making great beers. Within three years Great Divide was taking medals at the Great American Beer Festival, and it is now one of the most decorated microbreweries in America.

The brewery is constantly expanding and is still committed to supporting the local community.

But why does Dunn do it? Well, I like his mission statement: 'I wanted to capture the spirit of Denver's urban energy and Colorado's awe-inspiring mountains, by having an unwavering commitment to both experimentation and quality.'

KERNEL CENTENNIAL PALE ALE

Website: www.thekernelbrewery.com
Brewed in: London, UK
First brewed: 2009
Grains: Pale ale malt, caramalt
Hops: Centennial
ABV: 5.2%

Appearance: Peachy gold, bouncy white foam
Aroma: Elderflower, rose, geranium
Flavour: Floral, honeyed, pine needles
Great with: Roast pheasant, passion fruit fool, Caerphilly cheese

THE BEER

When a beer is marketed with the hop variety (Centennial) in its name, you really hope it does it justice – and I can assure you this beer doesn't just showcase the Centennial hop, it tickertape parades it up and down your tongue! (See photo on page 115.)

Full of huge floral elderflower, geranium and rose on the nose; on the palate a gentle honeyed note is added, which is followed by citrus and pine – all wrapped up in a full body that ensures not one of your taste buds is missed.

THE BREWERY

Evin O'Riordan is one cool hippy-looking dude, so the fact that his tiny brewery is on Druid Street in south-east London couldn't be more fitting! I first met Evin when he was working at London's famous foodie venue, Borough Market, and I must confess that when he handed me a bottle of his homebrew, my heart sank, as the three previous homebrews that I'd agreed to try had been fit only for cleaning the kitchen drains.

So, when I sampled Evin's beer I was incredibly surprised at how good it was. I was not that surprised, in fact was very happy, when he opened a brewery not long afterwards.

After a career working with cheese, O'Riordan had his beer epiphany when he was in the United States, helping open a cheese shop in 2007: 'I suddenly realized that people take beer as seriously there as I took cheese when I was working at Borough Market. I knew what cows the milk came from, what the weather was like when the cheese was made and how it was stored.

'When I came back from New York I also noticed that when we went to the pub after work we weren't really thinking about the beer; most of the time we were just drinking a brown bitter, which is not to be horrible about bitter, it just didn't make us think like those American beers did.

'That's not to say beer isn't first and foremost a social lubricant, but I wanted to drink something worthy of true attention.'

When he started looking for space to start his brewery, he soon found a place next to the famous Neal's Yard cheese maturation rooms. Now, with a cheesemaker on one side and ham curer on the other, it's not hard to see why Saturday open days at the brewery are so popular: beer, cheese and meat all in one place, what more could you wish for?

FLYING DOG DOGGIE STYLE CLASSIC PALE ALE

Website: www.flyingdogales.com
Brewed in: Frederick, Maryland, USA
First brewed: 1990
Grains: Crystal malt
Hops: Cascade, Northern Brewer
ABV: 5.5%

Appearance: Deep caramel, exuberant white head
Aroma: Lychee, passion fruit, grapefruit zest
Flavour: Refreshing peach, tangy grapefruit, pithy finish
Great with: Cajun chicken and mango salad, sweet BBQ ribs, New York cheesecake

THE BEER

When you first read the words Flying Dog Doggie Style Classic Pale Ale (see photo on page 114), you know you're probably in for an uncompromising experience – if you haven't already twigged that thanks to the label, an illustration by Ralph Steadman, Hunter S Thompson's partner in Gonzo journalism.

But you really can't be prepared for the flavours that this beer chucks at your taste buds; you get everything from lush tropical fruit flavours to dry pithy/zesty notes and huge citrus overtones – which somehow are here and gone in a heartbeat, leaving you desperately wanting more.

THE BREWERY

To misquote the American actor Oscar Levant, 'There is a fine line between genius and insanity, and Flying Dog has erased this line.'

This must be the most irreverent brewery the world has ever seen, but everything is done with such a natural nuttiness, ease and a skewed kind of class that you can't begrudge them their success.

The original brewpub, in Aspen, Colorado, was founded in 1990 by George Stranahan, whose motto for life is 'It's amazing what you can achieve if no one tells you that you can't'. Hats off to him, because the man has done everything from founding free-thinking schools and the Aspen Institute for Physics to becoming a professional photographer and surviving a 40-year friendship with Hunter S Thompson (perhaps the biggest feat of them all!).

He named the brewpub after an image of the mythical Flying Dog he noticed as he finished a beer after his perilous trek to K2 base camp in the Himalayas.

He decided he loved beer so much it was time he started making it. And when the brewery outgrew its Aspen home, the brewery successfully moved to Maryland with nary a murmur from the craft brewing scene and no interruption in quality.

Today Flying Dog brews, without doubt, some of the finest beers in the United States, from its Gonzo Imperial Porter (see page 176), Snake Dog India Pale Ale, In-Heat Wheat and Dogtoberfest to the 20th anniversary beer that I love so much, Raging Bitch (see page 207).

In fact, I should let Ralph Steadman's words, which have become the company's slogan, do the talking, as this is definitely 'Good Beer, No Shit'.

LITTLE CREATURES PALE ALE

Website: www.littlecreatures.com.au
Brewed in: Fremantle, Western Australia
First brewed: 2000
Grains: Pale, caramalt, wheat malt, kibbled wheat
Hops: East Kent Goldings, Cascade, Galaxy

ABV: 5.2%
Appearance: Apricot, fluffy foam
Aroma: Gooseberry, lychee, passion fruit
Flavour: Gooseberry fool, passion fruit, lime zest
Great with: Steamed lobster, Peking duck, passion fruit soufflé

THE BEER

In the UK, when I wax lyrical about the US craft beer scene to non-beer geeks, I tend to get funny looks or generally scoffed at; but when I start talking about the craft scene in Australia, people look positively stunned! But a craft beer scene there is, and it's growing at a rapid rate – and which has a lot to do with this one beer in particular.

The proliferation of craft brewing down under has seen the release of some fantastic beers. Few of them make it outside that massive and incredibly diverse continent, but when they do they are often spectacular, like Little Creatures Pale Ale.

For me, it's the Sauvignon Blanc of the beer world: it's got those stone fruit notes which you associate with that wine, as well as the slightly tart aspects of gooseberry and passion fruit, which add a lovely, mouthwatering sourness that makes you want to go back for more.

But the great thing is, all this big fruitiness is offset by the ever-so-slightly creamy nature of the beer, which isn't at all cloying; it just makes it even more of a satisfying sup.

THE BREWERY

The craft brewing world attracts some crazy people, and the idea of starting a brewery/restaurant in an old crocodile farm probably goes down as one of the more bizarre I've come across. But the wonderfully crazy people at Little Creatures sure know how to make good beer.

Established in 2000 by veterans of the brewing industry, Phil Sexton, Nic Trimboli and Howard Cearns, the brewery was originally heavily influenced by the burgeoning craft beer movement in the United States and the innovative use of flavours, particularly hops from America's Pacific Northwest.

At the time, the craft beer scene in Australia was very small and it has only really started to gain momentum and critical mass in the last few years. The company has been hugely successful and brewing giant Lion Nathan has passively invested in it. It is set to open its third brewery in 2011 on the other side of Melbourne from its White Rabbit brewery in the Yarra Valley. They describe White Rabbit as 'like a couple of Belgian hippies gatecrashing a lovely, traditional English tea party' – see, told you they were bonkers!

MORE TO TRY ...

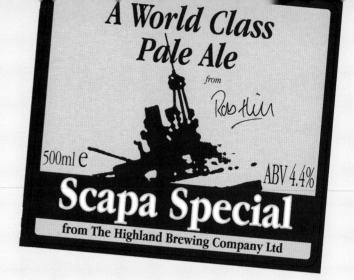

BrewDog Hardcore IPA

Website:	www.brewdog.com
Brewed in:	Fraserburgh, Scotland, UK
ABV:	9.2%
Appearance:	Bright orange, fluffy white head
Aroma:	Lime, caramel, grapefruit
Flavour:	Toffee, grapefruit, caramelized lime peel
Great with:	Citrus salmon, vindaloo, lemon curd and white chocolate cheesecake

In typical BrewDog style, this beer pulls no punches – it's rather like being assaulted by irate citrus fruit! It's tempered by a strong underpinning caramel/toffee body.

Coopers Pale Ale

Website:	www.coopers.com.au
Brewed in:	Adelaide, South Australia
ABV:	4.5%
Appearance:	Cloudy lemonade, brief rocky white head
Aroma:	Pears, fresh white bread, underripe peach
Flavour:	Green apple, brioche, green grapes
Great with:	barbecued prawns, chili halloumi, watermelon

Designed for discerning palates who want something with a bit of fizz, Coopers Pale Ale is as simple or as complex as you want to make it. Sweet pears, apples and grapes are there on both the nose and palate, underpinned by a lovely fresh bread note, which is enhanced if you roll the bottle before pouring, the Aussie way, to mix in the yeast of this bottle-conditioned beer.

Highland Brewing Scapa Special

Website:	www. highlandbrewingcompany.co.uk
Brewed in:	Scotland, UK
ABV:	4.4%
Appearance:	Peachy yellow, soft cream head
Aroma:	Cashew nuts, peach, raspberry
Flavour:	Granary bread, lychee, fresh-cut grass
Great with:	Steamed langoustine, roast grouse, cranachan (raspberries, cream, whisky and oats)

Intensely drinkable pale ale that will excite your palate too – peach and raspberry on the nose, a chewy, satisfying bready middle, and then ending so cleanly, smelling like fresh-cut grass just after rain.

Nøgne Ø Pale Ale

Web:	www.nogne-o.com
Brewed:	Grimstad, Norway
ABV:	6%
Appearance:	Straw-gold, white moussey head
Aroma:	Marigold, hay, nettle
Flavour:	Caramel, pear, grapefruit
Great with:	Gravadlax, venison carpaccio, pear tarte tatin

With abundant fruit and floral notes, this refreshing pale ale is as pleasing to the nose as it is to the palate. Full of ripe wheat field aromas, with added zing from the grapefruity finish.

Russian River Pliny the Elder

Website: www.russianriverbrewing.com
Brewed in: Santa Rosa, California, USA
ABV: 8%
Appearance: Dark caramel, voluminous foam
Aroma: Pine, caramel, grapefruit
Flavour: Clove, toffee, mixed peel
Great with: Hot dog with chilli, seafood gumbo, Époisses washed-rind cheese

Not a beer for the faint-hearted: Pliny is a beautiful drink, but if you're not already a fan of American-style IPAs, I suggest that you work your way up to this. On both the nose and palate, there is a wealth of pine, citrus and clove spice, offset by the slightest of sweet notes in the middle.

Sierra Nevada Pale Ale

Website: www.sierranevada.com
Brewed in: Chico, California, USA
ABV: 5.6%
Appearance: Ginger biscuit-amber, tight, light, white head
Aroma: Honeycomb, straw, nettle
Flavour: Ginger, fresh grass, orange blossom
Great with: Teriyaki chicken, mackerel ceviche, aged Gouda

This spicy/sweet, orange-scented temptress almost never fails to encourage people into the craft beer category. And while it's all sweetness and light up front, it has a dark side, too – an orangey/nettley punch at the end, which sucks all sweetness from your palate.

Stone Ruination IPA

Website: www.stonebrew.com
Brewed in: Escondido, California, USA
ABV: 7.7%
Appearance: Deep yellow, cloud-like white head
Aroma: Crushed nettles, honey, caramelized grapefruit
Flavour: Fresh-cut grass, bitter greens, lime skins
Great with: Slow-cooked pork shoulder, mackerel, nachos with jalapeños

When a beer is called Ruination, you should take it seriously. Unless you're planning to start chewing hops for fun, I suggest that you make this your last beer of the evening! It's mainly about the bitterness, but what impresses me is that it's so dry and bitter yet is still full of fresh grass and caramelized citrus fruit.

Worthington White Shield

Website: www.worthingtonswhiteshield.com
Brewed in: Burton upon Trent, West Midlands, UK
ABV: 5.6%
Appearance: Amber with billowing white foam
Aroma: Red apples, pepper, slight sulphur
Flavour: Spicy pepper, tart marmalade, juicy vinous notes
Great with: Malaysian rendang curry, extra mature Cheddar, apple crumble

The classic survivor from the heyday of IPA, Worthington White Shield never fails to please. It has an utterly unique bouquet of red apple and pepper, with the merest hint of sulphur from Burton's famous water. On the palate it has a real depth of juicy flavour, and finishes off with a pow of pepper and sharp marmalade.

Others to try

Brasserie d'Achouffe Houblon Chouffe, Belgium
Amarcord Volpina, Italy
Batemans Victory Ale, UK
Dogfish Head 90 Minute Imperial IPA, Maryland, USA
Firestone Walker Pale 31, California, USA
Goose Island IPA, Illinois, USA
Hart of Preston Nemesis, UK
Brasserie Le Paradis La P'tite Sylvie. Lorraine, France
Thornbridge Kipling, UK

BITTER

Poor old bitter, I think it's hugely unfair that this glorious beer style has spent so much of its life saddled with a moniker that conjures images of stick-waving old gits – in fact, I'll go so far as to proclaim this an outrage! Yes, ladies and gentlemen, an outrage! And why? Because I consider bitter my national drink and I will defend it to the very last. I glory in its varying shades of brownness; I adore that it's served cool, but not chilled; I revel in smacking my lips after that first glorious sip, and I wallow in its dry astringency, which makes me want to plunge back in for more.

GETTING BITTER

But why do I get so passionate about what a lot of people consider to be the ugly duckling of the beer world? Let me tell you more ... Even people who know what I do for a living express surprise when I order a pint of bitter, often saying, 'But that's an old bloke's drink!'

In Britain, bitter is very much part of the old-school rite of passage for the serious beer drinker. When you clearly enjoy it, you get some sneaking respect, an almost ephemeral nod: it's like earning your beer-drinking stripes.

And the reason I love this style is because when I finally drank a bitter I 'got', it was like someone had turned a light bulb on in my head. I suddenly understood the appeal of what I'd previously thought was a really dull drink – and I'm now hooked because it's a beer style I can enjoy without having to think about it.

I do apologize for not sounding very inspirational there, but it's true: we all say we could eat foie gras, truffles or lobster every day, but , when it comes down to it, a sandwich is what we fancy most lunchtimes and it's the same for bitter – it's the beer world's equivalent of comfort food!

The other great thing about ordinary and best bitters – although not the stronger ESB style – is that they generally start at around 3.5% ABV and rarely stray above 4.6% ABV, meaning that in the UK they are the most widely available beers you can drink all evening and still make your way home without feeling that late-night dancing and a kebab is the best plan ever!

Maybe I'm getting old (I'm not; mid-30s is not old, it's not!), but for me there is little time more satisfyingly spent than in the pub with a newspaper, and a pint of bitter sitting faithfully by my side.

But – and this is a big but – this is not a beer style that you should introduce to new beer drinkers if you want to get them enjoying more brews. In fact, if you want to convert people to liking beer, it's probably the very worst style to give them because, unless they were raised sucking Brussels sprouts rather than a bottle, virtually no one likes bitter when they first try it.

So if you're a newcomer to beer, I doubt you'll genuinely enjoy these beers as much as others. It's a bit like being ready for a steady relationship – I recommend coming back in six months after you've been out wildly experimenting!

Facing page: From lemony light to deep copper – bitter is not all dull brown and boring.

Below: Having fun with beer names is all part of the British tradition – done tastefully, it works well.

BITTER BACKGROUND

Bitter is a direct descendant of pale ale (see pages 116–120), but while today's pale ales make a feature of their blaring hops, bitter is totally about getting a drinkable balance.

The murky history of how beer terms have changed over the years means it's difficult to judge exactly when pale ale became colloquially known as bitter, but the first written mention of the term is in *The Times* on 5 September 1842. By 1864 there was even a musical hall ditty dedicated to the style, and the Bass brand in particular – although Bass was still labelling its beer 'pale ale'. When the public decided that bitter beer was the phrase they liked, brewers adopted it very quickly, but with a great deal of regional variation in terminology and preferences for colour and taste.

DOWN THE PUB

As a very British style of beer, bitter is found in nearly every pub in the land. Over the years various brewing powerhouses have created different designations for their bitters, and have in turn been affected by what locals call their beer.

For example, if you're in a pub in the London area where they are selling Young's beers (see facing page) you'd be likely to fall into the parlance of asking for a pint of 'ordinary' for the 3.7% ABV beer and 'special' for the 4.5% ABV brew. If you're up north, it's just 'a bitter'; in most parts of the country if you want the stronger style, it's 'a best'.

As a very general guideline, a standard or ordinary bitter will have less than 4% ABV, a special, best or premium bitter will rarely exceed 4.6%, while an ESB – extra special or extra strong bitter – will be 4.6 to 6% or higher.

The colour of the drink you are ordering may vary according to the brewery as well as the location – as a general rule, you'll find northern bitter to be a light straw colour and bitter pretty much gets progressively darker as you move down the country.

Also, despite it being quintessentially British, we are by no means the only country to brew bitter, but we are still the ones who do it the best – after all, what is it everyone says about Britain? Great pubs, warm beer and bad food! Well, I'm pleased to say the last two are nearly wholly incorrect these days, with fantastic cellaring skills, belting British cask ale and culinary classics at the heart of our great pubs.

YOUNG'S BITTER

Website: www.youngs.co.uk
Brewed in: Bedford, Bedfordshire, UK
First brewed: 1862
Grain: Pale ale malt
Hops: Fuggles, Golding
ABV: 3.7% cask, 4.5% bottle

Appearance: Light amber, low foam head
Aroma: Earthy, slight orange, granary bread
Flavour: Slightly fruity, gentle citrus zing, subtle astringent finish
Great with: Mild medium-hard cheese, fish and chips, roast beef and all the trimmings

THE BEER

This is probably the beer I drink the most of: it's like a comfy sweater for me and I love that it's available so widely across the world – I even saw some when I was in the Caribbean!

It might sound paradoxical to rave about something that is so subtle, but that's what makes Young's bitter so eminently drinkable: its soft earthy nose, redolent of its English hops, the slight bready note, a hint of orange zest and its delicious gentle astringency at the end all combine to create the perfect session beer. It's my go-to, don't think about it, drink-all-afternoon beer!

While this beer is no longer brewed just down the road from me in Wandsworth, London, I believe it to be better than ever now that it is brewed at the more modern plant of Charles Wells in Bedfordshire, under the new banner of Wells & Young's.

THE BREWERY

There's a long-running argument about which is the longest continuous brewing site in the UK: the Ram Inn site in Wandsworth, London – the original home of Young's brewery – or Shepherd Neame in Faversham, Kent. Both hold documented evidence showing that brewing on the site started in the mid- to late 16th century, so I'm not going to wade into this spat – but the history behind the former Young's brewing site is pretty darn long.

The Ram Inn was a coaching inn that gave its name to the brewery itself; it still exists as a microbrewery to this day, run by a former Young's brewer called John Hatch.

The Ram Brewery gradually expanded and in the mid-18th century was brewing porter, London's most popular beer of the time. In 1831 Charles Allen Young and his partner Anthony Fothergill Bainbridge bought the brewery; by 1864 they had turned to the production of increasingly fashionable lighter beers, laying the foundation for what was to become Young's bitter.

Charles' son, also called Charles, formed the limited company Young & Co. on his deathbed in 1890. This continued until 2006, when the need to move from its now inconveniently located and pretty dilapidated brewery to a new site resulted in the surprise merger with Bedfordshire brewer Charles Wells.

The move to the Eagle brewery in Bedford was greeted with much cynicism, because Charles Wells had been moving towards the contract production and brand promotion of some pretty big-brand lagers for quite some time. However, the Young's brands made a pretty seamless transition. Importantly the brewery continues to use the original yeast strain and the modern brewing facilities have made the beers more consistent and tasty than ever.

FULLER'S ESB

Website: www.fullers.co.uk
Brewed in: Chiswick, London, UK
First brewed: 1971
Grains: Pale ale malt, crystal malt
Hops: Target, Northdown, Challenger, Goldings
ABV: 5.5% cask, 5.9% bottle

Appearance: Ruby brown, medium cream head
Aroma: Fruit cake, warm fudge sauce, marmalade
Flavour: Dried fruits, cinnamon, orange pith dry end
Great with: Steak and ale pie, roast lamb, rhubarb and ginger crumble

THE BEER

The original and still, for my money, the best, Fuller's ESB has given a name to whole category of beers. However, like all originals, it is much aped, and, ironically, was disqualified from 2010's World Beer Cup as not being to style – which brings things back down to earth with a bump! But, regardless of what the judging panels of these competitions say, it's a truly spectacular beer.

The smell and taste always remind me of baking when I was a child: sticky alcohol-macerated raisins and sultanas, a wisp of spice that leads into some heady mixed peel aromas and brown sugar richness. In fact, this beer is so comforting it almost sends you into a trance.

Fuller's current head brewer John Keeling had a hand in its creation. He recalls: 'We were making an entirely different beer called Old Burton Extra, which was in decline, so we decided to bring on a strong bitter that we'd started brewing as a winter ale in the late 1960s/early 1970s.

In 1971 the final ESB was settled on and it was decided to make it a year-round beer. Many breweries were making an ordinary and a special bitter, which we had and still have in the form of Chiswick and London Pride, so we named this one ESB, extra special bitter. It was important to make sure we made it very different, so in the copper the hops are Target, Northdown and Challenger, the last two being added late to the copper. It's then dry-hopped in the fermenter with Target and in the maturation vessel with Goldings. And, as if that isn't enough, it's also then dry-hopped in cask with Goldings.'

THE BREWERY

Although the Griffin brewery in Chiswick, West London, can trace its origins as far back as the mid-1600s, the Fuller, Smith & Turner presence on the site dates from 1845. It is the only remaining historic family brewery in the whole of London. Descendants of the founding partners John Fuller, Henry Smith and John Turner are still involved in the business today.

GOOSE ISLAND HONKER'S ALE

Website: www.gooseisland.com
Brewed in: Chicago, Illinois, USA
First brewed: 2001
Grains: Pale malt, caramel malt, wheat, roasted barley
Hops: Styrian Goldings
ABV: 4.2%

Appearance: Bright amber, medium white foam
Aroma: Raisin, red apple, rye bread
Flavour: Green apple, chutney-like fruit, slightly burnt toast
Great with: Burgers, lamb kebab, Cheddar cheese

THE BEER

Described by its creator Greg Hall, who is no longer at the brewing helm of Goose Island: 'When you first see Honker's your mind just races over to a pub in England: it's got that sunset colour that you have to love about a pint of bitter in a proper pub, and that was the inspiration.'

Much tarter than your average British bitter, Honker's offers up a lovely rich, fruity nose with a hint of breadiness. That fruit expands over your palate and is joined by a pleasingly astringent roasty-toasty note with just a zing of green apple and grassy freshness to polish it off. Honker's is a rarity on the US craft beer scene for being incredibly popular despite its relatively low alcoholic strength.

THE BREWERY

If you are ever in Chicago, I heartily urge you to go to one of the Goose Island brewpubs or the brewery itself. Write off the afternoon, in fact the rest of the day and night, because once you get stuck into these beers you won't be able to stop. Goose Island was right at the forefront of the American craft brewing movement; when John Hall started his brewpub in 1988, he wanted to shake the Midwesterners from their mass-market beer torpor and treat them to a whole new flavour sensation, as well as educating them at the same time.

The brewpub was a huge hit, with people seeing their beer made right before their eyes, and by 1995 it couldn't keep up with demand. John and his son Greg, who had joined him to become brewmaster, decided to take the plunge into a larger brewery and bottling plant, and they purchased the Fulton Street site. A second brewpub was opened in 1999.

Along with a lovely line of soft drinks, including root beer, the brewery now produces over amazing 50 beers. In 2011 the brewery was sold to AB-InBev, the global giant responsible for Stella and Budweiser, among others. Let's hope they will keep the brewery's integrity.

MORE TO TRY ...

Crouch Vale Essex Boys Bitter

Website:	www.crouchvale.co.uk
Brewed in:	Chelmsford, Essex, UK
ABV:	3.5%
Appearance:	Pale brown, feathery head
Aroma:	Fruit cake, fudge, straw
Flavour:	Burnt caramel, hay, orange peel
Great with:	Pork pie, cheese and onion pasty, salted peanuts

Eminently drinkable; the low alcohol content and gentle flavours won't stand up to much more than a bar snack, but will make it a simple affair to sink a few pints at the end of a hard day.

Elysian The Wise

Website:	www.elysianbrewing.com
Brewed in:	Seattle, Washington, USA
ABV:	5.9%
Appearance:	Bright amber, tightly packed cream suds
Aroma:	Honey, citrus medley, grass
Flavour:	Hint of butterscotch, sage, grapefruit
Great with:	Hamburger, chickpea salad, banana split

This ESB was Elysian's very first brew back in 1996. The almost jewel-like colour beckons you into the sweet, grassy nose, followed on the palate by a hint of butterscotch, a herbal depth and super-zingy citrus end.

Firestone Walker DBA (Double Barrel Ale)

Website:	www.firestonebeer.com
Brewed in:	Paso Robles, California, USA
ABV:	5%
Appearance:	Light-struck copper, fleecy white head
Aroma:	Vanilla, white toast, mace
Flavour:	Brioche, strawberry, white pepper
Great with:	Mackerel on roasted tomatoes, baked aubergines, strawberry shortcake

Instead of being held in the more usual stainless steel vessels, 20 per cent of this beer is fermented in new American oak barrels, which accounts for its intensity of flavour. Warm vanillins, sprinkled with an earthy spice, fill your nose and continue on the palate, joined by a bready note and some jammy strawberry, which helps balance out the astringent peppery end.

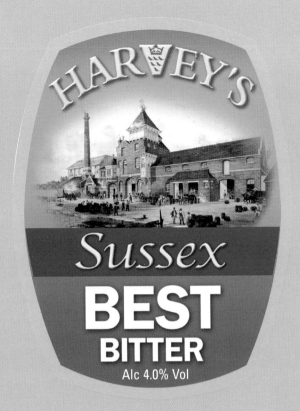

Marble Pint

Website: www.marblebeers.co.uk
Brewed in: Manchester, UK
ABV: 3.9%
Appearance: Stem ginger-orange, creamy white head
Aroma: Crushed nettles, ginger, hay
Flavour: Gingerbread, straw, green peppercorns
Great with: Sausage and mash, cheese bubble and squeak, spotted dick

It's a funny thing when a brewery suddenly catches everyone's attention after having quietly grafted away for ten years, but that's exactly what happened to Marble, and now they are brewing flat-out to keep up with demand for their excellent beers. While this beer's aroma and flavour descriptions might sound complex, all of the components are in balance, creating the perfect quaffing beer.

Oakham JHB

Website: www.oakhamales.com
Brewed in: Peterborough, Cambridgeshire, UK
ABV: 3.8%
Appearance: Lemony sunshine, small head
Aroma: Lemon, lime, raspberry
Flavour: Sharp lemon, kaffir lime, mown hay
Great with: Dry roasted peanuts, teriyaki chicken, young goat's cheese

JHB (Jeffrey Hudson Bitter) is one of the rare very pale gold bitters that's been brewed for decades, well before golden and blonde ales came into vogue. It is a truly refreshing brew. It's the consistent bitterness through this beer that makes it so thirst-quenching, and I love it.

Harvey's Sussex Best Bitter

Website: www.harveys.org.uk
Brewed in: Lewes, Sussex, UK
ABV: 4%
Appearance: Deep copper, loose feathery head
Aroma: Fresh-cut grass, baking bread, caramel
Flavour: Toasted granary bread, brown sugar, nettle
Great with: Roast beef, treacle tart, young Wensleydale

The recipe for Harvey's Sussex Best Bitter was resurrected in 1955 when wartime rationing ended. A benchmark against which to judge other bitters, its subtle, balanced sweetness and fresh crushed nettle-like end creates session beer perfection. When it's on the bar, it's nearly always my go-to beer for a first pint while I decide what I want next, which could very well be another one!

Others to try

Anderson Valley Boont ESB, California, USA
Deschutes Bachelor ESB, Oregon, USA
RCH Pitchfork, Somerset, UK
Ruddles County, Suffolk, UK
Timothy Taylor Landlord, Yorkshire, UK

TRAPPIST ALE & ABBEY BEER

From bubbly blondes and spritzy, slightly sour palate-teasers to delightfully dark, strong sipping beers, the Trappist and abbey styles are a broad church indeed. Most readily associated with Belgium, home to six of the world's seven Trappist breweries, they have an influence that has spread worldwide, with brewers seeking to produce similar products for the delight and delectation of beer lovers everywhere.

BLESS ME FATHER FOR I HAVE BREWED

Although people regularly seek to categorize Trappist and abbey beers, they defy categorization because Trappist beers range from an easy-drinking organic blonde ale at one end of the spectrum to strong dark ales at the other, and plenty in between.

However, there are so few genuine Trappist and abbey beers that it's worth addressing the story as a separate section, simply because it is so interesting and has given the world some beers that can only be described as divinely tasty. Prepare for tales of creation, destruction, greed, hope and charity – just like the Bible, this story has got it all! The word 'Trappist' generally conjures up pictures of hushed cloisters, gentle chanting, men in white robes and a life of contemplative abstention – not powerful and exciting beers, though that's exactly what Trappist beers are. Rich, hefty and complex, ranging in style from the tempting golden Westmalle Tripel to spicy Chimay Bleu, these brews are in a quite exclusive club, with only seven monasteries in the world – six of them in Belgium – producing beer.

The Catholic Church has never been shy on the drinking front and records show that monks have been brewing beer for more than 1000 years. However, the ales produced by today's Trappist monasteries have been in existence for only about 100 years – but this doesn't mean you should treat them with any less reverence.

Before we look at the beers, let me explain the Trappist ethos; it'll make you feel good when you're drinking these world-class brews.

To be a Trappist monastery, the monks must follow the Order of Cistercians of the Strict Observance, a contemplative religious order that consists of monasteries of monks *and* nuns – the latter being referred to as Trappistines. It's widely believed that the Trappists are a silent order: they aren't, they simply discourage idle chit-chat.

The Trappists, named after the abbey of La Trappe in Normandy, where they were founded in 1664, form part of the larger Cistercian family, which traces its origins to 1098, and the Cistercians were an offshoot of the Benedictines – are you keeping up with this religious family tree? The monks live by the 'Rule of St Benedict' – actually a book of more than 60 rules – which instructs its followers to fill their waking hours with being contemplative and productive, whether it's helping the monastery to be as self-sufficient as possible through farming or creating products that are sold to help fund the monastery and its good works.

Facing page: All across the world the Trappist brewing traditions, and its sister abbey beers, are revered.

Above: A beer a day allows monks to work, rest and pray.

And that final point is a poignant one. When I visited Orval (one of the Trappist monasteries that makes beer, see page 143), I was informed that some of the rural populations in the area were so poor that giving alms at the gate was not an unusual occurrence. So remember that when you buy a Trappist brew, you are helping people in need.

SEVEN HEAVENLY BREWERS

Most of the beers from the seven Trappist monasteries pack a punch, but I'd like to point out that, although drinking isn't a sin, drunkenness is, and the monks themselves drink Patersbier (Fathers' beer), which is no stronger than 3.5% ABV. These weaker brews are sometimes available to the public through nearby or on-site cafés like those at Chimay and Orval. It's highly unlikely you'll get to taste these beers unless you visit the monasteries – and I heartily suggest you do visit some of them, at least once in your life; Chimay, Orval and Rochefort, set in the Ardennes countryside, are particularly beautiful.

A lot of people use the term Trappist to mean a specific type of beer, but this couldn't be further from the truth. It simply means that the beer is brewed at the monastery, by or under the supervision of

Trappist beer styles

There are three distinct styles that the Trappists have made their own, and which are much imitated by brewers around the world:

Dubbel – a dark brown, quite fruity ale, often with caramelized banana and spicy notes, generally around 6–7% ABV.

Tripel – a style created by Westmalle in 1934 (the recipe changed slightly in 1956), this is a strong golden ale (around 9% ABV), with brisk, citrus and earthy spice aroma and flavour, and a hint of sweetness but a dry finish. The slightly lower alcohol **Blonde** ales are based on this style.

Quadrupel – now you're playing with the big beer! Super-strong, dark and often with sherry or madeira-like notes, viscous in texture, quite sweet and very relaxing to sip from either a classic chalice glass or a brandy balloon. Made into a brand by La Trappe in 1992 and now applied to all the strongest ales from the Trappist breweries,

Trappist monks. The Trappist breweries describe their beers in different ways and don't all brew the same range of beers; for example, Orval, in the south of Belgium near the French border, brews only one beer (see page 143), while La Trappe in the Netherlands offers nine beers.

LET THERE BE BEER ...

The Trappist breweries developed independently from each other and they don't all label their beers as Dubbel or Tripel. Chimay identifies its beers by the colour of the label: red 7% ABV, white 8%, blue 9%. Rochefort's beers are labelled 6, 8 and 10, referring to the density of the wort in Belgian degrees – this would take too long to explain and is not directly linked to the alcoholic strength; Rochefort 6 has 7.5% ABV, Rochefort 8 has 9.2% and Rochefort 10 has 11.3%.

Above: Belgium is not the only country to have monastic breweries. The beautiful Monastery of Christ in the Desert in New Mexico, USA, is winning high praise for its beers.

WHAT ARE ABBEY BEERS?

What sets abbey beers apart from the Trappist ales? Primarily, they aren't brewed in monasteries and aren't approved by the International Trappist Association – although some of them are made under a licensing arrangement that benefits the religious institution whose name they bear. Others are named after fictitious or long-defunct abbeys.

Most of them are similar in style to the Trappists – strong with a suggestion or more of sweetness, brown or blonde, 'Dubbel' or 'Tripel'. However, there has been a rash of brands that don't respect any heritage and have merely sought to capitalize on a growing demand for strong, Belgian-style ales. Belgian versions are usually labelled bilingually, as *Abbaye* and *Abdij*, but there's little to help the buyer decide which beers are worth trying. There is often an element of snobbery about abbey beers; some beer drinkers seem to think that if it's not Trappist it doesn't cut it, but I find that view a little odd because some of these beers have just as much history and complexity as the Trappist ales themselves, and some have a little more accessibility and drinkability to them. It doesn't help that it's not always clear whether an abbey beer actually contributes to any religious institution.

ABBEY BEERS OF BELGIUM

Probably the best-known beers of the abbey-style beers are those of Leffe, named after an abbey in southern Belgium and brewed under licence by global brewing giant AB InBev. While I rarely praise the corporate brewers, who are all about bottom line at the expense of flavour, the most widely available Leffe beers – blonde and brown – are reasonable introductions to the style and still plough profits back into the abbey. Grimbergen is a perfectly respectable range, brewed by Heineken for Grimbergen abbey just north of Brussels, but my personal favourite is the Maredsous range and the Brune in particular (see page 144), brewed for the abbey of the same name by Duvel-Moortgat.

I also very much rate the Affligem range: Blond, Dubbel and Tripel. The history of the Benedictine abbey of Affligem, founded in 1074, echoes that of many Belgian monasteries and sheds a lot of light on why many of them have outsourced their brewing to lay operations, been abandoned or no longer brew – a result of centuries of war, religious persecution or fire. After the French Revolution the brothers started brewing for themselves and did so right up until World War I, when the German army seized the vats to use the copper – an unforgivable act of religious and cultural vandalism that was repeated in other breweries. The monks bought new vessels in 1920 and brewed for the next 50 years until handing over operations to the villagers of Opwijk (pronounced *Op-wike*) to concentrate on its educational and cultural activities.

OUTSIDE BELGIUM AND THE NETHERLANDS

However, it's not just in Belgium that you'll find monastic connections to breweries. In the Czech Republic the Klasterni Pivovar, which is based at the Strahov monastery in Prague, produces the Saint Norbert beers.

There's even a Benedictine monastery in New Mexico, USA. The Monastery of Christ in the Desert in Abiquiu was founded in 1964; to date, its beers have been brewed under contract like Belgium's abbey beers, but in 2011 the brothers installed a new brewery in-house with the help of roving brewing consultant Brad Kraus. The Monks' Ale and Monks' Wit are brewed alongside some seasonal offerings.

Many craft breweries the world over, from the Americas to Australia and the UK to New Zealand, are taking great joy in looking at the abbey and Trappist beers and using them as divine inspiration for their own interpretations. Breweries like Sharp's in the UK (page 145), the much-loved Allagash in the US and Murray's Craft Brewing Co in New South Wales, Australia are just a few examples of this well-travelled style.

PRAY AND WORK

Beers aren't the only products of Trappist monasteries. Benedictine rules emphasize that communities should be self-supporting; there are 15 Trappist monasteries where the monks and nuns make and sell a range of products, from cheese, bread and pea soup to wines, liqueurs, cosmetics and floor-cleaning products! The Trappist label guarantees the origin of approved products.

ORVAL

Website: www.orval.be
Brewed at: Villers-devant-Orval, Belgium
First created: 1932
Grains: Pale malt, caramalt
Hops: Hallertau Herzbrücker, Hallertau, Strisselspalt
Other ingredients: Liquid brewing sugar
ABV: 6.2%

Appearance: Sunset orange, heavenly white foam
Aroma: Orange zest, coriander root, slight vinegar
Flavour: Tart marmalade, plummy fruit, zingy end
Good with: Port Salut-style cheese, rich beef stews, crème caramel

THE BEER

Only one beer is brewed at this Trappist abbey; a glorious golden orange sunset topped by a fluffy cloud. On the nose it is full of zingy citrus when it is young, but after some time in bottle it mellows to a warm, marmalade aroma that's got an underlying soft balsamic vinegar note. On the palate it is a joyous expression of tingly carbonation, tart zestiness and huge amounts of spicy, warming richness, ending in an exciting balsamic sourness provided by the *Brettanomyces* yeast used in the secondary fermentation in the bottle.

THE BREWERY

Orval Abbey is, like many other religious buildings, a triumph of faith in the face of adversity and human ability to destroy beauty.

Founded in 1070, it gradually became relatively prosperous until it was gutted by fire in 1252; it took another century for it to recover. Later it was all but completely destroyed during the French Revolution. In 1926, local landowners the de Harenne family offered the ruins of Orval and the surrounding land to the Cistercian Order so monks could return to the area – an amazing gift. The abbey was built upon the foundations of the 18th century building and was finally completed in 1936.

How did Orval get its name? Well, it's a very pretty story, and gives the brewery its emblem of a trout with a golden ring in its mouth.

In 1076 the area in which the monastery was established was the seat of the Countess Mathilda of Tuscany. One day the Countess was seated beside an exceptionally clear spring when her wedding ring slipped from her finger and dropped into the water. Appalled at its loss she offered up a prayer and suddenly, to her amazement, a trout rose to the surface with the ring in its mouth. Filled with wonder at this divine miracle, she cried out: 'Here is my golden ring! Blessed be the valley that has returned it to me! From now on I want it to be called the golden valley.' As she would have been speaking Latin, she would have said 'aurea vallis' rather than golden valley, and from 'aurea vallis', we get Orval – the golden valley. A lovely story and one that matches the great beauty of the beer itself.

Overseeing the production of this legendary beer since 1985 has been lay brewer Jean-Marie Rock, a man with an impish sense of humour but great respect for the role he holds. Having previously worked at other Belgian breweries (Palm and Lamot), he says: 'I don't feel any different working for Orval than I did for other breweries, I still have a boss. Being Orval's guardian makes me feel good, not god, but good!'

MAREDSOUS 8 BRUNE

Website: www.maredsousbieres.be
First brewed: 1958
Brewed in: Breendonk, Belgium
Grains: Pilsner, caramalt, roast malt
Hops: Styrian Goldings
ABV: 8%

Appearance: Chocolate brown, billowy white head
Aroma: Coffee, chocolate, caramel
Flavour: Fig, digestive biscuit, bitter chocolate
Great with: Beef Wellington, pâté, truffles

THE BEER

Maredsous 8 Brune is pure pleasure in a glass, but watch it: you'd never guess it has 8% alcohol! This deep brown beer is full of rich Camp coffee notes (roasted chicory roots, often used as a coffee substitute) combined with a fruity note from the yeast, and it has a pleasingly dry finish for an initially sweet beer – it really does tick a lot of happy boxes.

THE BREWERY

The Maredsous Abbey in Denée, near Namur, in the beautiful Ardennes region of Belgium is a relatively new religious establishment and part of the Benedictine order; it laid its foundations in the late 19th century and started brewing in the early 1900s. Shortly after this, Father Attout decided to develop the Brune as a Christmas beer, and the recipe was resurrected in 1958 for general sale.

The beer is no longer brewed at the abbey, because the monks needed more space for their school. Since 1963 the beers have been brewed by the mid-sized Belgian brewing concern Duvel-Moortgat (which also produces Vedett, Liefmans and, of course, Duvel – see pages 98 and 102). And it's great to know that Duvel-Moortgat still uses exactly the same recipes that Father Attout created for all the beers, including the Brune, because the more I read about him, the more I'm sure that he put a lot of time and dedication into their creation and wouldn't like any meddling.

He seems to have been an inspirational figure: besides creating these beers he was also responsible for nurturing the talent of Belgian architect Francis Bonaert, who attended the school at Maredsous, initially to study classics. Father Attout directed his burgeoning photographic talents and steered Bonaert towards a more artistic route. And, in a nice full circle kind of way, some of the profits from the beers go to the upkeep of the school, as well as the monastery and charitable works.

The trefoil outlined on the beer's label is said to symbolize happiness and the label also features the abbey's coat of arms, with the Benedictine cross and a branch of mistletoe. The abbey's motto is 'in viam pacis', which means 'on the path to peace'.

SHARP'S HONEY SPICE TRIPLE

Website: www.sharpsbrewery.co.uk
Brewed in: Rock, Cornwall, UK
First brewed: 2008
Grain: Pale ale malt
Hops: Northern Brewer, Perle, Willamette, Cascade
Other ingredients: Glucose, honey, citrus peel, coriander, ginger, nutmeg

ABV: 9.5%
Appearance: Deep gold, ebullient fine white foam
Aroma: Citrus, honey, herbal
Flavour: Honey ice cream, warming spice, gentle astringent finish
Great with: Roast poultry, pork belly, asparagus

THE BEER

Rich, complex and super-spicy, Sharp's Triple is very special. Tangerine and honey mingled with an almost rosemary herbal note with a kick of ginger assault the nose as you pour this awesomely big amber beer. When you raise it to your lips, you immediately encounter the citrus and honey notes you picked up on the nose, but it's all wrapped up in a creamy full-bodied hug enhanced by an enveloping, warming nutmeg and earthy coriander squeeze; your taste buds are drowsily, but gratefully, roused by a gentle bitter citrus zing.

THE BREWERY

Sharp's is a great example of a modern brewery thriving on old-fashioned passion. Founded by Bill Sharp in 1994 in the stunning coastal location of Rock in Cornwall, it was sold in 2003 to two guys who'd made their names in the chilled and frozen pasta business. Since then, the brewery has seen astronomical growth: its leading brand Doom Bar bitter (named after a sandbank in the nearby Camel estuary) is currently the second best-selling premium ale in the UK. In 2011 the brewery was taken over by international brewing group Molson Coors, with promises to leave head brewer Stuart Howe creating his speciality range of beers. Here's hoping they hold to that promise!

MORE TO TRY ...

Chimay Bleu

Website:	www.chimay.com
Brewed in:	Abbaye de Scourmont, Chimay, Belgium
ABV:	9%
Appearance:	Ruby-brown, billowing cream head
Aroma:	Fresh bread, geranium, chocolate
Flavour:	Rye bread, sandalwood, caramel
Great with:	Spicy charcuterie, oxtail stew, blue cheese

Chimay, in the Ardennes region of Belgium, is probably the most widely available of the Trappist beers. The Bleu is, for me, the pinnacle of the brewery's portfolio: complex, floral, sweet, woody and a perfect foil for a blue cheese like Roquefort.

Moonlight Brewing Twist of Fate Ale

Website:	www.moonlightbrewing.com
Brewed in:	Abbey de St Humulus, Santa Rosa, California, USA
ABV:	5.6%
Appearance:	Sun-struck copper, downy white head
Aroma:	Pepper, toffee, fresh hay
Flavour:	Sweet tobacco, bitter orange, pine
Great with:	Croque monsieur, roast monkfish, rum and raisin ice cream

Brian Hunt set up Abbey de St Humulus (the Abbey of Hops) after becoming an Abbot online for $20 – but he is devout that making good beer brings him closer to God, so I've included him with great affection. More quaffable than many abbey brews, Twist of Fate Ale has an enticing spicy/sweet nose, carried through to a richer, sweet tobacco-like initial flavour before the sassy end kicks in with a citrus, woody dryness.

Rochefort 10

Website:	www.abbaye-rochefort.be
Brewed in:	Abbaye Notre-Dame de Saint-Remy, Rochefort, Belgium
ABV:	11.3%
Appearance:	Liquid dark cherry chocolate, soft creamy head
Aroma:	Dates, brown sugar, Pedro Ximénez sherry
Flavour:	Caramelized figs, mace, oloroso sherry
Great with:	Fig and walnut salad, châteaubriand steak, blue cheese

Rich, complex, warming, spicy and satisfying – there's probably a joke about 'just how I like my men' in there somewhere! The enticing nose of chocolate-covered dates and brown sugar reminds me of rich sweet sherry; it follows through on the palate with caramelized figs, balanced in the middle by a woody spice, like mace or perhaps a hint of sandalwood; and ends silkily, on a long, fruity, oloroso sherry-like crescendo of flavour.

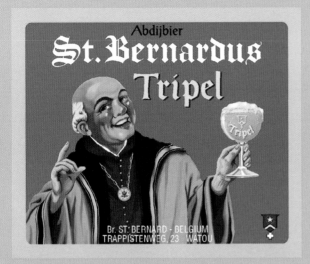

Flavour: Toffee, raisin, green peppercorn
Great with: Rib-eye steak, spice-crusted swordfish, Gouda

La Trappe is the only Trappist brewery outside of Belgium. It's also very innovative in comparison with the Belgian Trappists, with a portfolio of nine beers in 2011. The Dubbel is dangerously drinkable, with juicy, sweet raisin and plum aromas and flavours, balanced out with a bite of spice. A thoroughly enjoyable sipping beer, best served lightly chilled.

Westmalle Tripel

Website: www.trappistwestmalle.be
Brewed in: Onze-Lieve-Vrouw van het Heilig Hart, Westmalle, Belgium
ABV: 9.5%
Appearance: Pale orange-gold, cotton-wool-like white head
Aroma: Baked beans, cinnamon, hot orange marmalade
Flavour: Allspice, sandalwood, flamed orange peel
Great with: Asparagus and hollandaise, chicken kiev, Pont l'Évêque cheese

Westmalle Tripel was the original pale, strong 'tripel' and, most people agree, it is still the best. Intensely complex, spicy, yet refreshing, it manages to strike a balance of strength without being cloying. A huge hit of baked bean and tomato vine on the nose is swiftly joined by sweet, woody spices, and then it ends on a smell exactly like when you're making marmalade. All that enticing aroma follows through to the palate, with some additional sandalwood notes and a decent bitter orange kick, which is what makes it so dangerously quaffable!

St Bernardus Tripel

Website: www.sintbernardus.be
Brewed in: Watou, Belgium
ABV: 8%
Appearance: Cloudy amber, woolly white head
Aroma: Red apple, pears, old straw
Flavour: Lemon cordial, honey, dried orange peel
Great with: Fish pie, pumpkin and spinach curry, Gruyère

Fruitier than most tripels, this beer is redolent with apples, pears, lemons and oranges, with a candied, syrupy undertone on the nose. All of these exciting aromas are evident on the palate, along with a balancing bitterness like dried orange peel, with just a hint of liquorice joining it at the end.

La Trappe Dubbel

Website: www.latrappe.nl
Brewed in: Abdij Onze Lieve Vrouw van Koningshoeven, Berkel-Enschot, Netherlands
ABV: 7%
Appearance: Walnut brown with garnet highlights, amber foam
Aroma: Plum, caramel, pepper

Others to try

Achel Bruin, Belgium
Affligem, Belgium
Allagash Tripel, Maine, USA
Bosteels Tripel Karmeliet, Belgium
Iron Hill American Tripel, Delaware, USA
Westvleteren 12, Belgium

BARLEY WINE, SCOTCH ALE & OLD ALE

Are you ready to step up to the big leagues? Because this is where complexity of flavour and alcoholic strength are part of the territory.

Barley wines and Scotch ales are close relatives, high in alcohol, on the sweeter side of the flavour scale and full of delicious caramel and toffee tastes – but they should always be well balanced with strong undercurrents of berries and stone fruits and the skilful use of hop bitterness to stop them becoming too cloying.

Old ales are harder to pin down: historic versions of the style are full of all sorts of strange flavours like soy sauce and Marmite, with a noticeably sour end, but brewers have gone off on their own flights of fancy, and 'old ale' now generally refers to a strong beer that has been aged in the brewery for around six to 12 months to reach the perfect peak of maturity.

SWEETER SIDE OF LIFE

If beer styles were people, then barley wines and Scotch ales would be someone like George Clooney: respected by men and loved by women, growing old gracefully, with an air of sophistication, but retaining a puckish charm that could get you into trouble by convincing you to jump on a jet to Vegas instead of going home for dinner.

Barley wines and Scotch ales rarely stray below 6% ABV and can wander as high as 12% or even more. These beers inevitably yield some gloriously complex, sweet, flavours, but the great ones still offer a citrus zing or bitter chocolate finish that stops them from becoming too cloying. And, just like Clooney, they age well too.

As far as I can tell, there's nothing to say that the strong ales made in England have ever been wildly different from those brewed in Scotland. And, besides, any geographical or historical distinction between modern barley wines and Scotch ales is debatable: they are both viscous, strong and generally at the sweeter end of the beer spectrum. These days, the main differences are between breweries and their individual interpretations of the style.

Also, the terms barley wine and Scotch ale don't have much history to them. The phrase barley wine didn't enter common parlance until the early 20th century, when it came to be used for beers with more than 8% ABV. Brewers in the United States are not allowed to label their beer 'barley wine' and must use the term 'barleywine-style ale'.

Historically there have been various names for strong ales, such as 'doble-doble' in the 15th and 16th centuries. Later brewers sold their strongest ales as XXXX (X being the weakest). We can't be sure that these were similar to today's barley wines, but it's highly likely they bore more than a passing resemblance.

SHILLING ALES

In the explosion of craft brewing around the world, some brewers have latched onto the use of 'shilling' to denote what they call a Scottish, or Scotch, style of ale. The strongest versions are usually labelled 90/-, or 90 shilling ale, although some brewers make 120/- ale.

This seems to be little more than a fairly modern marketing ploy. In the 1970s, when the UK's cask ales began to fight back against the market domination of lager, Scottish brewers were looking for some sort of heritage to call on and adopted these phrases to denote a difference in strength.

These shilling designations were actually a pub trade term to denote the price landlords paid for the beer, which was certainly not something the public would have known. What's more, they weren't specific to Scotland but were used by brewers up and down the land.

Facing page: Barley wines, Scotch and old ales are comforting and uncritical companions to quietly relax with, just like a dog.

NORTH OF THE BORDER

In Scotland, the gentlest ales (under 3.5% ABV) are colloquially known as 'light'; those between 3.5 and 4% as 'heavy'; 'export' are around 4 to 5.5%; and the strongest ales, with more than 6% ABV, are often known as 'wee heavy'. The odd thing about Scotch ale, though, is that its namesake country has little to do with the proliferation of the style. The Belgians have been the greatest exponents of this style over the last century or so and, in more recent decades, it's a beer that craft brewers from the USA to Japan have embraced, occasionally using the term 'wee heavy' for their strong Scottish-style ales.

The Belgian connection dates from World War I, when several Scottish regiments were based in Belgium. An enterprising UK ex-pat, John Martin, began importing some strong Scottish ales to meet the demand from the homesick troops, and the brews soon found favour with the beer-loving locals too. He came up with the name Gordon Scotch Ale in 1924 and Gordon Scotch Ale has been brewed in Belgium since the 1960s.

Barley wines and Scotch ales made in the UK and Belgium emphasize the sweetness of the malt, balanced by alcoholic strength and a surprisingly high use of hops, which is scarcely perceptible due to the intrinsic sweetness of the base beer. The sweetness is often achieved by boiling the wort for longer than usual, which causes it to caramelize a little.

Today, barley wines and Scotch ales are seasoned travellers, embraced by breweries all over the world, including Japan, Canada, the USA, the Netherlands and New Zealand.

Above: Although Scotch ales have little to do with Scotland, they are still heavily advertised as if they are – so we're playing along!

OLD ALES

The word 'old' is used by brewers the world over in a nod to local traditions, but there is no historical or stylistic definition of old ales. Some are high in alcohol, with 6–8% ABV; others are lower; and many British brewers use 'old' to describe their 'winter warmer' – usually a deep red or brown ale, in which a deep sweetness of flavour, like liquorice or treacle, is most prevalent.

However, I would volunteer that this style developed from aged ales, which are documented to have had a sour edge, something I think the finest exponents of this style still have to this day. Although not all old ales are influenced by *Brettanomyces* yeast or *lactobacillus* or *pediococcus* bacteria, I do feel it's the one thing that can set great versions of this style apart, especially when the addition of these wild yeasts and other microscopic beasts can lift a good beer into greatness. However, there aren't that many of them out there.

DE MOLEN BOMMEN & GRANATEN

Website: www.brouwerijdemolen.nl
Brewed in: Bodegraven, Netherlands
First brewed: April 2008
Grains: Caramalt and pale ale malt
Hops: Nugget, Saaz
ABV: 15.2%

Appearance: Deep brown, vivacious creamy head
Aroma: Sweet sherry, dried fruit, peppery spice
Flavour: Fruit cake, sweet sherry, caramelized orange
Great with: Salty blue cheeses, balsamic-roast radicchio, gammon

THE BEER

This beer is well-named, as it will drop a flavour bomb on your taste buds. Inspired by English barley wines, and by the American penchant for putting twists on things, this hazy, orange-gold brew with its heady aroma immediately tells your senses you're in for something special.

The huge fruity notes that flow off it as its pours richly into the glass are akin to Pedro Ximénez sherry; prunes, dates, figs, raisins and a hint of spicy orange all follow through to the palate, along with golden syrup and a dark rum-like ginger-cake finish.

I have suggested some food pairings (above), but my favourite ways to enjoy this beer are either as a digestif after a meal or simply to sit back, relax and sip after a hard day, allowing it to blow all my cares away.

With a puckish sense of humour, the brewery names some of its beers after Dutch phrases or proverbs. I have to say that finding out the origin of this particular beer's name made my day! Bommen & Granaten (bombs and grenades) is taken from the phrase *duizend* (thousand) *bommen en granaten*, which originated from one of my childhood favourites, *The Adventures of Tintin*. Tintin's great friend, the salty sea dog Captain Haddock, regularly used the phrase 'ten thousand thundering typhoons!', which is roughly what this beer's name means when translated into English – brilliant!

THE BREWERY

Brouwerij de Molen is a precocious young brewery that began life in 2003 in a beautiful windmill named 'De Arkduif' after Noah's dove; the mill dates back to 1697. Since founder Menno Olivier made his home brewing hobby into a business, he now employs more than 15 people. Having joined forces with new co-owner John Brus in 2009, he is – as I write this in 2011 – leaving the mill for a new 25-hectolitre (550-gallon) brewery next door, although the pub and brewery shop will remain.

The new brewery will be state-of-the-art and environmentally friendly, reusing heat and water created by, or used in, the brewing process. It will continue to work with the Philadelphia Foundation, which helps mentally handicapped people learn necessary skills in the workplace.

Environmentally conscious, active in the community and successfully making great beer – Brouwerij de Molen is a model for modern brewers everywhere.

MOYLAN'S KILT LIFTER

Website: www.moylans.com
Brewed in: Novato, California, USA
First brewed: 1996
Grains: Crystal, Vienna, Munich, Special B and acidulated malts
Hops: East Kent Goldings

ABV: 8%
Appearance: Ox blood red, cheeky foam
Aroma: Sweet fruits, chocolate, sour cherry
Flavour: Toffee, liquorice, pine
Great with: Seafood gumbo, aged goat's cheese, New York cheesecake

THE BEER

This beer is as brash and hearty as a Scotsman wanting a pint. It swirls around your palate like a finely made kilt and finishes with a punch of flavour akin to a Glasgow kiss to your taste buds.

The nose almost reminds me of a panettone, with hints of chocolate, sour cherry and angelica in the mix; on the palate it has a pleasant balance of that fruit cake flavour, which is beefed up in the middle by a twist of liquorice and toffee and then, at the end, has a fresh, pine-like note that adds a pleasing astringency. The Kilt Lifter is by far and away Moylan's most popular and awarded beer, but it's much drier than you normally associate with this style. Head brewer Denise Jones explains why: 'Scotch ale, as a style, can be too cloying and sticky-sweet and this inhibits people from ordering more than one of these elixirs. Our goal is to brew it to a lower finishing gravity. While still malty and demonstrative of crystal malt character, the beer finishes drier, prompting the beer drinker to enjoy another. So far, the notion has paid off – Kilt Lifter is our top-selling brew around the USA and beyond.'

The demand for this beer is so high that it can now be found in 32 states and is exported to six countries – so with luck you should be able to get your hands on some!

THE BREWERY

A founding partner in Marin Brewing Co, Larkspur, California, in 1989, Brendan Moylan decided to move his family from San Francisco to Novato for a better quality of life, and opened his eponymous brewery/restaurant in 1991. Since then it has gone from strength to strength, winning numerous awards for its beers and keeping locals very happy with its food and drink.

GALE'S PRIZE OLD ALE

Website: www.gales.co.uk
Brewed in: London, UK
First brewed: 1920s
Grains: Pale, crystal and chocolate malts
Hops: Fuggles, East Kent Goldings
Adjuncts: Brewing sugar
ABV: 9%

Appearance: Deepest ruby brown, low tan foam
Aroma: Christmas pudding, molasses, balsamic vinegar
Flavour: Woody, spicy, sweet/sour
Great with: Strong Cheddar cheese, oxtail stew, dark bitter chocolate

THE BEER

If you like very fruity chutney made with balsamic vinegar, you'll love this; but maybe that's not selling it to you – please keep reading. This world classic opens with a distinct Christmas pudding, molasses and balsamic nose, which all follow through on the palate with an additional, almost ephemeral, woody spice, a hit of savoury balsamic and soy sauce with a sweet Pedro Ximénez complexity and a mouthwatering sour finish.

The recipe, and even some beer full of wild yeast and bacteria, was brought south from Yorkshire, to Gale's historic brewery in Horndean, Hampshire, in the 1920s.

THE BREWERY

Fuller's acquired Gale's in 2005 but closed the Horndean brewery because it was in such poor condition. Production moved to Fuller's Griffin brewery in Chiswick, west London, but before they left they brewed a huge batch of Prize Old Ale, to ensure the mysterious mix of yeasts and other beasts remained true to the original.

It's been a noble fight by the brewing team to keep the beer. Fuller's head brewer John Keeling thinks it's something the UK brewing has to be proud of, just as much as the Belgians should be proud of the lambic family of beers.

'The system at Gale's, with its wooden vessels, was impossible to clean properly. While that's a nightmare for most beers, in this case the completely wild system allowed natural micro-organisms to give the beer its unique quality; even when it was stored in stainless steel tanks, it didn't lose those brisk wild notes.'

It's a gentler beer now than it once was, due to the fact that some fresh beer is blended in that hasn't been inoculated with the original magic mix; however, it is still aged for a long time, so as to be true to the old ale style. 'We overbrew and hold some back, so we will always have a percentage of that original Gale's beer, slightly similar to the way that sherry is made,' says Keeling. 'Each vintage is aged for 18 months, which allows the micro-organisms to do their work.'

MORE TO TRY ...

Adnams Tally-Ho

Website: www.adnams.co.uk
Brewed in: Southwold, Sussex, UK
ABV: 7.5%
Appearance: Dark chocolate, light caramel froth
Aroma: Fresh mineral, cocoa, prunes
Flavour: Bitter chocolate, sour cherries, espresso
Great with: Wild boar, fruit cake, Stinking Bishop cheese

Tally-Ho is a deliciously morerish barley wine – the aroma is as rich as a big mug of cocoa with an additional prune-like fruitiness. The bitter chocolate flavour is overlaid with mouthwatering sour cherry and espresso coffee notes. This will excite your taste buds and warm your bones.

Anchor Old Foghorn

Website: www.anchorbrewing.com
Brewed in: San Francisco, California, USA
ABV: 8–10% (depends on year)
Appearance: Deep copper, spritzy white head
Aroma: Caramel, caramelized orange, crushed grass
Flavour: Toffee, bitter lemon, nettle
Great with: Roast pork, grilled cheese sandwich, Taleggio cheese

Born the same year I was (be kind), Old Foghorn is an American twist on a classic British barley wine. It smells similar, with its sweet caramels, sticky raisins and deep citrus aromas, but on the palate you get a much cleaner drinking experience, as it's got more bitterness from a higher addition of hops than its UK counterparts.

Bend Brewing Outback X

Website: www.bendbrewingco.com
Brewed in: Bend, Oregon, USA
ABV: 9.5%
Appearance: Dark ruby brown, feathery cream head
Aroma: Coffee, garibaldi biscuits, molasses
Flavour: Tiramisu, tea-soaked prunes, root ginger
Great with: Braised beef cheek, ratatouille, rhubarb and ginger crumble

Head brewer Tonya Cornett is one of the nicest people in the US craft brewing scene, and produces beers of the highest calibre, including this multi-award-winning old ale. The ruby depths hide a wealth of rich, but not cloying, aromas and flavours, which create a sweet but surprisingly astringent effect, finishing on a fiery kick of fresh root ginger.

Hogs Back AOverT

Website: www.hogsback.co.uk
Brewed in: Tongham, Surrey, UK
ABV: 9%
Appearance: Terracotta brown, creamy head
Aroma: Cherry cake, malt loaf, candied peel
Flavour: Black cherry compote, treacle, caramelized orange

Great with: Game pie, honey roast pumpkin, salty blue cheese

AoverT stands for 'aromas over Tongham', where this barley wine is made, because when it was first brewed a visitor mentioned how beautiful the brewery smelt that day. Deep berry and fruit cake aromas abound, making this the perfect foil for a full-flavoured blue cheese. A lingering but not overwhelming treacly sweetness finishes on an astringent citrus note.

Oskar Blues Old Chub

Website: www.oskarblues.com
Brewed in: Lyons, Colorado, USA
ABV: 8%
Appearance: Cola-brown, fluffy caramel head
Aroma: Cocoa powder, coffee, caramel
Flavour: Chocolate milk, peaty smoke, brown sugar
Great with: Baby back ribs, smoked trout, salty hard cheese

Oskar Blues is at the forefront of canned craft beer. Yep, you read that right (see page 33 for more on the benefits of canning), but the can is irrelevant to what Old Chub Scotch ale delivers. Its coffee, chocolate, caramel nose, with an ephemeral whiff of smoke, follows through on the palate with a creamy body and a delicately peaty finish.

Robinsons Old Tom

Website: www.frederic-robinson.co.uk
Brewed in: Stockport, Cheshire, UK
ABV: 8.5%
Appearance: Dark chocolate brown, creamy tan head
Aroma: Dark chocolate praline, mocha, raspberry
Flavour: Bitter chocolate, cinder toffee, redcurrants
Great with: Boeuf bourguignon, treacle tart, fondue

Old Tom is as easy to make disappear as the Cheshire cat on its label. Be warned, this brew has claws! Its alcohol is disguised under waves of dark chocolate and berry fruit aromas and flavours, and the dry, redcurrant end creates a drinkability that's quite astonishing in a barley wine of this strength.

Theakston's Old Peculier

Website: www.theakstons.co.uk
Brewed in: Ripon, North Yorkshire, UK
ABV: 5.6%
Appearance: Garnet red, loose, bubbly foam
Aroma: Red wine vinegar, redcurrant, sour plum
Flavour: Underripe red apple, balsamic vinegar, wood-sap dry
Great with: Beef and beer stew, sausages with sauerkraut, Cheddar cheese and chutney

Theakston's Old Peculier is one of those beers that can catch you completely off-guard. Like Gale's Prize Old Ale (see page 153), it is a rare surviving example of a British beer that has some balsamic notes to it – a genuine old ale. Vinegar, sour fruit and dry woodiness abound on both nose and palate, and it's surprisingly dry – a truly unique brew.

Others to try

Batemans Dark Lord, UK
Breconshire Rambler's Ruin, UK
Fuller's Golden Pride, UK
Gordon Scotch Ale, Belgium
Greene King Strong Suffolk, UK

MILD

Modern milds are some of my favourite beers; in the UK they are generally low in alcohol and merely kissed by hops, making them the perfect choice for the sneaky lunchtime pint. They offer the richness of flavour of a porter with the quaffability of a golden ale and the refreshing qualities of a bitter – all in one glass.

Although historically the designation of mild didn't mean low in alcohol, or even dark, this is the way most brewers make them nowadays, and I, for one, welcome their gentle ways as a break from some of the brewers' more exuberant offerings. But that doesn't mean they are *all* gentle beasts, so watch out, because milds they might be, but they're not always meek!

THE BEER

Mild is one of the most misunderstood of beers, and early in my career I was thoroughly misled by the myth that milds have to be dark and low in alcohol and with barely a hop cone waved at them. I now know better and I'd like to share my insight with you.

The word mild was historically applied to young or fresh beers that were 'mild of flavour' – you'll notice that there's no insistence on colour or alcoholic strength. You see, mild was 'fresh beer' and, as such, was less aggressive in flavour than its contemporaries; beers such as porters were described by writers of the day as being strong in flavour with a slightly sour edge to them, almost certainly as a result of collecting some *Brettanomyces* yeast, and possibly other spoiling bacteria, during their long cellaring period (see pages 166–167 for more on the flavours these micro-organisms give).

And although that might sound like a pretty horrible beer to us, it was fine with the drinkers of the day and they were used to it. The initial appeal of these fresh mild beers was probably their price point.

The removal of duty from beer in 1830 saw brewers expand their beer ranges and the gap between mild ales and porters in price diminished; previously porter had been the only accessible beer to the working classes, but now these fresher beers, which had previously been more expensive, came into reach of society as a whole. So, simple economics saw mild become more popular from the mid to late 1800s, while aged beers – and porter in particular – saw a decline; the common people were delighted to drink fresher beers and began to lose their taste for the sour side of brewing in favour of these sweeter, younger beers.

Facing page and below: Mild has always had a very traditional image, but that doesn't mean it isn't a fabulous drink, like the Hobsons below and on page 162.

Mild

3.2%

HOBSONS

DARK CHAMPION BEER

But mild's lower price point has been both a blessing and a curse for the style. It was certainly Britain's most popular drink up until World War II and was widely enjoyed by the working man. But with social change after the war, mild became a victim of fashion. Manual labour became stigmatized, office work became more attainable, and the aspirational sectors of society sought to shake off their blue-collar background and all its attached markers, including mild.

Mild's popularity was not just confined to the UK: the style travelled the world with British emigrants in the mid-1800s and records show that the USA (where mild is often known as brown ale), Canada, South Africa, Australia and New Zealand (where it's known as Kiwi brown) all had their own versions.

The great news is that all areas of the world are now rediscovering mild in all its glory. So make sure you give this meekly named beer a try, and you'll discover that it's anything but shy in the flavour department!

MOORHOUSE'S BLACK CAT

Website: www.moorhouses.co.uk
Brewed in: Burnley, Lancashire, UK
First brewed: 1979
Grains: Crystal, chocolate and pale ale malt
Hops: Fuggles, Willamette
ABV: 3.4%

Appearance: Deep brown, white head
Aroma: Mocha latte, Maltesers, dark chocolate
Flavour: Espresso coffee, liquorice, slight creaminess
Great with: Steak, chocolate, egg custard

THE BEER

I'm a very lucky girl because Black Cat was my introduction to the mild style of beer, and I've never looked back. On the nose it's enough to make any coffee junkie a fan for life, with rich mocha-like notes, tempered with a little bit of caramelly goodness, then on the palate it's so full of flavour and yet so refreshing! With espresso, dark chocolate, a slightly creamy body yet a lovely, clean refreshing and liquorice-like finish, it will leave you purring with anticipation for that next sip.

Although the word mild was removed from the name in 2000, to widen its appeal, that was the year Black Cat won the title Champion Beer of Britain – the first mild to do so in 27 years. And, Black Cat remains extremely popular – along with the rest of its witch-themed stable-mates, Pendle Witches Brew and Blond Witch – and in the USA it is considered the benchmark for the style.

THE BREWERY

You know they say it's good luck if a black cat crosses your path? Well, it certainly was for Moorhouse's brewery in Burnley. When Black Cat was born, it joined just one other beer in the Moorhouse's stable, the 3.7% session ale Premier Bitter. At that time the company's main focus was hop bitters (low-alcohol mild, stout and bitter) for export and use in shandy concentrates.

The beer was initially rustled up out of some concentrate liquorice that had been lying around the brewery. The brewery realized it was onto something when the beer sold out in double-quick time. The brewers started to experiment with more traditional ingredients, and when they included chocolate malt (a malt kilned at high temperatures) to provide the depth of colour and flavour, Black Cat as we now know it landed on the beer map on all four paws.

When the beer was launched it seemed like a slightly mad move because mild, along with other traditional ale styles in the UK, was declining against lager sales, and the beer initially struggled to find a foothold. But the north-west of England has always been loyal to mild, being unabashedly a place where the working man goes down the pub as often as possible – and the local watering hole is still the heart of the community.

What also helped Black Cat was that the major breweries had all but stopped brewing milds, so Moorhouse's was taking that niche market with the right level of operation to do so.

But even a lucky black cat needs a careful owner and Moorhouse's itself came very close to closing its doors in 1985, until locally born businessman Bill Parkinson stepped in to save it. Superstition is still paying off and the business is investing £4.2 million in a new brewery and visitors centre in 2011 alongside a brewing school for 2012.

NOLA BROWN ALE

Website: www.nolabrewing.com
Brewed in: New Orleans, USA
First brewed: 2008
Grains: Pale ale, caramunich, special roast, chocolate, black, kiln coffee and flaked barley malt
Hops: Perle, US Goldings

ABV: 3.9%
Appearance: Chocolate brown, wispy white head
Aroma: Chocolate, coffee, caramel
Flavour: Dark chocolate, digestive biscuit, blackcurrant
Great with: Steamed shellfish, jambalaya, milk chocolate mousse

THE BEER

NOLA Brown Ale is as smooth as a deep-South accent and as much fun as Mardi Gras, but will probably leave you with less of a hangover! A cheery chocolate milkshake aroma with a tiny hint of latte is carried through to the palate and joined by a darker chocolate flavour, a heavier hit of espresso, and a hint of fruity prune. Put all that together with the pleasingly dry and refined finish and you have a true Southern belle of a beer.

THE BREWERY

There are times when you have to say you respect not only a brewery's product but their ethos as well, and NOLA is definitely one of those cases.

NOLA Brewing, which stands for New Orleans Lager & Ale, arose out of one native's desire to help put something back into his home town following the devastating effects of Hurricane Katrina in 2005.

Owner and founder Kirk Coco, stationed in the Gulf of Arabia where he was serving his 11th year as a surface warfare officer in the US Navy, watched as this devastating storm flooded 80% of his home town. He immediately decided to come home to help rebuild and create jobs in his damaged community. Not entirely sure what he was going to do when he got there, he was enjoying a brew with fellow New Orleanian and home brewer Byron Towles when

they started musing on the question of why New Orleans didn't have great local microbreweries like Portland or Seattle to offer a variety of beer to a city full of brewing history?

The brown ale is a brave beer in a market that likes high-alcohol, highly hopped beers, but it must have impressed investors when brewmaster Peter Caddoo knocked up a batch in 2008 to show the money men – it looked like a winner and the first big batch was released on 3 March 2009.

Says Kirk: 'We wanted a brown ale that you could drink year round in New Orleans and enjoy it in our 100-degree, high-humidity weather. We tried a lot of different brown ales, but found an English-style mild went particularly well with our weather and food.'

TIMOTHY TAYLOR'S GOLDEN BEST

Website: www.timothytaylor.co.uk
Brewed in: Keighley, West Yorkshire, UK
First brewing record: 1928
Grains: Pale malt
Hops: Fuggles, Goldings
ABV: 3.5%

Appearance: Light gold, medium white foam
Aroma: Biscuit, brown sugar, autumn leaves
Flavour: Fresh bread, soft peach, mineral finish
Great with: Potted shrimps and toast, ploughman's, Wensleydale cheese

THE BEER

As gentle as a summer rainshower and just as refreshing, Timothy Taylor's Golden Best is probably the last remaining example of a golden mild from around the Pennines – other brewers like JW Lees and Theakston's no longer brew their versions.

This isn't a big shouty beer that will get people super-excited; it's more of a quiet companion in the pub that allows you five minutes of peaceful contemplation at the end of a busy day. Its sweet biscuity and bready aromas and flavours come from a specially supplied malt variety, Golden Promise. They're supported by a bit of earthy autumn leaf and gentle peachiness from those quintessential English hops, Fuggles and Goldings, leading through to a very clean, mineral-fresh end – which makes you smile just a little before taking another sip.

As I've said of many of the historic beer styles within this book, beer drinkers are seeking out almost extinct styles and resurrecting their popularity – much to the surprise, but definitely to the delight, of long-standing brewers like Taylor's Peter Eells.

'When I joined in 1984 the golden mild was called common ale and accounted for two-thirds of the brewery's capacity; but it dwindled in popularity and it was at a low in 2006 of just 10%. Recently we've seen a swing back towards the golden mild; it's now 15% of the brewing capacity and we're expecting it to grow quite significantly in the future.'

THE BREWERY

Perhaps most famed for its flagship beer Landlord, proclaimed by Madonna to be the Champagne of ales on a UK chat show, Timothy Taylor's is a Yorkshire institution.

Founded in 1858 by Timothy Taylor in Keighley, his beers soon proved so successful that he had to move to bigger premises just down the road and the brewery has been there since 1863, taking advantage of the soft Pennine spring water that it takes from source.

MORE TO TRY ...

Coopers Mild Ale

Website:	www.coopers.com.au
Brewed in:	Adelaide, South Australia
ABV:	3.5%
Appearance:	Dark gold, lively head
Aroma:	Light chocolate, straw, bread
Flavour:	Honey, milk chocolate, soft lemon
Great with:	Honey-roast nuts, chargrilled steak, flat fish

Although both Australia and New Zealand had a mild ale tradition in the past, the original dark style no longer really exists there, having adapted to local tastes into something more resembling a golden mild/lager hybrid, but its roots are still there in the lack of bitterness. The bottle conditioning gives it excellent depth of flavour and the low ABV makes it the ideal quaffing beer for hot temperatures.

Hobsons Mild

Website:	www.hobsons-brewery.co.uk
Brewed in:	Cleobury Mortimer, Worcestershire, UK
ABV:	3.2%
Appearance:	Mahogany with a downy tan head
Aroma:	Roasting coffee, milk chocolate, caramel
Flavour:	Iced coffee milkshake, nutmeg, bitter chocolate
Great with:	Toad-in-the-hole, grilled halibut, milk chocolate mousse

Hobsons Mild is a well-deserved former Champion Beer of Britain, and the brewery is committed to being as sustainable as possible, using local ingredients and supporting the community, which straddles the two counties of Shropshire and Worcestershire. This easy-drinking yet flavour-packed beer is a symphony of subtle chocolate, coffee and toffee aromas and flavours with a hint of spicy nutmeg.

Prospect Nutty Slack

Website:	www.prospectbrewery.org.uk
Brewed in:	Wigan, Lancashire, UK
ABV:	3.9%
Appearance:	Dark chocolate with cloud-like head
Aroma:	Treacle, coffee, aniseed
Flavour:	Molasses, mocha, liquorice
Great with:	Chilli crab, deep-fried pickled jalapeños, raspberry ripple ice cream

Owner Patsy Slevin swore she'd never expand from the tiny brew kit in her mother-in-law's garage, but she didn't reckon on demand for her beers and is now based where the Heinz pudding factory used to be in Wigan! So it's fitting that she's brewing a beer with so much sweetness to it, a sweetness balanced by a lovely liquorice character, moreish and satisfying.

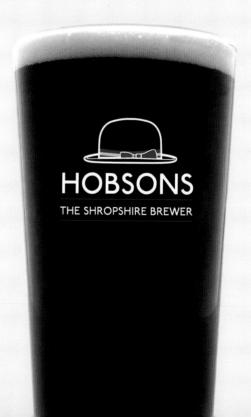

HOBSONS
THE SHROPSHIRE BREWER

Sarah Hughes Ruby Mild

Website:	www.sarahhughesbrewery.co.uk
Brewed in:	Dudley, West Midlands, UK
ABV:	6%
Appearance:	Deep ruby brown, low foam
Aroma:	Fruit cake, sour cherry, dark chocolate
Flavour:	Dandelion & burdock, cola, dry red wine
Great with:	Black pudding, gammon steak, raclette

This jewel-like stunner is full of dried fruit, vinous notes and sweetness, with just enough astringency to stop it becoming cloying; someone once described it to me as like taking a piece of fruit cake and dipping it in a dry red wine. As odd as it sounds, it's a very accurate description!

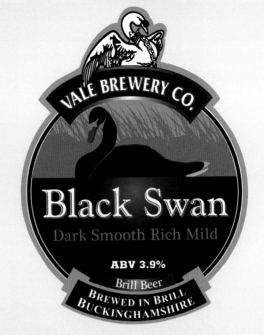

Silverton Brewery Bear Ass Brown

Website:	www.silvertonbrewing.com
Brewed in:	Silverton, Colorado, USA
ABV:	4.5%
Appearance:	Light bronze, lacy white head
Aroma:	Milk chocolate, caramel, digestive biscuit
Flavour:	Mocha, fudge, burnt toast
Great with:	Tempura fish, stuffed peppers, Emmental

The Bear Ass mild is a pretty rare flower on the American craft scene as it is low in hops and alcohol. Refreshing in its straightforward aromas and flavours, it offers a swipe of chocolate, biscuit and caramel across your nose and taste buds before leaving with a hint of bitter burnt toast and creamy coffee.

Vale Black Swan Mild

Website:	www.valebrewery.co.uk
Brewed in:	Brill, Buckinghamshire, UK
ABV:	3.9%
Appearance:	Darkest ruby brown, creamy caramel head
Aroma:	Dark chocolate, mocha, blueberry
Flavour:	Espresso, bitter chocolate, blackcurrant
Great with:	Fennel and orange salad, profiteroles, Comté cheese

The Black Swan mild is a drier, more astringent mild than most, which adds to its appeal as a thirst-quenching session beer. It's got all the chocolate and coffee that you'd expect from a dark mild, except here they are darker and more obvious in their roasted nature. Add a dry blackcurrant finish and you've got one special beer.

Others to try

Avery Ellie's Brown Ale, Colorado, USA
Beer Valley Gone Fishin Mild Ale, Oregon, USA
Brains Dark, UK
Ilkley Black, UK
Otley Dark-O, UK
Yards Brewing Co. Brawler, Pennsylvania, USA

PORTER & STOUT

Are you afraid of the dark? Or do you embrace the depths of porters and stouts? I ask because it can be a very divisive area of the beer world: to some people, porters and stouts are dark, handsome seducers, tempting their taste buds with a siren call of rich coffee and chocolate flavours, dried fruits, refreshing astringency or subtle smokiness. To others they look like a horrifyingly heavy drink that will make them drowsy and fat in two seconds flat!

I should be clear here that sure, a big stout will feel more satisfying to drink than most beers, but it's supposed to. A great stout is something to be savoured, not sucked down without being tasted because it's barely above freezing. And a well-crafted porter should be refreshing because, despite its dark and brooding appearance, porters were created as quaffing beers.

So, just as you shouldn't judge a person by their colour, you also have to get to know porters and stouts individually; and I'm willing to bet the more time you spend in their company, the more you'll realize you've made a friend for life.

AND THAT'S WHEN THE ARGUMENT STARTED...

In beer circles, asking people what they think the difference is between porters and stouts is more guaranteed to start an argument than coming home four hours late, drunk, on your anniversary!

Why? The truth of the matter is that, throughout most of their history, there seem to have been only subtle variations between porter and stout. And these days, brewers call their beers whatever they like, so one man's porter can be another man's stout. However, old brewing records and treatises suggest that porters should be medium to dark brown and have a slightly thinner, more drinkable body and a distinct hop character; they may also have a slightly smoky tart edge to them. Stouts tend to be darker brown to black with a rich, creamier, rounder flavour. In modern times, this is due to the use of grains that give more body, like wheat and oats.

And although the recipes for these beers tend to call for a lot of hops, the star of the beer should always be the flavours coming from the dark and roasted malts. If you can taste the hops more than you can the base malt flavours of chocolate, raisins, toffee, burnt toast and coffee of the beer then, personally, I think the brewer has missed the point of this beer style!

Facing page: Don't be afraid of the dark – these beers aren't all heavy and frightening. They can, in fact, be remarkably fun and refreshing.

Below: A porter pushing some stout around the Guinness brewery at St James's Gate in Dublin.

History in the making

Porter, which first started to develop in the 1700s in London, is arguably the most important British beer style ever to have been created. Prior to its ascendancy, beer was a hotch-potch of regional variations, a combination of hopped and un-hopped beers and countless different terms for what, for all we know, could have been the same or different brews. Porter was the first style of beer to be industrially brewed with a focus on consistency and quantity.

But how did porter first come into fashion? Well, the most common story is that it evolved from something called 'three threads', which was popular in London alehouses in the early 1700s. It was made by blending beers from vats of different ages to create a personal blend. How strong this personal blend was probably depended on how much was in the drinker's pocket. Now, while the three threads market was undoubtedly something brewers would have been looking to cash in on, it's believed that a happy mistake by some London brewers, using a hitherto undiscovered combination of dark and paler malts, recreated in one brew the most favoured combination of three threads, and for less money. Funnily enough, that idea caught on!

The beer was originally known as Entire Butt, a butt being the largest size of beer barrel at 108 gallons, to show that it was a single brew rather than a blend of beers, but this name was quickly usurped, as the beer found huge success with the porters who kept goods moving in the streets and rivers of the capital.

Below: Fuelled by porter these hard-working lifters and shifters kept the streets of London moving.

And although we're very used to the concept of economies of scale these days, the efficiency of brewing the single beer meant that it stayed relatively stable in price, making it even more attractive to the working classes, and others. As the industry grew, so did the economies of scale and porter's dominance of the beer market, first in London and then throughout the British Isles.

The biggest impact that porter brewing had on the whole brewing industry was the move from delivering beer to each and every individual pub for maturation in the cellar to mass-maturation in large vats in the breweries themselves. This meant that beer became a cheaper product for the licensees to buy, and also meant they didn't need to keep in their cellars beer that wasn't ready to sell.

What did this early porter taste like? Well, it's difficult to tell exactly, as controls on the brewing process were only as good as the science of the day would allow, but myriad texts and old treatises describe it as having a sour edge to it, which most likely came from it being infected by wild *Brettanomyces* yeast (you can learn more about these on page 24) during the long maturation period. London's Meantime Brewing Co deliberately introduces these yeasts for its historic version of porter.

Porter's gradual decline in popularity can be traced to advances in brewing technology in the early 1800s. First, the introduction of thermometers and cooling coils gave brewers more control over the brewing process. At the same time, hydrometers (which measure the density of a liquid compared to water – the measurement is known as original gravity) revealed which malts yielded the highest amount of fermentable sugars for brewing purposes. The new technology allowed brewers more control over how much of that sugar the yeast ate and meant that they could create sweeter beers designed to be served young; these

Above: A drayman delivering a barrel of porter to a licensee who appears to be sampling the wares!

quickly found favour and became known as milds (for more on mild, see pages 156–158).

This new technology, combined with a leap forward in the use of paler malts resulted in a whole new trend towards paler beers that were also cheaper to brew and therefore financially accessible to all classes of society. The quality of the water in the Burton upon Trent area in the Midlands proved more suitable to the paler styles and, as more and more people became enamoured of the paler beers the mantle of brewing capital of the world passed from London to Burton, leaving porter to go into an almost terminal decline until its recent huge resurgence.

Meet the family

Stout

Loved the world over because of its Irish connection with the culture of the craic, today's dry stouts are generally distinguished by their black body, white head and a full, rounded flavour.

Porter

Dark brown, black with a ruby gleam, with coffee or chocolate aromas but a refreshingly drinkable dryness and typically around 5–6% ABV – today's brewers interpret the style in a multitude of ways.

Export stout

A strong brew, generally above 6.5% ABV, designed for export. However, the beer is now often brewed under the same name in the countries it was once exported to, such as Nigeria and Sri Lanka. Guinness Foreign Extra Stout is widely available; other examples include Jamaica's 7.5% ABV Dragon Stout.

Milk stout

Why milk? Well, to create a sweeter beer the brewer adds lactose (the sugar present in milk) into the brew; the ale yeast, *Saccharomyces cerevisiae*, can't ferment lactose, so it hangs around to sweeten the beer instead of being turned into alcohol. This style first went into commercial production in 1907 by Mackeson of Hythe in Kent, England. Bottles originally bore the claim 'each pint contains the energising carbohydrates of ten ounces of pure dairy milk'; Mackeson's really took off when the once-mighty London brewer Whitbread took over and started exporting it all over the country and then the world.

Oatmeal stout

Along with roasted barley and dark malts, this style uses either malted or unmalted oats, and was deemed by its brewers in the early 1900s to be refreshing, strengthening and restorative for invalids. It is still occasionally available today: good examples are Samuel Smith's Oatmeal Stout from Yorkshire, England, and Rogue's Shakespeare Oatmeal Stout from Oregon.

Imperial/Baltic porter

While it might appear that the American craft brewing movement (with its penchant for putting the word Imperial in front of anything brewed to a high strength) invented Imperial porter, it was brewers in the Baltic states, seeing how popular British Imperial stouts were in the mid-18th century, who first produced their own versions. Zywiec, in Poland, began brewing strong porter in the mid-19th century and is still going strong (see page 177).

Russian Imperial stout

The beer that has spawned thousands of extreme offshoots, revived by the American craft brewing movement and now produced the world over. Typically high in alcohol with expensive dark chocolate and vinous notes.

Smoked porter

Historically most early porters would have had a smoky edge to them. Some modern breweries, such as Alaskan (see page 176) and Okell's from the Isle of Man, make more of a feature of this characteristic.

Your health!

So many myths abound about stout it's ridiculous: just the other day I had to refute the claim that it was good for pregnant women for about the thousandth time. But since the striking 'Guinness is good for you' advertising campaigns in the 1920s and the widely held beliefs that oatmeal stout, milk stout or 'Invalid Stout' could cure whatever ailed you, it's hardly surprising we're still feeling the repercussions of those urban myths.

Stout contains no more iron than any other beer and its health properties are no greater than any other brew, so why did it gain this reputation? It probably dates back to the time when porter began to far outstrip the sales of any other beer in Britain in the mid-1800s. It was likely that some people felt better after drinking any form of beer: it was better than drinking water in the days before towns had a safe water supply; the alcohol would have given them a pleasant buzz; and besides providing valuable carbohydrates the roughly filtered beer would have retained some fibre.

Other strong voices of the day fuelled the myth; the mid-19th-century doyenne of all things domestic, Mrs Beeton, is partially responsible for the fact that some doctors, even in the 21st century, advise women to drink stout when pregnant or anaemic – although what she actually recommended was a mixture of stout and porter for breastfeeding mothers.

And, of course, the famous adverts of 'Guinness for strength' and 'Guinness is good for you' – classics every one – were born from market research into what people thought of stout, and the health attributes they associated with it.

In short, the myth that stout is better for you than any other type of beer is bunkum, but don't let that put you off trying it, in moderation and only for the benefits that all great beer offers to your health!

GUINNESS
IS GOOD FOR YOU

STOUT

From a historic point of view, the term stout was derived from 'stout porter'. The word stout used to mean strong, not short and slightly pudgy the way we use it today, and it was originally used as a term for any beer that was high in alcohol, whether light or dark in colour: this usage was first recorded in the 1630s. However, by the early to mid-1800s the term had been widely adopted by the porter brewers and that's how it entered common parlance. So where and when did stout diverge from the London porters? Well, in 1817 Daniel Wheeler invented black patent malt, by kilning it in a similar piece of kit to a coffee roaster. The introduction of the hydrometer around this time meant that brewers could measure how much sugar yield they got from their barley, and as taxes on the raw materials continued to rise it became more important for the brewers to get the most from their malts, which meant using more pale malts as they gave out more sugar. When Wheeler created this incredibly dark malt, of which only a small amount was needed, both the London and Irish brewers seized upon it with alacrity, so why did stout become synonymous with Ireland and Guinness?

Quite simply, where the London brewers used this black malt, the lion's share of the malt line-up was pale, with a small proportion of brown and a tiny addition of patent malt (1–2%) to create the colour of beer the market demanded – a dark, reddish tan.

Over in Ireland, however, it's recorded in the Guinness brewing records that by the 1820s, Guinness at least (which became the market leader) was using only pale malt with less than 4% patent malt, but that was enough to make the beer a very dark brown-black colour and this led to the visual identification of stout as we perceive it today.

Above: Sit down together and enjoy a pint of the black stuff.

The story of Guinness is, for many people, the story of stout. Founded in 1759, Guinness was originally an ale brewer but soon switched to porter production when it became clear that the Irish had taken the style to their hearts; like other porter brewers, Guinness also made a 'stout' or stronger version of their regular porter. Dublin water, like London water, was perfect for making dark beer. The business continued to expand and even stronger versions of the stout were brewed for export around the world. By the 1880s Guinness was the world's largest brewer. It eventually lost this position to American brewers, but there's no denying that Guinness's continued investment in stylish advertising and innovative dispense methods, designed to make the beer more fizzy or smoother or colder or fresher, have also played their role in making stout Ireland's national drink and a style enjoyed the world over.

RUSSIAN IMPERIAL STOUT

It all started when Peter the Great, during his 1698 visit to England, fell in love with all things British and took everything from barbers to shipbuilders back home with him. Although it's recorded that his favourite drink was brandy with pepper it's also said that he enjoyed British beers, especially the strong or 'stout' ones (remember, stout didn't refer to the same beer it does today). Allegedly, the first shipment of beer sent over spoiled on the 1600km (1000-mile) journey; the Barclay brewery of London swooped to the rescue of British brewing pride by providing a very strong beer that had a high level of preservative hops for the second effort – and the rich brew was an instant hit.

Records show that Peter's successor, Catherine the Great (1762–96), was also a lover of the darker styles of beer – and not just those from London. In 1784 William Bass, a brewer in the thriving brewery town of Burton upon Trent, having seen the money to be made in Russia and Baltic states, started to export ale directly via Hull; the company did so up until 1822, when Russia introduced ruinous taxation on British beer and UK brewers abandoned this market. However, some survivors limped on and the Barclay brewery, eventually taken over by Courage, continued to produce Imperial Russian Stout until the mid-1990s. Bedford brewer Wells & Young's now owns the rights to Courage and plans to brew it again. This luscious, warming style has seen a massive resurgence of late, with beers such as the US's Three Floyds Dark Lord and North Coast Brewing's Old Rasputin and the UK's Dark Star Imperial Stout (see page 175).

ODELL'S CUTTHROAT PORTER

Website: www.odellbrewing.com
Brewed in: Fort Collins, Colorado, USA
First brewed: 1993
Grains: Pale ale, Munich, crystal, chocolate and caramalt; roasted barley
Hops: Columbus, East Kent Goldings
ABV: 4.8%

Appearance: Raisin brown, medium caramel foam
Aroma: Coffee, blackcurrants, sultanas
Flavour: Mocha, spiced chocolate, espresso
Great with: Mid-strength blue cheese, raisin bread, dark meaty stews

THE BEER

A genuinely refreshing dark beer, it's always one of my go-to beers when the dark side beckons. Overflowing with fruity aromas, almost like a good fruit cake smothered with blackcurrant jam, this beer soothes your soul the minute you pick it up. From that intoxicating scent it builds on the palate with additional creamy coffee and milk chocolate notes, which strengthen into a spicy chocolate length and dry espresso finish.

THE BREWERY

Doug Odell is one of the US brewing scene's seriously good people. A softly spoken man with a ready smile, he loves nothing more than outdoor adventure, damn fine beer and giving back to the community – making his success thoroughly deserved.

When I first held a 'meet the brewer' event with Doug and his beers in the UK, everyone went mad for them, especially the St Lupulin summer ale, but the Cutthroat Porter has always been my favourite. It has won more awards than any other in what is an incredibly polished and balanced stable of beers – and rightly so.

Originally brewed in 1993 for the famous, but now defunct, Mountain Tap Tavern in Fort Collins, Colorado, Doug figured if the beer was being brewed for the bar they could name it too. Jim Parker, the proprietor, was an avid fly fisherman, so he named it after the Cutthroat trout, an indigenous fish to western North America and the state fish of Colorado. (Who knew that individual states have designated fish?) It was a success at the Mountain Tap and after about a year Odell's began general distribution; it was an easy decision for Doug to make, as it filled a hole in the portfolio. 'I knew, at that time, we weren't going to brew both a porter and a stout, so I tried to write a recipe that incorporated attributes of both styles – although it does lean more towards the lighter brown style of London porter with its drinkability.'

DOROTHY GOODBODY'S WHOLESOME STOUT

Website: www.wyevalleybrewery.co.uk
Brewed in: Stoke Lacy, Herefordshire, UK
First brewed: 1987
Grains: Pale ale malt, flaked barley, roasted barley, crystal malt, chocolate malt
Hops: Northdown
ABV: 4.6%

Appearance: Deepest brown-black, mousse-like cream foam
Aroma: Coffee, prune, chocolate
Flavour: Melted dark chocolate, raisin, espresso finish
Great with: Jerk chicken, shepherd's pie, chocolate brownie and ice cream

THE BEER

When former Guinness brewer Peter Amor decided to launch a brewery, it was unsurprising that a complex stout would find its way into the brewery's repertoire. Ridiculously enticing on the nose, this bottle-conditioned beer smells exactly like you dream a stout should: coffee notes curl their way around your senses as you pour, with a hint of something sweet and prune-like, joined by a sensuous swirl of chocolate. On the palate it has a silky yet refreshing mouthfeel that brings with it all the flavours you've smelt, along with a slightly stronger fruity, raisin note and a pleasingly dry, espresso-like finish.

THE BREWERY

The Wye Valley brewery, a family business, has been a success from the start, consistently winning awards. It was founded as a microbrewery in 1985 and is now a medium-sized affair, and Peter has handed over the day-to-day running of the brewery to his son Vernon.

Besides well-loved traditional British bitters like Butty Bach and the blonde stunner HPA (Hereford Pale Ale), the prettiest of the Wye Valley pack is definitely offshoot brand Dorothy Goodbody's.

The slightly saucy Dorothy is the product of owner Peter Amor's imagination. The story goes that Amor discovered a remarkable set of manuscripts detailing the eventful village life of Dorothy Goodbody, a local hop-grower's daughter. Set in the early 1950s, they depict a time of innocence and purity, centred on the charming Herefordshire community of Dormington – a prime English hop-growing area. Dorothy developed her interest in brewing when she began courting the head brewer at the local brewery – and the rest, as they say, is history!

DARK STAR IMPERIAL STOUT

Website: www.darkstarbrewing.co.uk
Brewed in: Partridge Green, Sussex, UK
First brewed: 2005
Grains: Pale ale malt, flaked barley, roasted barley, crystal malt
Hops: Target, Hallertau Magnum, East Kent Goldings
Adjuncts: Muscovado and white sugar

ABV: 10.5%
Appearance: Almost black, creamy tan head
Aroma: Winey, dark chocolate, cherries
Flavour: Port, dark chocolate ganache, sour cherry
Great with: Strong cheese, truffles, chocolate-dipped cherries

THE BEER

Head brewer Mark Tranter says the idea for the beer was born on a dark and stormy night; is he being facetious? You never know with that man!

It's a hugely complex and rich beer, almost irresistible to drink straightaway, but it will repay you beautifully if you age it for as long as you can resist. The hugely vinous and port-like nose laced with rich dark chocolate and a hint of coffee is very alluring; on the palate it is almost like a chocolate liqueur filled with kirsch bursting in your mouth, with a gorgeously dry and refreshing finish.

But how did the beer come to be born? Tranter explains: 'We'd been talking about classic beer styles and I think our Sussex neighbours Harvey's had just started brewing their Imperial stout. Courage had recently stopped brewing their version, which I was sad about because it was one of the first beers that had really blown me away. We had a spare day in the brewing roster and Imperial stout just sprang to mind.

'I didn't research the recipe much but we'd had some experience of brewing fairly strong beers, although nothing over 8%, and there weren't many examples in the UK for us to try, so we just went for what felt right.

'We were thrilled with it straight out of the gate and we've stuck to our original recipe, but the way it ages makes every year seem different when you taste and compare bottles from different years.

THE BREWERY

Dark Star brewery is one of the UK craft brewing scene's big successes. From its beginnings as a Brighton brewpub in 1994, it has moved home twice. In 2010 it churned out in excess of two million pints, and shows no sign of slowing down any time soon – and nor does demand for its innovative, yet remarkably suppable, beers.

Dark Star's beers are known for big flavours, bold branding and refreshing drinking. The brewery's signature beer is Hophead, the 3.8% ABV pale, golden ale so packed full of fruity, floral aromas and flavours it's hard to believe it's such a sessionable strength. Dark Star American Pale Ale is a 4.7% ABV US-style beer that won Best Golden Ale at the Champion Beer of Britain 2009 competition.

Darker offerings include a much-vaunted Espresso Stout, which uses locally roasted coffee in its production but at just 4.2% ABV is still eminently drinkable.

MORE TO TRY ...

Alaskan Smoked Porter

Website:	www.alaskanbeer.com
Brewed in:	Alaska, USA
ABV:	6.5%
Appearance:	Dark chocolate, bubbly tan head
Aroma:	Hot chocolate, mocha, burnt toast
Flavour:	Dark chocolate, sour cherry, espresso
Great with:	Smoked salmon, blue cheese, vanilla ice cream

Dark as night and sinfully tasty, this smoked porter is released in limited amounts every year on 1 November. It's worth getting a number of bottles as it ages very well indeed. The brewery smokes a small proportion of the malt in a food-smoker over local alder wood, and this lends a subtle, fruity smokiness to the underlying dry coffee and chocolate flavours.

Birrificio Del Ducato Verdi Imperial Stout

Website:	www.birrificiodelducato.com
Brewed in:	Roncole Verdi di Busseto, Emilia-Romagna, Italy
ABV:	8.2%
Appearance:	Black with ruby highlights, caramel cloudy head
Aroma:	Toffee, liquorice, roasting coffee beans
Flavour:	Tobacco, rose, espresso
Great with:	Honey-drizzled Grana Padano cheese, osso bucco, chocolate brownies and vanilla ice cream

From the village where the composer Verdi was born, this imperial stout is a big cuddle in a glass. It demands that you relax and let yourself be soothed by its enticing coffee and toffee nose, and then be caressed by its deliciously sweet, yet balanced, tobacco and floral flavours, before diving head-long into a lingeringly bitter coffee end.

Flying Dog Gonzo Imperial Porter

Website:	www.flyingdogales.com
Brewed in:	Maryland, USA
ABV:	9.2%
Appearance:	Espresso, billowing off-white head
Aroma:	Pencil shavings, roasting coffee, dark chocolate
Flavour:	Raisin, chocolate-covered coffee beans, marshmallow
Great with:	Herbed salami, barbecued steak, chocolate soufflé

Gonzo Imperial Porter is one complex, and potentially dangerous, dude. Full of assertive coffee and chocolate, it has an additional layer of complexity with some herbal, woody dryness and a sweet high note of marshmallow.

Left Hand Black Jack Porter

Website:	www.LeftHandBrewing.com
Brewed in:	Colorado, USA
ABV:	6.8%
Appearance:	Nearly black, small white head
Aroma:	Liquorice, tar, smoke
Flavour:	Dark chocolate, liquorice, molasses
Great with:	Barbecue ribs, smoked eel, aged goat's cheese

Like all the Left Hand beers, Black Jack keeps your tongue and senses busy. You know it's a complex beast when you bring it to your nose, with its strong aromas of smoke and liquorice. The liquorice follows through on the palate with a molasses bitterness, tempered by a slight chocolate sweetness.

Meantime London Porter

Website: www.meantimebrewing.com
Brewed in: London, UK
ABV: 6.5%
Appearance: Ruby brown, low foam
Aroma: Caramel, mocha, smoke
Flavour: Tobacco, milk chocolate, filter coffee
Great with: Roast partridge, Camembert, pumpkin pie

The caramel, mocha and smoke on the nose continue into the body, and a sweet tobacco and rich filter coffee bitterness creates a pleasingly astringent finish.

Mikkeller Beer Geek Breakfast

Website: www.mikkeller.dk
Brewed in: Anywhere (cuckoo brewer)
ABV: 7.5% (many variations differ in ABV)
Appearance: Dark chestnut brown, billowing tan head
Aroma: Fresh granary bread, fresh espresso, geranium
Flavour: Burnt toast, coffee, burnt caramel
Great with: Honey-roast ham, smoked trout, tiramisu

This was brewer Mikkel Borg Bjergsø's attempt at making an oatmeal stout by throwing pilsner, oat, smoked, caramunich, brown and chocolate malts with roasted barley and flaked oats into the brew – but he was disappointed. However, the addition of caffeine makes everything clearer: in this case, he applied it to his beer and hey, presto!

Sambrook's Powerhouse Porter

Website: www.sambrooksbrewery.co.uk
Brewed in: London, UK
ABV: 4.9%
Appearance: Deep cherry-wood brown, medium rocky head
Aroma: Digestive biscuit, Mars bar, cappuccino
Flavour: Toasted granary bread, toffee, coffee liqueur
Great with: Blackened salmon, roast venison, cherry cheesecake

A relatively new brewery, founded in 2008, Sambrook's has hit the refreshing yet satisfying qualities of a porter on the nose with this beer. The cheeky chocolate digestive and sweet confectionery aromas are pleasingly offset by the bitter coffee and cherry spirit twist when you drink.

Zywiec Porter

Website: None available
Brewed in: Cieszyn, Poland
ABV: 9.5%
Appearance: Liquorice black, mocha cloud-like head
Aroma: Tar, cola, burnt toast
Flavour: Dark chocolate, golden rum, espresso
Great with: Braised pork knuckle, pickled cabbage, chocolate torte

An historic survivor – which has annoyingly been withdrawn from the UK by Heineken – this is a beer to sip, savour and coo over. Imbued with astringency and bitterness from the heavily roasted malts, but balanced by an almost liqueur-like sweetness, all of which marry harmoniously with the hefty alcohol content to create a warming drink.

Others to try

Fuller's London Porter, UK
Minoh Stout, Japan
Rogue Shakespeare Oatmeal Stout, Oregon, USA
Brasserie de la Senne Stout Erik, Belgium
Brasserie Trois Dames Bise Noire, Switzerland

FRUIT, FIELD, SPICE & ALL THINGS NICE

Tradition and innovation both play a part in the incredible range of ingredients that are used in beer today, from pumpkins and blackberries to unusual grains like quinoa and rye, from plants such as heather and juniper to kitchen spices – not to mention exotic ingredients like lemongrass or Italian chestnut honey.

Although most of these beers use barley as their main source of fermentable sugars, the additional flavours, textures, aromas and excitement that can be brought to beer by the judicious use of quality ingredients is limited only by the brewer's imagination. Many 'serious' beer drinkers dismiss beers that use unusual ingredients – but this means they're missing out on lots of tasty fun. However, buying and drinking these beers is most definitely a voyage of discovery; the best advice I can give you is to ask for recommendations from knowledgeable friends and bar staff or reputable beer sellers.

So, are you ready to leave your inhibitions at the door and dive into the world of some weird and wonderful brews? Well, come on then, we're going in!

Facing page: The truly awesome array of fruits, vegetables, spices and confectionery used creatively in beer is limited only by the brewer's imagination.

FRUIT AND VEGETABLE BEERS

Brewers have always reached for nature's bounty or, to be more truthful, mankind has always tried to make alcohol from anything to hand that even faintly looked like it might ferment. Partly that will have helped us save precious grains in the brewing process, but mostly it's because we like drinking, and the more alcohol we can make, the better!

From dates in ancient Egyptian beers via cherries in both English and Belgian beers to the pumpkin beers brewed by early American settlers and revived by craft brewers since the 1980s – if it adds flavour and contains starches or sugars that might ferment and create alcohol, we've brewed with it.

However, I'd like to think we're a little more refined these days and the main reason for using fruit and vegetables in our beers is to add some exciting flavours. Occasionally, as in the case of the work Guinness is doing in Africa with the root cassava, brewers are seeking a more sustainable and environment-friendly source of fermentable sugars.

So whether it's a blueberry beer from Canada like Folie Douce from Les Brasseurs RJ, a vegetable beer from the USA like Saranac Pumpkin Ale (see page 190), a Chocolate Orange Stout like the one from Amber Ales in the UK or the delicious and beautifully berried Ducassis from the Belgian Brasserie des Géants, there's plenty out there to try.

CREATING A BUZZ AROUND SWEETER BEERS

As an evolutionary imperative we seek out sweet things: as hunter-gatherers, before we had shops and food available 24/7, one of the most recognizable markers for identifying something nutritious was sweetness, so we guzzled it down whenever we could.

It's a habit that we have never quite grown out of, and part of the reason we're all getting a little thicker around the waist than we should be, so it's not that surprising that getting a little added sweetness in our beer seems as pleasing to us now as finding a honeycomb was when we were still wearing animal hides.

The use of honey in beer can be traced back to the Sumerian civilization of ancient Mesopotamia. A Hymn to Ninkasi (the Sumerian goddess of brewing) written on a clay tablet dating from 1800BC goes: 'Ninkasi, it is you who hold with both hands the great sweet wort, brewing it with honey and wine.'

Many people mistake honey beers for mead, another drink with a very long history. Mead is far simpler to make than honey beer: it's just honey, yeast and water with a little bit of additional nutrition for the yeast, left to ferment.

Below: Honey would have been used historically and is being skilfully reinterpreted by modern brewers like California's Bison Brewing.

It's worth noting that different honeys will give different flavours, depending on what the bees have been feeding on. The honey in most brews is added during the fermentation period, when the yeast is highly sated with the sugars from the wort and will hungrily latch onto the more simple sugars from the honey; this ensures that not too much of the honey's sugars hang around to make the beer too sweet. Honey beers are usually on the sweeter side, although the best are always balanced by alcohol and use of bitterness from the hops.

The brewer's choice of honey, how much and when they choose to use it, means that some honey beers can be as soft as the fur on a bumblebee's bum, like Sleeman's Honey Brown Lager from Canada, while others can sting your senses into action, like Thornbridge's Bracia (see page 191), made in England with Italian chestnut honey.

When it comes to other sweet stuff, chocolate can be introduced into beer in various ways. Some brewers use cocoa nibs (shelled, roasted cocoa beans – a pure form of cocoa) to give a chocolatey edge. Some dispense with that formality and stick some chocolate in the brew, such as Young's Double Chocolate Stout (which also uses chocolate flavouring) – it's a bit sweet for my taste, but it's a worldwide hit. There are also brews like Brooklyn's Black Chocolate Stout that do not include any chocolate, but skilfully use the chocolate flavours that can be extracted from dark-roasted malts, known as chocolate malts, to achieve their flavour – but that's covered in the porter and stout section (see pages 164–172).

Above: Young's Double Chocolate Stout uses real chocolate and essence to achieve a truly chocolatey flavour.

Groovy grains

The majority of the world's beers use malted barley as their main ingredient: it provides the sugars and enzymes that create the most efficient fermentation. Roasted barley and wheat (malted or unmalted) may be added in various proportions for colour, flavour and mouthfeel. But there are other grains that proudly play their part in the brewing world.

Rye – it takes dedication to brew with rye because it makes the mash into something resembling wallpaper paste and it takes a very long time for the fermentable sugars to be released to create a wort. Not many breweries regularly give rye a starring role. Used in Finnish sahti (flavoured with juniper) and the fascinating Russian rye bread beer kvass, rye adds a spicy note to beer. A more mainstream example is Schremser's Bio-Roggenbier.

Sorghum – many breweries in Africa use this indigenous grain. It is gluten-free and can be used to make coeliac-friendly beers, which is a great breakthrough for beer-loving sufferers of this condition. However, it lacks the enzymes that barley has to extract fermentable sugars, so these have to be added.

Quinoa – this isn't a true cereal grain, but it's a pretty hardy South American crop grown for its nutritious seeds. They are high in protein, which makes for cloudy beers, but that's fine for brews that don't need to be clear, or those that are well filtered. It doesn't make a major contribution to the flavour, but as it's full of protein it does offer a richness of mouthfeel to the brew, as seen in the Dutch Mongozo range and some coeliac-friendly ranges that use this seed.

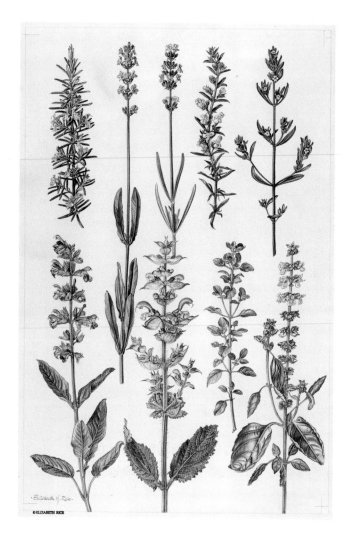

Above: Rosemary and other herbs would historically have been used to flavour beer.

SPICE WORLD

Whereas the historic use of herbs, spices and other ingredients like flowers embodies the phrase 'necessity is the mother of all invention', the use of such ingredients nowadays is more about 'when art best imitates nature'.

Before the use of hops, all sorts of diverse and interesting things were used to try and preserve or flavour beer, often attempting to cover up any spoilt notes. Heather was used in Stone Age Scotland, spruce in 18th-century America, and the traditional Finnish speciality sahti beer uses juniper berries instead of hops. Until the advent of quick and available transport, the ingredients used would have been from the local area. Finding flavours from nature was, and still remains, part of the brewer's craft.

Here are some plants that have historically been used to flavour beer. You may notice among them several 'medicinals', including wormwood, a hallucinogenic ingredient in the much-maligned spirit absinthe, a favourite of French writers and painters in the late 19th century, including Van Gogh.

Bogbean (also known as bog hop)
Bog myrtle (also known as sweet gale)
Broom
Camomile
Chilli
Dandelion
Eyebright
Fennel seeds

Ground ivy
Hay
Heather
Juniper
Laurel berries
Lemon balm (Latin name *Melissa officinalis*)
Liquorice
Mint
Mugwort

Myrtle
Nettles
Rosemary
Rowan
Saffron
Sage
Spruce
Wormwood
Yarrow

Today we don't need to use any of these botanicals to disguise the flavour of spoilt beer, or to attempt to preserve it. Instead, we add them because they bring a joy, a difference and an exciting edge to our drinking experience – and because they offer a seasonal edge to brews.

Particularly around Christmas time, many breweries bring out spiced beers that give a nod towards the tradition of mulled wine (warmed wine with botanicals and citrus fruits added). For example, Wales's Waen Brewery (whose Blackberry Stout is featured on page 188) produces the wonderfully named Mary Mother Mild, with clove and cinnamon in its dark depths; Italy's Baladin makes Nöel, with rich chai-like flavours; and Schlafly's Christmas Ale is a seriously spicy little number full of cardamom and clove from St Louis in the USA.

Above: Festive brews are often made with spices like cinnamon, cloves, allspice and ginger – a bit like mulled wine.

Above: Otley's Thai-bO – it pays to be as experimental in your drinking as brewers are in their creating of such beers.

But it's not just during the festive season that spices make an appearance in the beer universe: spiced beers can offer a refreshing kick to the palate in warmer weather. Probably the most widely used is ginger, whether it's subtly as in Left Hand's Good JuJu from Colorado, USA or big and almost hot in beers like Marble Ginger from Manchester, England. I've seen beers made with even more exotic spices, such as pink or Sichuan peppercorns, chilli, liquorice and star anise.

Herb and spice beers need not be big and shouty. Buckbean's Orange Blossom Ale from Nevada (page 189) is one of the most breathtakingly subtle beers I've ever tried. Others are more upfront, yet balanced: one of the UK's favourite flavoured bottled beers is the elderflower-scented Badger Golden Champion, made by Hall & Woodhouse of Dorset.

TO TRY OR NOT TO TRY

A lot of beer drinkers will tell you that beers that use unusual or downright weird flavourings are gimmicky, or just no good – I would disagree. The use of top-quality ingredients and flavourings can bring a lot to a brew, and these beers can also be a gentle introduction to the world of beer for anyone who has been put off by more traditional styles.

That said, there is one sector of the flavoured beer world I would like to flag up as potentially disappointing – and this is beers that use syrups and concentrated flavourings. There are *always* exceptions to the rule, such as the Badger beer I mentioned earlier, which uses elderflower flavouring, but it does so subtly. The beers I'm talking about are the ones that smell like the perfume counter from five paces and are so obviously designed to taste as little like beer as possible that's it's difficult to define them as such. While everyone's palate is individual, I have found, in general, that if you really like good beer these are not for you. They can nonetheless prove to be good gateway drinks for people who say they 'don't like beer'. When you're experimenting, the key is to go somewhere where everybody knows their beers.

But after that note of caution, don't be put off by what sound like utterly mad beers. I know from experience that it really pays to experiment in my own brewing adventures. I've collaborated with the Otley Brewing Company in Wales to create thai-bO, using kaffir lime leaf, galangal, lemongrass and lime skin, which they can't sell enough of when it's available. As a consequence I've learned not to judge beers by their label, like the Hell or High Watermelon Wheat Beer (see page 187).

WILLIAMS BROS FRAOCH HEATHER ALE

Website: www.williamsbrosbrew.com
Brewed in: Alloa, Scotland
First brewed: 1990
Grains: Pale malt, caramalt, wheat malt
Hops: First Gold
Adjuncts: Heather, bog myrtle, ginger
ABV: 5%

Appearance: Pinky-brown, negligible head
Aroma: Floral, marshmallow, spice
Flavour: Floral sweetness, slight caramel, spicy bitter finish
Great with: Burgers, pork vindaloo, lavender pannacotta

THE BEER

Fraoch (pronounced *froo-ach*, the second syllable is soft, as in Bach) is complex, but it is a very clean reflection of its ingredients: you know there's something very floral going on, with a hint of spice in the background on both the nose and the palate. With a deep amber colour, a real outdoorsy, floral, herbal aroma, deliciously fulfilling, gently caramel centre and a lip-smackingly dry finish, which really does conjure up the glorious Scottish highlands.

Heather beer's history goes all the way back to 2000BC, the approximate date of a neolithic drinking vessel found on the Isle of Rum; the cup contained traces of a brew made from grains, heather and other herbs. Legend also links heather ale with the Picts, who ruled parts of Scotland from the late Iron Age until the 10th century.

The Williams brothers tell the story that in 1988 a woman walked into their homebrew shop in Partick, bearing a translation of a 17th-century recipe for 'leanne fraoch' (heather ale), which she had inherited from her Gaelic family. She wanted to try to recreate the recipe made famous by the legend of a Pictish king who supposedly threw himself off a cliff after his son had been captured and tortured by the Scots king in an attempt to coax the recipe from the Picts. The legend was retold in the poem 'Heather Ale' (1880) by Robert Louis Stephenson.

Bruce Williams did a lot of research into the history and origins of the beer. Today's Fraoch is made with heather in the mash tun; the hot brew is then infused with more heather flowers for an hour before being fermented.

Hops were not part of the historic recipe, but are included to appease the USA's Food and Drugs Administration, which would otherwise consider it liquor.

THE BREWERY

The brewery was a natural extension of Bruce Williams' interest in beer.

Along with his brother Scott he opened a tiny five-barrel plant, producing heather ale for a handful of Scottish pubs. Demand grew and the brothers moved several times before they settled in Alloa, once home to at least nine major breweries that exported beer throughout Europe.

The brewery also produces also Alba, a rich, tawny ale brewed with pine and spruce sprigs; Grozet, a refreshing gooseberry wheat ale; Ebulum, an elderberry black ale; and Kelpie, a seaweed ale, alongside a range of more contemporary styles.

BISON BREWING HONEY BASIL ALE

Website: www.bisonbrew.com
Brewed in: Berkeley, California, USA
First brewed: 1995
Grains: Pale malt, munich, caramalt
Hops: Pacific Gem
Adjuncts: Honey, basil
ABV: 6%

Appearance: Yellowy-gold, exuberant white head
Aroma: Sweetly herbal, honey, hint of biscuit
Flavour: Slightly earthy, spicy honeyed centre, zingy herbal finish
Great with: Lemon and garlic chicken, salmon, frozen honey yogurt

THE BEER

The first year I judged at the Great American Beer Festival in 2009 was such an eye-opener for me; I had tried some American craft beers, but the staggering array at the festival was like letting a kid loose in a sweetshop. In fact, there might still be nail marks in the wall at Denver International Airport where I had to be dragged onto the plane. And in all that sensory stimulation, Bison's Honey Basil Ale still stood out.

With its gentle golden hue and sweet, herbal-floral aromas, it took me straight to a walk in an English garden after the rain. It surrounds your senses before you've even taken a sip, but as you drink it fills out, those pretty flavours expanding into robust herbal flavours, bringing with them a slightly earthy note and finishing with a flourish of lime-like zing.

Originally a seasonal brew, the demand for this thirst-quenching sessionable beer has grown to the point where it has become a mainstay of the Bison stable. But where did the idea come from? Co-owner and brewer Daniel Del Grande puts it far more eloquently than I ever could: 'We seek a beer that leaves us intoxicated by its fragrance, euphoric from its spiciness, and smiling from ear to ear.'

THE BREWERY

To say that Bison is committed to treading lightly on the Earth's surface is a bit like saying I'm partial to a pint: this company is totally committed to sustainable, ecologically sound, environmental best practice.

For fun, Del Grande, a qualified civil engineer, has created a 'reactor' to brew bio-diesel, a fuel made from cooking oil, for the brewery's vehicles.

The brewery has also founded a carbon-offset program called 'Drink Neutral', which encourages consumers to offset the carbon footprint of their drinking through its packaging and website – the first such program that I'm aware of for a brewery.

When you walk away from the store with a carrier of beer, all the cardboard is 100% recycled and the bottle is carbon offset. That's not just treading lightly, that's leaving no footprint other than an impressive flavour.

All the brewery's beers are organic – and trust me when I assure you there's no compromise on flavour. Bison's Chocolate Stout has been likened by one US critic to Barry White's voice in a bottle and the Barleywine Ale manages to warm you from the tips of your toes to the top of your head.

21ST AMENDMENT HELL OR HIGH WATERMELON WHEAT BEER

Website: www.21st-amendment.com
Brewed in: Cold Spring, Minnesota, USA
First brewed: 2000
Grains: Pale malt, wheat
Hops: Magnum
Additional ingredients: Fresh watermelon purée

ABV: 4.9%
Appearance: Lemony-gold, tight white foam
Aroma: Floral, fruity, ozone
Flavour: Lightly biscuity, sea-air fresh, slightly sour watermelon finish
Great with: A hot summer's day

THE BEER

Describing this beer is like trying to paint a picture with water: you make all the brushstrokes and then the original thought disappears. Although this tastes like a beer, it's a real original. First off, it comes in a can (see page 33 for why cans are good for craft beer). There's not too much about it on the nose; there's a definite tropical fruit of some sort, a hint of creamy oat biscuit aroma, but not a lot else.

When you drink it, your mouth goes mad! It's like summer has decided to turn up and celebrate its arrival on your tongue! From a lovely, fresh, wheat beer base rises up a glorious, light, watermelon touch that's just incredible. And I nearly never tried it ... Why? For the very reasons that Shaun O'Sullivan, co-owner of the brewery, points out: 'So many people think it's going to be like a boiled sweet, overly perfumed and sickly sweet, but it's not, it's subtle but it's still recognizable as watermelon.

'This started off as a homebrew by co-owner Nico. Watermelon is in

the same family as cucumbers, so it has that really refreshing quality – and this beer is not high in alcohol. One of the great things about it is when these big craft beer drinkers, who came in for their massively strong double IPAs but who end up on this, sidle up to me, all embarrassed, and whisper in my ear that they like the beer.'

THE BREWERY

Readers outside the US may not know that the 21st Amendment to the Constitution ended Prohibition in 1933. It's also the name that Shaun O'Sullivan and business partner Nico Freccia chose when they opened their brewpub/restaurant in the South Park region of San Francisco in 2000. Such is the demand for the beers that they now brew all their canned beers at a production brewery in the town of Cold Spring, Minnesota. However, the soul of these products remains in the brewpub, where Shaun and Nico still brew special batch beers solely for the pub/restaurant.

WAEN BREWERY BLACKBERRY STOUT

Website: www.thewaenbrewery.co.uk
Brewed in: Powys, Wales
First brewed: 2009
Grains: Pale, crystal and chocolate malt; roast barley
Hops: Bramling Cross
Additional ingredients: Blackberries
ABV: 3.8%

Appearance: Purple-black, loose creamy foam
Aroma: Chocolate, blackcurrant leaves, Horlicks
Flavour: Espresso, blackberries, bitter chocolate
Great with: Venison stew, chocolate fondant, gentle blue cheese

THE BEER

With many dark beers it can be hard to tell whether fruit is added or whether the flavour is the product of a skilful use of the base ingredients; when it comes to Waen Brewery's Blackberry Stout, I'm delighted to say it's both. When you bring this to your nose the initial information is definitely chocolatey, coffee and a little sweet, then you take a second sniff and you realize that, in the background, there are some deliciously juicy fruity aromas that have shyly been waiting for the malts to stop shouting so they can say hello. And this delicate, ephemeral fruit continues gently getting your attention on the palate as well: juicy raisins, sticky blackcurrant jam and fresh, tart blackberry all float above a sea of refreshing mocha-latte flavours, with just enough of a dry, tart twist at the end to make this probably the most refreshing stout I've ever drunk.

The creator and owner of the Waen Brewery, Sue Hayward, explains her inspiration for this fantastic beer: 'How did I come up with this? Well, I wanted something with blackberries because I love 'em! I thought a stout was the obvious choice because it's luscious and gorgeous and that it would use the dark, rich tartness to good effect. The blackberries also add a velvetiness to the beer that we weren't expecting – in fact, I'm feeling thirsty just talking about it.'

THE BREWERY

The tiny Waen Brewery, owned by John and Sue Hayward, started brewing in 2009 and has quickly gained acclaim. They wanted to install the brewery at their hilltop home – shared with their children Oscar and Hermia, dog, cats, ducks, pigs and sheep – but decided to make life easier for prospective customers by renting a small unit nearby. Visitors are welcome – but are advised to phone first, as it's rather a long way off the beaten track.

MORE TO TRY ...

Buckbean Orange Blossom Ale

Website: www.buckbeanbeer.com
Brewed in: Reno, Nevada, USA
ABV: 5.8%
Appearance: Light amber, rocky white head
Aroma: Jasmine tea, orange blossom, sugar
Flavour: Orange blossom, slight caramel, jasmine tea
Great with: Sushi, tea-smoked salmon, milk chocolate

If something can taste pretty, then it's this beer; this is what I imagine drinking jasmine tea in a Japanese peace garden is like – with added alcohol! The subtle, sweet aromas and flavours derived from real orange blossom are simple, delicate, joyous and unique.

Hop Back Taiphoon

Website: www.hopback.co.uk
Brewed in: Salisbury, Wiltshire, UK
ABV: 4.2%
Appearance: Pale lemon, soft low foam
Aroma: Lemon peel, biscuit, lemongrass
Flavour: Coriander seed, lime peel, lemongrass
Great with: Salt and chilli deep-fried tofu, griddled squid, soft sheep's milk cheese

This was the first beer I heard of that used lemongrass, and while there are other examples these days, this is still a fantastic drink. The zippy lemon notes are lightly underpinned by a biscuity/bread and earthy coriander in both the aroma and taste, but it's the finish that's so special: long, limy and refreshing. Don't be tempted to pair it with recipes using lemongrass, however, as they'll cancel out the beer's flavour.

Birrificio Italiano Cassissona

Website: www.birrificio.it
Brewed in: Lurago Marinone, Lombardy, Italy
ABV: 6.5%
Appearance: Pinkish amber, lively cloud-like head
Aroma: Geranium, raspberry, tangerines
Flavour: Black grapes, sweet biscuit, blackcurrant liqueur
Great with: Saltimbocca, fig and mozzarella salad, melon medley

Like a great table wine, this beer allows the most delicate of fruity flavours to float over your palate, enhancing your drinking or eating experience. Made with blackcurrant syrup, Cassissona broadcasts its enticing floral and berry aromas, with a hint of citrus, and keeps this going on the palate to a refreshing black grape, biscuit and blackcurrant dryness that makes you want more.

MAUI BREWING CO.

1814

CoCoNut PorTeR

...LIKE HOT CHICKS ON THE BEACH

Rise Bryggeri's Ærø No. 5 Valnød Hertug Hans

Website:	www.risebryggeri.dk
Brewed in:	Ærøskøbing, Denmark
ABV:	6%
Appearance:	Reddish-amber, fluffy cream head
Aroma:	Maple syrup, pecan, peanut butter
Flavour:	Oak, maple syrup, walnut skins
Great with:	Pistachio and herb-crusted rack of lamb, turbot, pecan pie

When someone asked me to try a walnut beer I must confess I was wary. I'd tried peanut butter beer in the USA and I frankly thought it was absolutely disgusting, but I'm pleased I took the plunge because this is special! Imagine the incredibly enticing aroma of a pecan pie, take away the cloying sweetness and make it into a really refreshing beer with hints of chocolate – meet Ærø No 5. It's not that easy to find but is well worth hunting down.

Maui CoCoNut Porter

Website:	www.mauibrewingco.com
Brewed in:	Hawaii, USA
ABV:	6%
Appearance:	Coffee brown, silky caramel head
Aroma:	Coffee, toffee, coconut
Flavour:	Chocolate, espresso, toasted coconut
Great with:	Blackened mahimahi, beef goulash, coconut ice cream

The good people at Maui Brewing Co are as lovely as you would expect laid-back folk from Hawaii to be, and also create gorgeous canned craft beers (a good thing, trust me, see page 33). CoCoNut Porter is probably their most feted beer, made with real toasted coconut. It's truly gorgeous – like eating a bitter chocolate-covered coconut ice.

Saranac Pumpkin Ale

Website:	www.saranac.com
Brewed in:	Utica, New York, USA
ABV:	5.4%
Appearance:	Pumpkin orange, downy white head
Aroma:	Cinnamon, brown sugar, cloves
Flavour:	Allspice, vanilla, ginger
Great with:	Roast turkey, nut loaf, pecan ice cream

If you've ever had an American pumpkin pie, then just translate that into beer form and here's the end result. It smells and tastes of the spices traditionally used to make pumpkin pie, including cinnamon, allspice, cloves and vanilla – probably because it's brewed with them. A hefty belt of warming ginger and a lively, spritzy carbonation ensure the beer never becomes over-sweet.

Shmaltz He'brew Origin Pomegranate Ale

Website:	www.shmaltz.com
Brewed in:	Saratoga Springs, New York, USA
ABV:	8%
Appearance:	Reddish-amber, foamy cream head
Aroma:	Raisins, milk chocolate, pomegranate molasses
Flavour:	Rose, chocolate, pomegranate juice
Great with:	Chargrilled halloumi, cous cous salad, milk chocolate mousse

The kosher beers from Shmaltz Brewing come with a hefty dose of Jewish humour and buckets of flavour. The pomegranate juice for this beer is squeezed by hand, a labour of love if ever I heard one, and it's well worth the effort for the perfumed fruitiness and tongue-tickling astringency it brings.

Thornbridge Bracia

Website:	www.thornbridgebrewery.co.uk
Brewed in:	Bakewell, Derbyshire, UK
ABV:	10%
Appearance:	Deepest chocolate brown, fudge-coloured fluffy head
Aroma:	Linseed oil, bitter chocolate, plaster
Flavour:	Intense chocolate, bitter orange, chestnut honey
Great with:	Dark chocolate

Bracia is a unique beer and I'm sorry if the notes above make it sound unappetizing, but explaining chestnut honey if you've never smelt it before is an uphill task. However, this would definitely be on my list of desert island beers – its dark, chocolatey, liqueur-like medicinal depths are truly remarkable. If you see it, buy it.

Others to try

Great Northern Wild Huckleberry Wheat, Montana, USA
Lammin Sahti, Finland
Marble Ginger, UK
Otley thai-bO, UK
Schremser Bio-Roggenbier, Austria

VINTAGE & WOOD-AGED BEER

Wood-aged and vintage beers are the sophisticated bloke or woman-about-town of the beer world; if they were people you'd expect to find them in an exclusive club with leather chairs and a roaring fire, casually chatting about their weekend in Monte Carlo. These beers deserve your respect, and anyone who's drinking one is either to be envied or quickly cultivated as your new best friend – in the hope that they'll share!

I've put these two categories together not only because there is often some crossover but also because of their sheer complexity and, often, because of the pretty hefty levels of alcohol they contain!

Also, as a general rule, both vintage and wood-aged beers are designed to grow in complexity and interest as they age; like good wines they can be cellared like good wines and brought out for special occasions.

NO AGE LIMIT

I often get a bemused reaction when I say to people they can cellar certain bottled beers and age them, but over the last ten years I've learnt that beer will produce some of the most amazing, and unexpected, flavours as it ages. It also goes through peaks and troughs, with years when it's wonderful to drink and others when it's not so good.

I've drunk beers more than 130 years old, which have become akin in flavour to a madeira wine or a rich, dark, sweet sherry but still maintained an identity all of their own. I've drunk beers that are 30 years old that have developed soy-like characteristics but have a fresh hit of mint on the end. I've drunk beers that are five years old that have deepened in sweet complexity and have become so Christmas cake-like you feel like donning a Santa hat!

Facing page: Whether barrel-aged, carefully matured by the brewery or crafted for keeping, these beers can be truly spectacular.

Below: A cooper's craft – the UK's only remaining cooper at work at the Wadworth brewery in Devizes, Wiltshire.

Above: Fuller's produce a vintage ale every year, and these beers are rapidly becoming collectors' items.

OXYGEN – FRIEND AND FOE

What happens to beer as it ages? While oxygen is the enemy of beers designed to be served fresh, such as cask ales or bottled lagers, it can, over time, create fantastically complex and interesting flavours in stronger beers.

The process of oxidation can enhance and develop the characteristics of the beer created by the malts used at the beginning of the brewing process. Here's the basic science (I promise it won't take long). Melanoidins are brown polymers (large molecules) formed when sugars and amino acids combine at high temperatures where there's a low water presence – for example, when browning a piece of meat or malting a grain of barley. The melanoidins present in the malts react with the oxygen to produce a range of flavours, from sweet almonds to prunes.

Glutamic acid (one of the amino acids present in malted barley) can also give a sense of soy sauce in aged beers; this savoury flavour, known as umami, often becomes more pronounced as beer ages.

BUYING VINTAGE BEER

Not many breweries label their beer with a 'vintage' year. UK brewers Fuller's (see page 199) and JW Lees (see page 200) do so; in Australia there is Coopers Vintage Ale; and San Francisco's Anchor brews a different secret recipe Christmas Ale every year. Until it ceased brewing in 1999, Thomas Hardy's Ale was highly sought-after by collectors in the UK and USA.

Creating your own vintage beer

First off, there's absolutely no point in trying to put a mass-produced, pasteurized, filtered beer (like big-brand lagers) down to age. These beers are designed to be drunk as quickly as possible and you will never get the complexity of flavour you're looking for; in fact, if you try and age cheap, light beers, you'll end up with something worse than you started with!

However, there are a number of beer styles that can gain in complexity with age: generally these are beers with more than 6.5% alcohol, and you can often learn more from the label. If a brewery suggests that you can age its beer give it a go: a few pounds, dollars, euros or yen is not a massive investment but could yield incredible results.

Here are some styles that should repay aging for a year or two:

- Imperial stouts and porters
- Old ales
- Strong festive ales
- Wild ales
- Barley wines
- Scotch ales
- Top-strength Trappist and abbey ales
- Wood-aged beers

There are a number of factors that affect beer in its bottle:

- **Oxygen**: Oxygen can have a delicious effect on beer sitting quietly in its bottle. But this does not apply to all types of beer: some styles are intended to be enjoyed fresh, including most lager and wheat beer, golden, pale, bitter and mild ale, and oxygen will destroy any delicate hop aromas or characteristics.
- **Yeast**: Many people think that only bottle-conditioned beers (where the brewer bottles the beer with live yeast to allow it to finish its maturation in the bottle) are good for aging; in my experience this is not necessarily the case. I've tasted beers ten years old that don't have any yeast in the bottle and that have developed magnificently, gaining complexity and layers of flavour. However, bottle-conditioned beers are designed to mature in the bottle, so they are more likely to become more interesting as they age.
- **Light and temperature**: Keep your beers in a cool, dark place. You don't have to have a cellar (although that's useful if it's clean); a cool cupboard or larder would be perfect. While most beer will need to be kept upright in order to protect the seal on the crown cap, beers with corks must be stored on their sides for exactly the same reason you lay down wines: if the cork dries out, you lose your seal and the flavour is compromised or destroyed.

Above: Keep beer in the right conditions and you could be experiencing it in a totally unique way with your 'vintage'.

So, how do you know when to drink vintage ale at its best? Well, my recommendation is to keep an eye out for reviews and look at the brewery's website – or even contact the brewery on a yearly basis to find out what they think is drinking well. If they've bothered to create this incredibly complex product that is designed to be aged, they will almost certainly want to interact with the people buying it. I also recommend that you buy at least three or four bottles so that you can follow the progress of the beer yourself.

WOOD-AGED BEERS

The beers currently being produced through wood- and barrel-aging are more fun than a bag full of monkeys on helium! From whisky to sherry casks, port, rum, brandy and bourbon barrels, brewers are no longer satisfied with bunging their beers into a boring old metal cask or keg: they want ever more flavour for ever more exciting beers.

Once, the majority of beers were fermented and matured in wooden barrels. The barrels were made by craftsmen known as coopers, but the

Below: Rolling out all stages of 'coopering' a barrel. These men would once have been employed by the breweries.

Roll out the barrel,

We'll have a barrel of fun

Roll out the barrel,

We've got the blues on the run

Sing boom tararrel,

Ring out a song of good cheer

Now's the time to roll the barrel,

For the gang's all here.

Beer Barrel Polka

[English lyrics by Lew Brown, c.1939]

centuries-old trade of coopering fell into decline in the 1970s as wooden barrels were replaced by metal casks and kegs. Now, wood is back, big time!

We looked at the yeasts and other beasts that a barrel can bring with it in wild beer (see pages 58–61); these micro-organisms have a radical effect on the beer, creating sour flavours that can be deeply refreshing. But if fresh new wood is used or the barrels are thoroughly cleaned to remove all yeasts and bacteria, the wood itself can make an enormous contribution to the complexity of a beer's flavour.

The aging of alcoholic drinks in barrels that have been previously used for something else is nothing new. Whisky has been 'finished' in different casks (such as those previously used for sherry) since the early 1990s and cider has a long history of using spirits and fortified wine barrels to offer additional layers of flavour.

The difference between wood- and barrel-aging is straightforward: to call something barrel-aged it must be aged in an actual barrel. Wood-aged simply means that some form of wood has been applied during the aging process. In the wine world, and now the beer world, this often means using

Below: Aging beer can be done in any size of barrel, from a tiny pin (4.5 gallons) to an enormous hogshead (56 gallons).

Right: While wood chips are frowned on in the wine world, the relatively short amount of time beer needs to be exposed to them means it has none of the same 'cheap' connotations.

MADE IN WOOD

Maturation in barrel isn't the only way that beer can pick up flavours from the wood. American brewery Dogfish Head in Milton, Delaware, is returning to pre-Prohibition brewing methods by constructing 10,000-gallon (380-hl) wooden brewing vessels. One is made from Palo Santo wood (see page 199) and the brewery has two further vessels of the same size in oak. A handful of other American brewers, including Three Floyds, near Chicago, and Firestone Walker in Paso Robles, California, are now using historically based wooden brewing vessels for the flavour they bring to their beers.

wood chips. In a similar way to using mesquite wood chips on the barbecue to flavour your food, brewers can use wood chips in beer. These chips come in different flavours, generally achieved by toasting the wood to various degrees, which will then give vanilla, mocha, coconut or spicy notes.

Some brewers have developed machines that will push the maturing beer through a pump primed with these chips. (These contraptions were originally developed to push extreme hop flavours into beer but brewers soon side-stepped into using them for wood chips, nuts, fruits and other flavourings.) American Sam Calagione, owner of the Dogfish Head brewery in Delaware, famously has one of these machines on the bar for a bit of theatre when serving the beer; he fills it with anything from hops to apricots.

Because of the often limited availability of used barrels, like sherry, and the natural impulse of brewers to create seasonal specials, I can't tell you definitively what flavours you will get from any given beer aged in wood – so much depends on the original style of beer, its alcoholic strength, the size of the barrel and what it held before being used for beer, and how long the beer is aged. However, most wood-aged beers will have a strong personality and a good backbone of alcohol, which are needed to balance the flavour of the wood.

In the following few pages I've picked some of my favourite barrel-aged beers, but I have to warn you they are, to many beer geeks, the equivalent of a naughty magazine and could get your pulse seriously racing! So, turn the lights down low, get comfortable and enjoy!

MORE TO TRY ...

Allagash Curieux

Website:	www.allagash.com
Brewed in:	Portland, Maine, USA
ABV:	11%
Appearance:	Hazy gold, massive rocky white head
Aroma:	Vanilla, coconut, red apple
Flavour:	Coconut milk, toasted almond, bitter honey
Great with:	Moroccan-spiced lamb cutlets, honey roast duck, baked Alaska

Definitely one for the sweet of tooth, Allagash Curieux is a viscous delight. Full of coconut, vanilla and sweet nut notes from its eight weeks in a Jim Beam bourbon barrel, it is delicious on its own, poured into a large goblet, but comes alive with any food that has a caramelized or aromatically spicy edge.

Dogfish Head Palo Santo Marron

Website:	www.dogfish.com
Brewed in:	Milton, Delaware, USA
ABV:	12%
Appearance:	Dark hot chocolate, loose tan head
Aroma:	Vanilla, balsamic vinegar, dark chocolate
Flavour:	Mocha, caramel, whisky
Great with:	Best enjoyed in a brandy balloon on its own

Those crazy bods at Dogfish Head are always looking to innovate and here's an example: they've built enormous 10,000-gallon (380-hl) tanks of 'holy wood' (Palo Santo) from Paraguay to age this beer! The resulting brew is simply amazing and unlike anything else I have ever tasted. It throws off rich, woody vanilla aromas leading into silky caramel flavours over which lie mellow balsamic notes and a whole host of other subtle complex flavours.

Fuller's Vintage Ale 2010

Website:	www.fullers.co.uk
Brewed in:	London, UK
ABV:	8.5%
Appearance:	Deep amber, low off-white foam
Aroma:	Rye bread, mace, cherry
Flavour:	Toasted raisin bread, sour cherry, orange blossom
Great with:	Peking duck, macaroni cheese, cherry cobbler

When a brewery releases a different vintage ale every year it's really hard to pick one. They all have their merits and beers age like wine – some years they're up, some years they're down. So I suggest you buy several bottles of this gently carbonated, fruit and spice-laden beauty now, keep it somewhere cool and dark and 'sample' it once a year. It's a tough task but I'm sure you're up to it!

Goose Island Bourbon County Stout 2009

Website:	www.gooseisland.com
Brewed in:	Chicago, Illinois, USA
ABV:	13%
Appearance:	As dark as brown can get, thick head of caramel-coloured foam
Aroma:	Vanilla, Bourbon whiskey, dark chocolate
Flavour:	Praline, Bourbon whiskey, espresso
Great with:	Black pudding Scotch egg, cherry ganache, strong blue cheese

Brutally dark, wickedly delicious and so naughty it's incredibly nice, this is a saucy minx of a beer. She'll waft her perfume at you through a gleaming head of foam, beckoning you into perfumed depths full of vanilla, chocolate and hard spirits, and leave you wanting more.

Harviestoun Ola Dubh 12

Website:	www.harviestoun.com
Brewed in:	Scotland, UK
ABV:	8%
Appearance:	Engine oil, tan cloud-like head
Aroma:	Vanilla, whisky, Marmite
Flavour:	Bitter chocolate, burnt toast, liquorice root
Great with:	Fruit breads, chilli con carne, blue cheese

Ola Dubh means 'black oil' in Celtic and the 12 signifies not the age of the beer, nor its alcohol content, but the age of the Highland Park whisky barrels in which it is aged. There's a definite spirit note on the nose, but this doesn't dominate the palate, allowing you to enjoy the bitter chocolate and liquorice character of the beer without the whisky overwhelming it.

JW Lees Harvest Ale

Website:	www.jwlees.co.uk
Brewed in:	Manchester, UK
ABV:	11.5%
Appearance:	Reddish amber, thick honey-coloured head
Aroma:	Raisin, crème caramel, caramelized orange
Flavour:	Golden rum, Pedro Ximénez sherry, orange bitters
Great with:	Apricot and prune stuffed lamb loin, Christmas cake, blue cheese

Lee's Harvest Ale is a true British classic; it's much underrated in its homeland but is venerated elsewhere in the world – odd but true! The astonishing bouquet of sweet raisin, soft caramel and burnt orange scarcely prepares you for the flavour of this viscous beer: it's as if someone has gently warmed golden rum, sherry and orange bitters in a pan with some golden syrup and made it alcoholic. Sound good? It is. Especially with salty blue cheese.

Orkney Brewery Dark Island Reserve

Website:	www.sinclairbreweries.co.uk
Brewed in:	Orkney Islands, UK
ABV:	10%
Appearance:	Ruby red, white rocky head
Aroma:	Fruit cake, toffee apple, allspice
Flavour:	Caramelized figs, orange liqueur, cinnamon
Great with:	Foie gras, rare pigeon breast, strong soft cheese

The 'Extraordinary Orcadian Ale' Dark Island Reserve was one of the first whisky-aged beers of note in the UK. It spends three months in single malt Orkney whisky barrels and the result is as pleasing as it is complex. From the minute you pour this ruby beauty into a glass, it exudes fruit and woody spice aromas and flavours. You just know that if you'd been traipsing around the Orkneys in the cold and then came home to a bottle of this with a cheese plate beside it, all would be right with the world.

St Erik's Dubh

Website:	www.galatea.se
Brewed in:	Stockholm area, Sweden (cuckoo brewer)
ABV:	10.7%
Appearance:	Deep black, fluffy caramel-coloured head
Aroma:	Liquorice, ash, peat
Flavour:	Ashy, bitter liquorice, smoky whisky
Great with:	Smoked herring, juniper-smoked venison, praline dark chocolates

Brewer Jessica Heidrick started brewing this Imperial stout as a bit of fun, but it's been such a hit that, as I write this, she's got the fastest-growing beer in Sweden without even having a brewery of her own! This glorious Imperial stout is aged separately in Bowmore and Laphroaig whisky barrels and then blended to reach the right balance of smoke and sweetness.

Others to try

The Bruery Coton, California, USA
Coopers Vintage Ale, South Australia
Mikkeller Big Worse Barley Wine Bourbon Barrel
   Edition, Denmark
Stone Oaked Arrogant Bastard Ale, California, USA
Traditional Scottish Ales 1488 Whisky Ale, UK

THE LUNATIC FRINGE

In this section the lunatics have taken over the asylum! Here you will find beers so high in alcohol they'll make your mind boggle, flavours to make your head spin and taste sensations like nothing you've ever had before!

This is where brewing's most skilled artisans display their unlimited imagination to produce some brain-blowingly unique products – you just have to be open-minded enough to give them a whirl.

You'll notice that I haven't put a food match with these beers. This is simply because I think most people will be quite content with the flavour experience of just sipping these madhouse inmates without letting anything else get in the way.

So, I have to warn you, it's a full moon in the world of brewing and these guys have been howling at it – are you ready to enter beer bedlam? Right then, let's go!

ROGUE MORIMOTO SOBA ALE

Website: www.rogue.com
Brewed in: Newport, Oregon, USA
First brewed: 2003
Grains: Crystal malt, Munich malt
Hops: Crystal
Other ingredients: Roasted soba
(buckwheat, technically a flower seed)

ABV: 5%
Appearance: Soft beige, medium-cream head
Aroma: Oat cake, lime leaf, fresh bread
Flavour: Honey, water biscuits, orange marmalade

THE BEER

This beer messes with your head. I don't know why, but its flavour delivers in an almost back-to-front fashion! When you first take a sip your tongue is working hard to find the flavour: all it gets is a small bready note and then a very gentle bitterness which slides down your throat,

And then, according to the laws of science and experience, that should be it – but no! Out of nowhere, you get a hit of fresh soba noodle. It's like inhaling the steam you get when you're cooking a pan of noodles, but it's strong, it's not subtle, and your tongue simply can't figure out why this is happening. Frankly, it's a bit trippy!

THE BREWERY

The idea for Rogue was born when Jack Joyce, Bob Woodell and Rob Strasser were approached by Jeff Schultz, Bob's accountant and an avid home brewer, with the idea of opening a local brewery. In 1988 in Ashland, Oregon, along a very scenic little stream called Lithia Creek, a 10-barrel brew system was set up in a basement with a pub located above. However, while the product was good, the old adage of 'location, location, location' was one the four men had failed to fully take into account and things were not looking too good.

So, Jack Joyce went off to Newport in search of a new venue. While looking around the historic bay front area he found himself seeking shelter from a horrendous blizzard and taking refuge in a place called Mo's Clam Chowder. The owner, Mohave Niemi, then introduced him to a suitable space on the proviso that a picture of her in the bath was displayed in perpetuity in the bar, and that the brewery gave back to the local fishing community. The brewery was opened in its new venue and Mo in all her glory is still immortalized there today. Since then, Rogue has gone from strength to strength, winning awards year after year.

SAMUEL ADAMS TRIPLE BOCK 1997

Website: www.samueladams.com
Brewed in: Boston, Massachusetts, USA
First brewed: 1994
Grains: Pale ale malt, chocolate malt
Hops: Tettnang, Hallertauer
Adjuncts: Maple syrup

ABV: 18%
Appearance: Darkest mahogany, little to no head
Aroma: Smoke, soy sauce, espresso
Flavour: Oloroso sherry, Marmite, sandalwood

THE BEER

You just have to take the merest whiff of this ruby-black beer to know that you're dealing with something beyond the realms of anything usual.

The initial notes are of a smoky, peaty whiskey, from the few months the beer spent in whiskey barrels. As you delve deeper with your nose, you start to pick up Marmite, soy, chocolate, espresso and sour cherry, which all follow through to the palate, where they are joined by layers of oloroso and Pedro Ximénez sherry, ending in sweet complexity almost like aged Caribbean rum and finishing on a gently dry, almost sandalwood, note.

Living embodiments of how aging can change and benefit a beer, all three of the Sam Adams Triple Bock vintages (1994, 1995 and 1997) are some of the most exciting, interesting and complex beers I've ever drunk. The 1997 is currently my favourite, but who knows how the others will have developed by the time you're reading this? Try them and find out!

It's well worth investigating all the Samuel Adams speciality beers: find out more about them and the brewery at their website.

THE BREWERY

In 1984 Jim Koch's head and heart told him it was time to show the USA that beer could be better than the commodity brands available. He raided the recipe books his father had from the old family brewery, which had closed during Prohibition. And while Jim's father, Charles, thought his son had lost the plot, he chose for him a favourite family recipe, which his great-grandfather, Louis Koch, had made at his brewery in St Louis, Missouri in the 1870s. The following spring, Jim Koch filled his old consulting briefcase with bottles from his sample brew and started going door to door asking Boston bars and restaurants to serve the beer that he had named Samuel Adams Boston Lager®.

He chose that name because Samuel Adams was a revolutionary thinker who had fought for independence. Most importantly, Samuel Adams was also a brewer who had inherited a brewing tradition from his father.

The brewery has since become one of the largest independent breweries in the United States and now brews everything from the easy-drinking Boston lager to the truly epic Utopias at 27% ABV.

BROUWERIJ BOSTEELS DEUS

Website: www.bestbelgianspecialbeers.be
Brewed in: Buggenhout, Belgium
First brewed: 2002
Grains: Malted barley (secret blend)
Hops: Styrian Goldings, Saaz
Adjuncts: Candy sugar

ABV: 11.5%
Appearance: Ginger gold, mousse-like white foam
Aroma: Bitter orange, caramel, fresh-cut grass
Flavour: Grapefruit, toffee, nettle

THE BEER

I'm not going to expand on the tasting notes above because I'd like you to know more about the production method of this remarkable beer. It is brewed in a fairly standard fashion and then goes through a secondary fermentation in conditioning tanks. It is then shipped by tanker to a cellar near Epernay in Champagne, France, where it is re-fermented with Champagne yeasts in the bottle at 12°C (54°F) for nine months. Then, just like the celebrated sparkling wine, the bottles are tilted, neck downwards, and gently rotated for several weeks (a process traditionally called *remuage*). The yeast that gathers in the neck of the bottle is frozen and removed (*dégorgement*) before the bottle is corked, caged and foil-sealed, in the same way as a Champagne wine would be – and, personally, I think it tastes a hell of a lot better!

THE BREWERY

The Bosteels brewery has been in the village of Buggenhout for over 200 years. Established by Evarist Bosteels in 1791, it has been a growing family concern ever since, passing from son to son. It is currently under the management of seventh-generation Antoine Bosteels. As well as the outstanding Deus, the brewery also makes the acclaimed abbey-style Tripel Karmeliet and the ever-popular Kwak, with its saddle-cup style glass, hundreds of which are stolen from bars by students and beer enthusiasts every year!

DOGFISH HEAD MIDAS TOUCH

Website: www.dogfish.com
Brewed at: Milton, Delaware, USA
First brewed: 1999
Grains: Pale ale malt
Hops: Simcoe
Additional ingredients: Orange blossom honey, Muscat grape juice, saffron

ABV: 9%
Appearance: Amber gold, medium-white foam
Aroma: Melon, honey, biscuit
Flavour: Sultana, golden syrup, saffron

THE BEER

Midas Touch highlights the immensely long history of beer and its importance in so many civilizations. The recipe is based on a chemical analysis of the contents of clay jars taken from the tomb of King Midas! The vessels, dating from the 8th century BC, were found in a royal burial chamber in Gordium, Turkey, and were eventually analysed by archaeologist Dr Patrick McGovern. He discussed his findings with Dogfish Head founder Sam Calagione and the rest, as they say, is history!

Lusciously juicy, fruity and with a strong honeyed, mead-like character, this is a window on the past using modern brewing methods, and is as fascinating as it is tasty.

THE BREWERY

Owned by Sam Calagione, one of the biggest characters in the US brewing scene, Dogfish Head is a hive of the kooky and creative. In 1995 it began with the opening of Dogfish Head Brewings & Eats, Delaware's first brewpub, in the beach community of Rehoboth Beach.

As the smallest commercial brewery in the USA, brewing 12-gallon (45-litre) batches of beer, they brewed three times a day, five days a week. This allowed them to brew myriad different recipes and add all sorts of weird ingredients.

The brewery moved in 2002 to Milton, Delaware, into a converted cannery and Dogfish Head has been busy breaking boundaries ever since.

FLYING DOG RAGING BITCH

Website: www.flyingdogales.com
Brewed in: Frederick, Maryland, USA
First brewed: 2010
Grains: Crystal malt
Hops: Warrior, Columbus, Amarillo

ABV: 8.3%
Appearance: Fake tan orange, bouncy white foam
Aroma: Passion fruit, lychee, bitter orange
Flavour: Caramel, melon, pine needles

THE BEER

As you'll know if you've read the pale ale section (see page 126 for more on the brewery), Flying Dog doesn't hold back. For its 20th anniversary it pulled out all the stops to produce a truly sublime beer. But, be warned, Raging Bitch is a beer that slaps you upside the head if you even look at it wrong!

It is based on the brewery's excellent Snake Dog India Pale Ale, and for the 20th anniversary brew they decided to apply more of everything by ramping up the hops and using a particularly pungent strain of Belgian yeast.

Trust me that this is one angry lady. Once she gets in that glass she starts throwing passion fruit, lychees, mango and melon at your nose, and when she's finished there she starts trying to shove caramelized oranges down your throat – but all in a loving kind of way!

In all seriousness, this is a brew of exceptional flavour. Don't let the angry words fool you; tickle this bitch's tummy and she'll roll over!

WHERE TO FIND THE BEST BEER

This is just a small selection of what I consider to be some of the best beer bars, brewpubs and brewery tours around the world. I know there are hundreds, if not thousands, more: this is just a place to start. I probably don't need to tell you that the internet is an awesome resource. Many of the websites given here will include links to help you find even more great beer.

See also page 32 for further information on national beer drinker bodies and other useful websites.

BEER BARS

AUSTRALIA
Dragonfly Bar, Adelaide www.dragonflybar.net.au *Upbeat, groovy bar with super-friendly staff and a decent range of Australian beers.*
The Local Taphouse, Melbourne and Sydney www.thelocal.com.au *Excellent service, beers and passion for all things brewed, always busy and with a fun vibe at both sites.*
The Royston, Richmond, Melbourne www.roystonhotel.com.au *Wide range of Australian craft beers, focusing on local but also national, very friendly.*

AUSTRIA
Bierometer, Vienna www.bierometer.at *Cavernous bar based in an old gas works, for boisterously good fun where you can swing your Stein.*

Krimpelstätter, Salzburg www.krimpelstaetter.at *Lovely and atmospheric old place with an emphasis on local beer and food; very warm welcome.*
Stiftskeller, Innsbruck www.stiftskeller.eu *Right in the centre of Innsbruck; updated traditional beer hall.*

BELGIUM
Bier Circus, Brussels (no website) *Amazing selection of Belgian beers and meatloaf to die for (or possibly from, given the portion sizes). Go hungry and thirsty!*
Moeder Lambic, two sites in Brussels www.moederlambic.eu *Wide range of Belgian beers, specializing in wild ales; great bar snacks. Moeder Lambic Fontainas is close to Cantillon.*

CZECH REPUBLIC
U Medvidku, Prague www.umedvidku.cz *With the tiny brewery on the second floor, the souvenir shop and the Budweiser Budvar bar on the ground floor, it's a one-stop beer experience in central Prague.*

FRANCE
Academie de la Bière, Paris www.academie-biere.com *With a cracking selection of French and international beers, this is your first stop for top brews in Paris.*
Le Hochepot, Lille www.lehochepot.fr *Delightful French brasserie/bar; local beer and food beautifully showcased on its menus.*

GERMANY

Alt-Berliner Weissbier Room, Nikolai district, Berlin www.prostmahlzeit.de *Slightly updated take on a traditional Berlin backstreet boozer; you can try the best Berliner Weisse alongside some sturdy food.*

Sophien'eck, Central Berlin www.sophieneck-berlin.de *Not strictly a specialist beer bar but warm, comfortable and almost vaudeville in feel, it has a great range of beers and lovely food.*

ITALY

Bir & Fud, Rome www.birefud.blogspot.com *A civilized haven tucked in a side street, it does exactly what it says on the tin.*

The Football Pub, Rome www.football-pub.com *Don't be fooled by the name, this venue has superb, hand-picked beer, from both home and away.*

La Ratera, Milan www.laratera.it *Although Spartan, it is renowned for its beer and food pairing and decent range of Italian microbrews.*

JAPAN

Biervana, Akasaka, Tokyo www.biervana.com *Plenty of national and international beers on tap; one of the most diverse beer bars in Tokyo.*

Harajuku Taproom, Harajuku, Tokyo www.bairdbeer.com/en/taproom/harajuku-taproom *Great for light bites like yakitori; serves Baird beers; lively, good fun.*

NEW ZEALAND

Brew on Quay, Auckland www.brewonquay.co.nz *Über-stylish craft beer bar; international and local beers, strong range of ciders too.*

The Bruhaus, Wellington www.thebruhaus.co.nz *More than 150 local and international brews by the bottle and 28 taps offering local craft beer.*

HasigoZake, Wellington www.hashigozake.co.nz *Edgy craft beer bar; home-grown and international beers.*

Pomeroy's Old Brewery Inn, Christchurch www.pomeroysonkilmore.co.nz *British-style pub with a great range of craft brews.*

Sprig & Fern, various sites www.sprigandfern.co.nz *Less a chain and more a collection of friendly local bars with fantastic beers from the Sprig & Fern brewery.*

UK

Bunch of Grapes, Pontypridd, Wales www.bunchofgrapes.org.uk *One of the Otley brewery's three pubs in Wales, serving all their brews and great local food, such as laverbread.*

Cask Pub & Kitchen, Pimlico, London www.caskpubandkitchen.com *Large range of international beers; good food, large portions; good atmosphere.*

Euston Tap, Euston, London www.eustontap.com *Teeny bar just outside busy London train station; interesting mix of international beers.*

The Harp, Covent Garden, London www.harpcoventgarden.com *Higgledy-piggledy, quaint, friendly pub in the heart of London; superbly kept beer range, mostly English.*

North Bar, Leeds, Yorkshire www.northbar.com *Continental-style bar, international beers, enthusiastic staff, great atmosphere.*

The Rake, Borough Market, London www.utobeer.co.uk *Edgy, bustling, eclectic, tiny beer bar in the heart of London's best food market.*

The White Horse, Parsons Green, London www.whitehorsesw6.com *Old coaching inn, super-slick service and massive range of perfectly kept international beers; high-end beer-matched food.*

USA

Barcade, NYC www.barcadebrooklyn.com *Classic video games, awesome craft beer on tap and a suitably darkened room for you to indulge your inner child – what more do you want?*

Beer Table, Brooklyn, New York www.beertable.com *More a tasting than a tap room, rotating quality beer and small plates of comfort food. Another site in Grand Central Station is planned.*

The Bier Baron, Washington D.C. www.bierbarondc.com *Formerly known as the Brickskeller, this has been the beer bar in D.C. since 1957, with over 1000 beers.*

Blind Tiger, NYC, New York www.blindtigeralehouse.com *Service can be a little slow, but the beer – including often hard-to-find rarities – is worth waiting for.*

Falling Rock, Denver, Colorado www.fallingrocktaphouse.com *One of my favourite bars in the world; amazing beers, awesome owners and top beer grub.*

The Horse Brass, Portland, Oregon www.horsebrass.com *British-style tavern with incredible beer; turned into a classic by the late Don Younger, who was much loved on the US beer scene.*

Monk's Café, Philadelphia www.monkscafe.com *If you crave Belgian beer while on US shores, here's the place to head, with a sprinkling of US craft beers for good measure.*

Rattle 'n' Hum, NYC www.rattlenhumbarnyc.com *Great place for meet the brewer events; also stocks cask-conditioned beers, a rarity in the US.*

BREWPUBS

Beer doesn't get any fresher than when it's brewed on-site and at a brewpub you're normally dealing with incredibly passionate and knowledgeable staff, which can make your beer journey much more fun! Here are a few of my recommendations across the globe.

AUSTRALIA

Lord Nelson Hotel, Sydney www.lordnelsonbrewery.com *The oldest, and some would argue still the best, in Sydney, with award-winning beers, contemporary food and accommodation and an old-world feel.*

Mildura Brewery, Mildura, Victoria www.mildurabrewery.com.au *Set in a magnificent art deco building in a rather out-of-the-way location, a beautiful and thriving brewpub, matching contemporary cuisine to great beer.*

AUSTRIA

Branger Brau, Unterperfuss, Innsbruck www.brangeralm.at *Charming brewpub in the suburbs of Innsbruck.*

Fischer Brau, Vienna www.fischerbrau.at *Vienna's oldest brewpub, very pretty; refreshing beers served with a big smile.*

CANADA

L'amère à boire, Montreal www.amereaboire.com *Czech and English-inspired beers and hearty food served in cosy surroundings.*

Brutopia, Montreal www.brutopia.net *A must-visit in downtown Montreal; three bars on three floors; beers brewed in-house.*

Grizzly Paw, Canmore, Alberta www.thegrizzlypaw.com *Cracking Canadian micro-brews and good food.*

CZECH REPUBLIC

Pivovarsky dum, Prague www.gastroinfo.cz/pivodum *Eclectic beer selection paired with traditional Czech dishes, delightful ambience.*

Strahov Monastery Brewery, Prague www.klasterni-pivovar.cz *Monastic brewpub opposite Prague Castle; delicious beer and filling food.*

FRANCE

Les 3 Brasseurs, many sites in France, Canada and French-speaking territories www.les3 brasseurs.com *Extensive brewpub chain.*

Le Frog & Rosbif, various sites www.frogpubs.com *Tongue-in-cheek take on a British pub; a range of beers brewed on-site.*

Brasserie Kohler Rehm, Strasbourg www.kohler-rehm.com *Indulge in the local food and on-site brews.*

GERMANY

Brauhaus Joh. Albrecht, Hamburg www.brauhaus-joh-albrecht.de *Just by the town hall, one of the cutest in-house breweries I've ever seen. It's lovely!*

Brauerei Eschenbräu, Berlin www.eschenbraeu.de *Interesting venue with open vessels for brewing so you can really see what's going on; compact beer range, but a good one, even so.*

Brauhaus GeorgBraeu, Nikolai district, Berlin www.georgbraeu.de *Massive brewpub in the historic centre of Berlin with exceptionally quaffable beers and food that uses virtually every part of the pig!*

Isar Bräu, just outside Munich www.isarbraeu.de *A brief ride on the S-bahn, this is well worth the trip: relaxing environment, great beers.*

Brauhaus Mitte, Berlin www.brauhaus-mitte.de *Weirdly, it leads into a shopping centre, but has excellent German food and top-quality quaffing beers. I like the maibock a lot.*

Ball-& Brauhaus Watzke, Dresden www.watzke.de *There are several Watzke sites but the ballroom and brewery is definitely the most impressive.*

ITALY

Birrificio Lambrate, Milan www.birrificiolambrate.com *Lively brewpub just by Lambrate metro station.*

Birrificio Torino, Torino www.birrificiotorino.com *Stylish brewpub in the centre of Turin.*

NEW ZEALAND

Hallertau, Riverhead, Auckland www.hallertau.co.nz *Beer brewed on-site; great food.*

Malthouse, Wellington www.themalthouse.co.nz *Run by a riotous Scotsman; fantastic selection of world beers and home-grown stunners; formerly home to the Tuatara brewery (see page 101).*

The Mussel Inn, Onekaka, Golden Bay www.musselinn.co.nz *Anywhere with an on-site brewery that also serves bowls of 'sossys' (sausages) earns my vote!*

UK

Beacon Hotel, Sedgley, West Midlands www.sarahhughesbrewery.co.uk *A rare Victorian brewery; brilliant British beer.*

John Thompson Inn, Melbourne, Derbyshire www.johnthompsoninn.com *Idyllic setting in the English countryside; accommodation and great beer.*

Marble Arch, Manchester www.marblebeers.co.uk *Odd sloped floor; great beer and food.*

The Old Brewery, Greenwich, London www.oldbrewerygreenwich.com *Stunning high-end venture from Meantime Brewery, complete with microbrewery.*

Old Cannon Brewery, Bury St Edmunds, Suffolk www.oldcannonbrewery.co.uk *Beautiful view of the brewery from the bar, tasty beers.*

Zerodegrees, various sites www.zerodegrees.co.uk *Reliably good beer and food; best for big parties.*

USA

21st Amendment, San Francisco, California www.21st-amendment.com *Innovative brewing; killer Sunday brunch.*

Goose Island, Chicago, two sites www.goose island.com *If you're in Chicago, don't miss these two top brewpubs serving up Goose Island standards and specials.*

Gordon Biersch, various sites across the US www.gordonbiersch.com *European-style beers; fusion menu.*

Heartland Brewery, several sites around NYC www.heartlandbrewery.com *Very quaffable regular beers and slightly off-the-wall seasonals, great places to watch the world go by, friendly staff and regulars.*

Piece, Chicago, Illinois www.piecechicago.com *Fantastic beer that's won multiple World Beer Cup and Great American Beer Festival medals served alongside giant pizza; sports on the screen; a must-visit.*

Pizza Port, various sites, California www.pizzaport.com *Award-winning beers in classic Californian settings; lovely people who brew them too, utter bliss!*

Rock Bottom, various sites across the US www.rockbottom.com *Great beer, classic American food, sports on the screen; rather like Cheers!*

Wynkoop, Denver, Colorado www.wynkoop.com *Classic brews, hearty food, fantastic ambience.*

BREWERY TAPS AND TOURS

These are places where you can see how the beer is made, generally on a much larger scale than a brewpub, and have a drink afterwards – heaven!

AUSTRALIA

2 Brothers, Melbourne www.2brothers.com.au *Fantastic venue where you can get 'the keys to the brewery' to hire the brewery tap and brewery for the evening – think of the fun!*

BrewBoys, Croydon Park, Adelaide www.brewboys.com.au *A basic brewery tap but stuffed full of tasty beers and good fun.*

Little Creatures, Fremantle, Western Australia www.littlecreatures.com.au *The quintessential Aussie beer experience: visit the brewery and then lunch by the water.*

Redhill Brewery, Red Hill South, Melbourne www.redhillbrewery.com.au *Influenced by British, German and Belgian brewing, this place offers its own Aussie spin on it all, and serves top nosh too.*

AUSTRIA

Augustinerbräu Kloster Mülln, Salzburg
www.augustinerbier.at *The only monastic
brewing site in Austria and probably one
of the best beer halls in the world.*

Ottakringer, Vienna www.ottakringer.at
*Second largest independent brewery in Austria,
showcases some unusual regional specialities
such as Zwickl.*

Stiegl, Salzburg www.stiegl.at *Enormous
brewery tour and tap; quite an experience
at Austria's largest independent brewer.*

BELGIUM

Brasserie Cantillon, Brussels www.cantillon.be
*Joyously chaotic, family run; amazing beers;
charcuterie and cheese made with the beers.*

De Halve Moon, Bruges www.halvemaan.be
*The only remaining brewery in the centre of
Bruges; Bruges Zot is probably its most famous
beer; warm welcome; good food.*

CZECH REPUBLIC

Budweiser Budvar, Ceské Budejovice
www.budvar.cz *The most high-tech brewery tour
I've ever been on; unfiltered, unpasteurized
must-try beer.*

Pilsner Urquell, Pilsen www.pilsnerurquell.com
*The home of golden lager; magnificent old
brewery and cellar brewery tap where you must
try the unfiltered, unpasteurized beer.*

FRANCE

Brasserie Artisanale La Choulette, Hordain
www.lachoulette.com *Visit a genuine farmhouse
brewery and make sure you try the Bière des
Sans Culottes while you're there.*

Bières Mandrin, La Brasserie Artisanale du
Dauphiné, Grenoble www.mandrin.biz

*Unique beers, including one with walnuts;
brewery tours are daily but contact for details.*

Brasserie Artisanale St Alphonse, Vogelgrun,
Alsace www.brasseriesaintalphonse.com
*Only open Saturday mornings; a friendly
welcome and the three beers produced are very
tasty indeed.*

GERMANY

They're welcoming and fun and full of food and
good cheer but there's not a huge amount of
difference between the big brewery tours in
Germany, so I've listed the main ones, with
websites:

Augustiner, Munich www.augustinerbraeu.de
Ayinger, Aying www.ayinger-bier.de
Erdinger, Erding www.erdinger.de
Hacker-Pschorr, Munich
www.hacker-pschorr.de
Hofbräuhaus, Munich www.hofbraeuhaus.de
Klosterbrauerei Andechs, Andechs
www.andechs.de
König Ludwig, Kaltenberg www.kaltenberg.de
Löwenbräu, Munich www.loewenbraeu.de
Paulaner, Munich www.paulaner.de
Schneider, Kelheim www.schneider-weisse.de
Spaten, Munich www.spatenusa.com
Unions-Bräu Haidhausen, Munich
www.unionsbraeu.de
Weihenstephan Brewery, Weihenstephan
www.brauerei-weihenstephan.de
Veltins, Meschede-Grevenstein www.veltins.de

ITALY

Birreria Baladin, Piozzo www.baladin.it
*Home of the mad scientist of Italian brewing,
Teo Musso.*

Birrificio Italiano, Lurago Marinone
www.birrificio.it *Great beers, great pub.*

POLAND

Tyskie Brewery, Tychy www.tyskie.pl *Long and informative brewery tour, not the most exciting beer in the world but fun and incredibly friendly.*

Zywiec Brewery, Zywiec www.zywiec.com.pl *Interesting blend of old and new, with skittles, hearty grub and beer at the end! Not easy to get to, but a fun day out.*

UK

Adnams, Southwold, Suffolk brewery tours.adnams.co.uk *If you want to visit the seaside and throw in a brewery tour then Adnams is your pick! Lovely beer, beautiful pubs, gorgeous scenery and a distillery too.*

Black Isle Brewery, Ross-shire, Scotland www.blackislebrewery.com *Beautiful organic brewery in the wilds of Scotland.*

Black Sheep, Masham, Yorkshire www.blacksheepbrewery.co.uk *A haven of great beers on the banks of the River Ure in glorious Yorkshire.*

Fox & Crown, Nottingham www.alcazarbrewery.co.uk *In the shadow of Nottingham Castle is Alcazar Brewery's tap; beautiful city and great beers.*

Fuller's, Chiswick, London www.fullers.co.uk *The only remaining family brewer in London, beautiful heritage site, great beers, warm welcome and great pubs in the neighbourhood, too.*

Greene King, Bury St Edmunds, Suffolk www.greeneking.co.uk *Warm welcome and generous tastings at the end of the tour.*

Harvey's, Lewes, Sussex www.harveys.org.uk *There's a waiting list for Harvey's brewery tours, so ring ahead to secure your place.*

Hook Norton Brewery, Hook Norton, Oxfordshire www.hooknortonbrewery.co.uk *Fantastically welcoming family brewery in the heart of the Oxfordshire countryside.*

Moorhouse's, Burnley, Lancashire www.moorhouses.co.uk *In an old Lancashire mill town; great beers and hospitality, where the brewery tap regulars are a show on their own.*

Okell's, Isle of Man www.okells.co.uk *Tours run between May and October; you get a great insight into brewing, plus quite a few hours in the bar afterwards.*

St Austell Brewery, St Austell, Cornwall www.staustellbrewery.co.uk *This is both a museum and a brewery tour: very interesting and very good beer.*

Wadworth, Devizes, Wiltshire www.wadworth.co.uk *With a horse-pulled dray, on-site sign writers and the country's only remaining brewery cooper, Wadworth is a true slice of brewing history; the beer's good too!*

USA

Brooklyn Brewery, Brooklyn, New York www.brooklynbrewery.com *A tour and tasting at Brooklyn is worth it if only to meet the legendary brewery cat, Monster! It's where all the experimental and high-end stuff is made, so book early!*

Great Divide, Denver, Colorado www.greatdivide.com *I recommend having a few tasters in the tap before taking the tour, and then a few more afterwards!*

Left Hand, Boulder, Colorado www.lefthand brewing.com *The offbeat folks at Left Hand are super-welcoming and their beers are sublime; easy to get a bus here from Denver.*

Odells, Fort Collins, Colorado www.odellbrewing.com *Well worth the short journey from Denver, Odells has one of the most elegant and balanced beer ranges in the US.*

Stone Brewery & Bistro, Escondido, California www.stonebrew.com *Stone is focused on making beer an esoteric experience: high-end food and far-out beer.*

OTHER BREWERY TOURS
Belgian brewery tours www.podgebeer.co.uk
UK brewery tours www.visitabrewery.co.uk
Portland area tours www.brewbus.com
San Diego www.brewerytoursof sandiego.com
San Francisco www.bayarea brewerytours.com

UNIQUE BEER EXPERIENCE
Bamberg, Germany. *This place is a legendary beer town. A UNESCO world heritage site, it's not only stunningly beautiful, it is also jam-packed full of everything any beer tourist could ever want. I refer to you Ron Pattinson's www.europeanbeerguide.net/bamburg for everything you need to know.*

BEER BLOGS

My beer blog
www.girlsguidetobeer.blogspot.com
Pete Brown UK blog
www.petebrown.blogspot.com
Adrian Tierney-Jones UK blog
www.maltworms.blogspot.com
Jay Brooks UK blog
www.brookstonbeerbulletin.com
Mark Dredge UK blog
www.pencilandspoon.com
Tim Hampson UK blog
www.beerandpubs.wordpress.com
Stuart Howe's brewing blog
www.brewingreality.blogspot.com

Stan Hieronymous US blog
www.appellationbeer.com
Randy Mosher US blog
www.radicalbrewing.com
The late **John White**'s comprehensive beer site
www.whitebeertravels.co.uk
The late **Michael Jackson**'s website
www.beerhunter.com
Japanese beer culture www.beerjapan.com
Swedish beer blog www.beersweden.se
Laurent Mousson Swiss blog
www.libieration.blogspot.com
Knut Albert Norwegian blog
www.knutalbert.wordpress.com

Below: The author enjoying a session at The Rake in London's Borough Market.

BEER FESTIVALS

A beer festival can be a great voyage of discovery for beer novices and seasoned geeks alike, but can sometimes be a little daunting to even the most seasoned visitor.

TOP TIPS

My recommendation is to look at these events as a marathon, not a sprint: plan ahead, pace yourself and keep yourself fuelled with water and food (little and often).

1 If you can, check out the festival website and plan your first few beers in advance, then freestyle from there
2 Buy a festival guide: big events can often have the most unintuitive floor plans and it's easy to get disorientated
3 Take water, or buy a bottle in the festival (some have water stations) – you'll need it
4 Eat something while you're going round: it's not only a smart idea for staying sober, it also helps reset your palate
5 Don't try and drink pints, or litres, of every beer: go for smaller measures, which means you'll get to taste more beers
6 Go with a group of friends, to make it way more fun
7 Look for tutored tastings, meet the brewer events or beer and food pairings: there are often some really cool things happening that you might not get elsewhere
8 Plan your journey home and be safe

MAJOR BEER FESTIVALS

The box, see right, lists some of the biggest festivals around the world, but don't forget that there are many smaller-scale festivals throughout the year, so keep a lookout for events happening near you.

For a comprehensive guide to beer festivals around the world, try this website: *www.beerfestivals.org* Other websites such as *www.ratebeer.com* and *www.beeradvocate.com* also have calendars of events.

BEER FESTIVALS

Beervana, Wellington, New Zealand
www.brewersguild.org.nz

Belfast Beer & Cider Festival, Northern Ireland
www.belfastbeerfestival.co.uk

Bokbierfestival, Amsterdam, Netherlands www.pint.nl

Easter Beer Festival, Cork, Eire
www.FranciscanWellBrewery.com

Fête de la Bière, Martigny, Switzerland www.fetedelabiere.ch

Great American Beer Festival, Denver, CO, USA
www.GreatAmericanBeerFestival.com

Great British Beer Festival, London, www.gbbf.camra.org.uk

Great Canadian Beer Festival, Victoria, British Colombia
www.gcbf.com

Great Indian Beer Festival, Mumbai, India www.gibf.co.in

Great Japan Beer Festival, Tokyo, Japan www.Beertaster.org

Italian Beer Festival, various cities, Italy www.degustatoribirra.it

National Winter Ales Festival, Manchester, UK
www.camra.org.uk

Oktoberfest, Munich, Germany
www.oktoberfest.de

Salone del Gusto, Turin, Italy
A large brewer presence attached to an awesome food festival www.salonedelgusto.com

Stockholm Beer Festival, Sweden
www.StockholmBeer.se

Zythos Beer Festival, Sint-Niklaas, Belgium www.zbf.be

BEER VOCABULARY

See also Basic Beer Terms and Get your Inner Geek on, pages 40–41.

ABV (alcohol by volume) alcoholic strength: tells you what percentage of the liquid in the glass is pure alcohol

Acetaldehyde a compound that gives off green apple aromas

Acetic vinegary

Adjunct anything providing fermentable sugars that isn't malted barley

Aftertaste any lingering flavours or aromas after swallowing

Ale a term for warm-fermenting beers. See page 25

Alpha acid the bittering compounds in hops

Altbier German beer made with a warm fermentation and cool maturation. See page 88

Astringency has a drying effect on your palate

Attenuation degree to which the yeasts eat the malt sugars. See page 41

Barley the grain most commonly used to brew beer

Barley wine strong, generally quite sweet, warm-fermented beer. See page 149

Barrel beer container; in the brewing industry the brewer's barrel is a standard measurement of output: in the US, it is 31.3 US gallons; and in the UK, it's 36 UK gallons (43.2 US gallons)

Beer a word to describe any fermented/alcoholic product that uses cereal grains

Bitter a quaffable English style of warm-fermented beer. See pages 130–132

Bitterness the cleansing sharpness at the end of a beer; it's a matter of personal taste how much bitterness is pleasing

Blanche French for white, used for Belgian and French wheat beers. See page 72

Blonde generic term for light-coloured beer, often used specifically for a Belgian style. See page 98

Bock strong, often sweetish, high-alcohol style of lager

Body the feel of the beer, whether it is light, heavy, viscous, clean or cloying

Botanicals added herbs, spices, seeds and other natural plant flavourings, as opposed to synthetic

Bottle-conditioned the bottle contains yeast for secondary fermentation. See page 40

Bottom-fermented an outdated and misleading phrase, often used for lager. See pages 23–24

Brettanomyces a strain of wild yeast, desirable in some beers, not in others. See page 24

Burton snatch a sulphurous note that comes from the water chemistry, sometimes naturally, sometimes added deliberately. See page 41

CAMRA the Campaign for Real Ale, Britain's renowned beer campaigning body

Carbonation the fizz in beer

Cask ale cask-conditioned beer that goes through a secondary fermentation in the barrel. See page 40

Conditioning see *maturation*

Copper the brewing vessel in which the wort is boiled and hops and other flavourings are added. See page 17

Craft beer/brewing describes a beer or brewery that uses quality ingredients and isn't a large or multi-national brand

Decoction a stage in the brewing process when part of the mash can be removed from the main mash tun or lauter tun and heated to a higher temperature and then returned to the main mash; the aim is to increase extraction of sugars

Diacetyl a chemical compound that smells of butter or butterscotch/toffee, pleasant when balanced, unpleasant when not. See also page 38

DMS dimethyl sulphide, gives off the aroma of cooked corn, can be very strong in big brand lagers where a high amount of adjunct corn or maize is used

Draught beer beer that comes from a tap – rather than a bottle or can

Dry-hopping when hops are added at the maturation stage. See page 41

Dubbel a Belgian-style dark brown beer, generally around 7% ABV. See page 140

EBU/IBU the measurement used for actual levels of scientific bitterness, which often don't have anything to do with what you perceive when you drink the beer

Esters fruity aromas and flavours in beer

Ethanol the intoxicating alcohol in beer

Fermentation the process of transforming sugar into alcohol by the action of yeast. Yeast eats the sugar and produces alcohol and carbon dioxide as by-products.

Filtration a process that can be rough or very fine; removes particles from beer but can also remove flavour when done excessively

Finings a natural product derived from fish swim bladders, called isinglass, which clears cask ale in the barrel. Synthetic, vegetarian-friendly, options are available

Firkin 9-gallon (UK) barrel

Framboise/Frambozen wild ale made with raspberries. See page 63

Geuze/gueuze a Belgian beer blended from 1-, 2- and 3-year-old wild ales. See page 63

Gravity see *Original Gravity*

Green beer not fully matured and therefore not ready to be drunk

Grist the mix of grains that goes into the mash

Gruit herb mixture used to flavour beer, historically used in place of hops

Gypsum also known as calcium sulphate, naturally found in some water sources, or may be added to ensure clarity of beer

Head the fluffy white bit on the top of your beer

Hefeweissbier an unfiltered, and therefore cloudy, wheat beer. See page 72

Helles a very pale style of German lager

Hogshead 56-gallon (UK) barrel; the largest barrel sent out of a brewery, although it's now rarely seen

Hopback a secondary vessel that can be used to impart additional hop aroma; not every brewery uses one. See page 21

Hoppy an unhelpful phrase used in the brewing industry to describe the myriad flavours and aromas you get from hops

Hops the brewer's seasoning, a plant that provides bitterness and aroma and helps preserve the beer

Hydrometer see *saccharometer*

Imperial originally used for the very strong porters and stouts that were shipped from England to the imperial Russian court in the 18th and 19th centuries (see page 172), the term is increasingly being applied to any extra-strong version of a beer, such as imperial IPA and even imperial pilsner

IPA India Pale Ale, a strong style of British beer that was originally shipped to the colonies. See pages 112–120

Isinglass see *finings*

Keg a method of dispense under pressure and with added carbon dioxide

Keg beer not always a bad thing, particularly if unpasteurized (see *pasteurization*)

Kilderkin 18-gallon (UK) barrel

Kölsch German beer made with a warm fermentation and cool maturation. See page 88

Kriek wild ale made with cherries. See page 63

Lager a cool-fermented and cool-matured style of beer. See pages 80–89

Lambic a spontaneously fermented wild ale. See page 63

Lauter a secondary mash tun with a wider circumference

Light strike the detrimental effect light has on the hop compounds in bottled beers, particularly in clear or green glass, leading to unpleasant aromas and flavours

Liquor hot water used in the brewing process

Malt grains that have been partly germinated; the germination process is then arrested by heat and the grains are toasted to varying degrees to provide different colours and flavours. See page 15

Malty a pointless phrase used in the brewing industry to describe any of the vast range of flavours that come from the malts used in the brewing process

Mash the porridge-like mixture of malted and unmalted grains and adjuncts with hot water, from which fermentable sugars are extracted. See page 17

Mash tun the vessel in which the grains are mixed with the hot liquor (water) to extract sugars from the grist mix. See page 17

Maturation the time beer needs to reach its full potential: this can be two weeks, two years or more

Mild a style of beer that uses few hops, often on the sweeter side. See pages 156–159

Nitrogen a gas used to dispense smoothflow beers from a 'nitrokeg'; most commonly found with Guinness

Old ale a traditional British strong dark beer. See page 150

Oloroso a dark, nutty sherry, used as a tasting reference for beers, often when they've been extensively aged

Original gravity the amount of fermentable sugars in the wort, which gives an indication of how much alcohol the final beer will have

Oxidation the effect of oxygen on beer: can be good or bad

Palate your personal set of taste buds and olfactory system

Pale ale describes two styles of beer: old-fashioned British pale ales are bottled versions of the brewery's standard bitter; New World pale ales are highly aromatic. See pages 112–121

Pasteurization the process of heating a product to sterilize it after its production process is complete; detrimental to flavour

Pilsner a light, golden style of lager, developed in the Czech town of Plzen (Pilsen). See page 83

Porter the dark, drinkable beer that powered the industrial revolution in London and beyond. See pages 166–168

Racking transferring fermenting beer into another vessel, leaving the spent yeast behind

Saccharometer a large weighted glass bulb with a thin stem with calibrated markings, it is suspended in a tube of wort by brewers to assess how much sugar there is in the wort

Saison beer a Belgian style of farmhouse ale, highly aromatic. See page 106

Sediment should only normally be found in the bottom of cask and bottle-conditioned beers; this is primarily yeast but can also be proteins, particularly in aged beers

Session beer a quaffing beer, generally considered as anything below 4% ABV, but higher in some countries

Single variety a beer that uses one specific malt or hop variety (or both)

Shandy a mixture of lemonade and beer

Stock ale a strong beer designed to be kept; historically was also blended with younger beers in pubs

Stout short for stout porter, a dark beer that is a favourite worldwide, synonymous with Ireland.

See page 171

Top-fermented a misleading phrase, often used to describe beers made with a warm fermenting yeast. See page 23

Trappist a protected designation referring to all products produced by Trappist monasteries, including beers. See pages 138–141

Tripel a strong golden ale, a Belgian style that was created at Westmalle Trappist brewery. See page 140

Trub a brewer's term used to refer to all the left-over yeast and hops in brewing vessels

Ullage the head space in a barrel; also a term for waste beer

Umami the fifth sense of taste, refers to richness and savoury flavours. See page 47

Unfiltered beer beer that is served deliberately cloudy: it may contain yeast or may have been allowed to settle naturally or through the use of finings

Vat/VAT a vat is a vessel in which brewing can take place; VAT is the dreaded Value Added Tax, which is levied on the alcohol industry by the UK government

Wheat can be used in small quantities in the brewing process to add body and increase head retention

Wheat/Wit/Weiss terms for beers using a high proportion of wheat (usually 35% and above) in the brew. See page 68

Wort sweet liquid produced by mixing grains (usually malted grains) with hot water; the start of the brewing process

Yeast single-cell organism, which turns sugars into alcohol and carbon dioxide. See pages 22–24

Zymurgy the technical name for the branch of science that looks into the fermentation process

INDEX

AUTHOR ACKNOWLEDGMENTS

"Twas a woman who drove me to drink. I never had the courtesy to thank her." WC Fields

And on the subject of thank yous, I have many to make. First Maggie Ramsay, Fiona Holman and the Anova crew, thank you for babysitting me through my first book. Mum & Dad, Bernice & Michael Cole, you've never put limits on what I could achieve, thank you, I love you. Melanie Arnold, you're a proper big sis, love you; bro-in-law Keith, thanks for cricket, it goes so well with beer! Josh & Kate Arnold, I love you, please hurry and get older; I want to buy you your first pint! The Connolly clan, I feel the love from Canada. Pam & Stan Eaton, love you, thanks for introducing me to great beer! Mike & Jo Eaton, for showing me you can make dreams a reality.

Collaboration brewers Matt Clarke, Stuart Howe (thank you for all your help on this project); the Otley boys, Buster Grant (and Jo) and Mark Tranter. Also, Kelly Ryan, David Grant, Chris Miller, the Freedom crew, Andreas Failt, Steve Holt, Paul Halsey, Florent Vialan, Matt Jackson, Jaclyn Bateman, Steve Grossman, Matt Brynildson, Bill Jacobs at Piece, Greg Hall, Chris Swersey and Bob Pease, Chris Black at Falling Rock, Doug Odell, Eric Wallace, Tomme Arthur, Jeff Bagby, Glyn Roberts, Denise Herman and Tony Lennon. Dan Fox, Richard Dinwoodie and Mike Hill, I adore you all. And Glenn Payne – mwah, mwah, mwah! My fellow hacks, especially Garth Williams, Dave Tooley, Tim Hampson, Roger Protz, Jeff Evans, Adrian Tierney-Jones, Pete Brown, the late John White, Mike Bennett, Oz Clarke and Charles Campion. Joanna Dring, Vanessa Hollidge, R&R Teamwork and a big shout out to Tony Johnson. Mitch Steele, Stan Hieronymous, Jay Brooks, Jaime Jurado and others for helping me piece together the fractured history of US IPA. Also, Thomas Hummel for your sensory science genius. Euan Austin and Brendan Weibel for modelling for me. Thanks to the Twitterverse for its support, everyone who has ever come to my tastings and beer blogging community.

My lovely mates: Christine 'Booshi' Warren, Bertie Bussett, Nicola Swann & Nicola Connors, Paul 'big bro Stuart, Miya Canty, Meri Mance, Greg Start, Angharad Davies, John Comyn and Tim Moule. To anyone I've forgotten, I'm sorry and I really didn't mean to – but you know who you are! Last, and opposite of least, Ben, I love you.

PICTURE ACKNOWLEDGMENTS

The author and publishers would like to thank all the brewers and breweries who have helped with sourcing images for this book.

Other images:

Anova Books (photography by Yuki Sugiura) front cover and pages 1, 2-3, 4, 15, 27, 30, 31 (both), 32, 34, 36 (all), 37, 38, 39, 40, 45 (all), 47, 50, 51, 52, 58, 68, 69, 75, 80, 96, 97, 112, 115, 130, 131, 132, 145, 148, 150, 158, 169, 184, 188, 192, 194, 200, 204, 205, 215, 216

Alamy pages 70 Joris Luyten/Cephas Picture Library, 86 (above) Bill Bachman, 138 David Gee 2, 141 Sheryl Savas

Beergenie.co.uk pages 16, 183

Bridgeman pages 54 *A man in a landscape, raising a beer glass* (oil on panel) by Staverenus, Petrus (fl.1635-p.1666) Private Collection/ Johnny Van Haeften Ltd., London; 167 *The Porter Brewer's Draymen from Ackermann's 'World in Miniature'* (litho) by Shoberl, Frederic (1755-1853) (after) London Library; 172 *The First Russian Fleet* by Samsonev, Alexei (b.1968) Roy Miles Fine Paintings; 178 *Still Life of Fruit and Nuts on a Stone Ledge* (oil on panel) by Mignon, Abraham (1640-79) Fitzwilliam Museum, University of Cambridge; 182 *Rosemary and other herbs* (w/c) by Rice, Elizabeth (Contemporary Artist) Private Collection

CAMRA page 89

Cephas Picture Library (Nigel Blythe) page 146

Melissa Cole pages 12, 20 (left), 21, 24, 60, 87, 195

Corbis pages 17 Frank Conlon, 18 Patrick Ward, 23 Bettmann, 55 relaXimages, 59 Ludovic Maisant, 81 Dirk Olaf Wexel, 83 Ken Scicluna, 84 Bettmann, 86 (left) ImageChina, 105 Swim Ink 2, LLC, 139 Owen Franken, 156 Radius Images, 164 Clare Roberts/Eye Ubiquitous, 165 Hulton-Deutsch Collection, 170 above Richard Cummins, 170 below Richard Klune, 171 Catherine Carnow, 193 Homer Sykes, 197 Yves Herman/Reuters

Brasserie Dupont page 117

Duvel page 98

English Heritage page 120

Charles Faram and Co, the Hop Man page 20 (right)

Getty pages 42 Oli Scarff, 85 Universal Images Group/Hulton Archive, 121 Fotosearch Archive Photos, 196 Walter Nurnberg SSPL

Guild of Fine Food 41

Mary Evans Picture Library pages 71 Interfoto/Sammlung Rauch, 116, 118, 119, 166 Illustrated London News

Gary Moyes back cover and page 6

Shutterstock pages 5, 8-9, 12-13, 13, 14, 19, 22, 25, 26, 28-29, 35, 56-57, 104, 185, 198, 202